NORTH CAROLINA STUDIES IN THE
ROMANCE LANGUAGES AND LITERATURES
Number 268

PUERTO RICAN CULTURAL IDENTITY AND THE WORK OF LUIS RAFAEL SÁNCHEZ

UNIVERSITY OF NORTH CAROLINA AT CHAPEL HILL
DEPARTMENT OF ROMANCE LANGUAGES

DATF ┌

NORTH CAROLINA STUDIES
IN THE ROMANCE LANGUAGES AND LITERATURES

Founder: URBAN TIGNER HOLMES

Editor: CAROL L. SHERMAN

Distributed by:

UNIVERSITY OF NORTH CAROLINA PRESS

CHAPEL HILL
North Carolina 27515-2288
U.S.A.

PUERTO RICAN CULTURAL IDENTITY AND THE WORK OF LUIS RAFAEL SÁNCHEZ

B Y

JOHN DIMITRI PERIVOLARIS

CHAPEL HILL

NORTH CAROLINA STUDIES IN THE ROMANCE
LANGUAGES AND LITERATURES
U.N.C. DEPARTMENT OF ROMANCE LANGUAGES

2 0 0 0

Library of Congress Cataloging-in-Publication Data

Perivolaris, John.
    Puerto Rican cultural identity and the work of Luis Rafael Sánchez / John Dimitri Perivolaris.
    p. cm. – (North Carolina studies in the Romance languages and literatures; no. 268).
    Includes bibliographical references.
    ISBN 0-8078-9272-6
    1. Sánchez, Luis Rafael – Criticism and interpretation. 2. Literature and society – Puerto Rico. I. Title II. Series.

PQ7440.S235 Z78 2000
863'.64–dc21   00-062500

Cover design: Heidi Perov

ISBN 0-8078-9272-6

IMPRESO EN ESPAÑA

PRINTED IN SPAIN

DEPÓSITO LEGAL: V. 4.197 - 2000

ARTES GRÁFICAS SOLER, S. L. - LA OLIVERETA, 28 - 46018 VALENCIA

1002711240

As late multinational capitalism commodifies every remaining aspect of human relations in every last refuge, establishing an international market of messages in which all the old power relations continue, albeit more invisibly than ever, it becomes ever more difficult for local identities to be forged and preserved.

(Martin, 364)

Aquí en Puerto Rico, colonia sucesiva de dos imperios e isla del Archipiélago de las Antillas.

[Here in Puerto Rico, successive colony of two empires and island of the Antillean Archipelago.]

(Sánchez, *La guaracha de Macho Camacho* 13)

I should constantly remind myself that the real *leap* consists in introducing invention into existence.

(Fanon 229)

CONTENTS

ACKNOWLEDGMENTS

A study of this kind always takes the form of a series of peripatetic dialogues. I should like to thank the following traveling companions, without whom my research would have been too lonely and silent a journey to be enjoyable. Firstly, Verity Smith, who provided the first maps and has supported my work since then, Paul Julian Smith who as my doctoral supervisor always guided me away from dead ends and directed me along new avenues, John King who, as an inexhaustible source of advice, information, enthusiasm, and contacts, introduced me to new friends and colleagues in my now beloved Puerto Rico. Of those who helped me on the island, persons too numerous to mention, I should like to take this opportunity to thank Juan G. Gelpí, the scholars of the University of Puerto Rico at Río Piedras, the staff of the Seminario de Federico de Onís and the José M. Lázaro Library, all of whom were generous with their time and the assistance they offered me on research visits to Puerto Rico during the autumn of 1993 and summer of 1999. These were generously funded by the British Academy, with help from the University of Cambridge of awards to me from the Jebb Fund and J. B. Trend Fund. I am also grateful to my colleagues at the Department of Spanish and Portuguese Studies, the University of Manchester, for allowing me the time to make my second trip toward the end of the busy examinations season.

Special thanks go to Ángel G. Quintero Rivera ("Chuco") for helping me organize the preliminaries of my first trip, and Luis Rafael Sánchez for his friendship since we first met over a stylish breakfast at The Metropolitan. But, of my *amigos boricuas*, I am most deeply indebted to Carmen Vázquez Arce, who allowed me access to her extensive Luis Rafael Sánchez archive, her unpublished but influential 1984 doctoral thesis, "Salsa y control: el discurso expositivo de Luis Rafael Sánchez," and the manuscript to her 1994 study of Sánchez's short stories, *Por la vereda tropical.* Her work and encouragement have proved indispensable. I relished writing the first drafts of the third and fourth chapters of this study in her enchanting tower of the penguins.

The encouragement, experience, professionalism, and wisdom of the following was a boon: Arcadio Díaz Quiñones, Aníbal González, my editor Carol. L. Sherman, her staff, and the anonymous reviewers of the manuscript. Funding from the Modern Humanities Research Association and the University of Manchester was indispensable in the preparation of this for publication.

Lastly, I should like to thank my friends at the University of Cambridge for their ideas and support, especially Conrad James for introducing me to a broader Caribbean culture, my colleagues at the School of European Studies, University of Cardiff, where a generous Research Fellowship allowed me the time and space to make progress with this book, and especially the students of my "Twentieth-Century Hispanic Caribbean Literature" course at the University of Manchester. I dedicate my work to all those I have mentioned, those I have not mentioned because of a lack of space, and to my lifelong traveling companions, Charlotte and Electra. The latter, my daughter, has traveled the road between crawling and running while I have been redrafting this book at a snail's pace. This study is also dedicated to my father, Dimitri John Perivolaris, who passed away just before its publication.

Earlier versions of some of the chapters contained herein were read at the following places: Chapter 1: The 1995 Latin American Studies Association Conference, Washington DC. Subsequently published in the *Journal of Hispanic Research,* 3 (1994-95): 397-414. Chapter 2: The Fifth Studies in Latin American Popular Culture Conference, New Orleans, 1996. Chapter 3: The Eighteenth Annual Conference of the Society for Caribbean Studies, Oxford, 1994. Chapter 4: The Modern Hispanic Research Seminar, Queen Mary & Westfield College, London, 1996. The observations on *La importancia de llamarse Daniel Santos* were subsequently incorporated in my essay "Little Stories of Caribbean History and Nationhood: Edgardo Rodriguez Julia and Luis Rafael Sanchez." *The Cultures of the Hispanic Caribbean.* Ed. Conrad James and John D. Perivolaris. London: Macmillan, 2000.

J. D. P.

Cambridge, San Juan, Cardiff, Stansted Mountfitchet, Nottingham, Manchester, 1995-2000.

ABBREVIATIONS

The following abbreviations have been used in the bibliography:

C	*Claridad* (San Juan, PR)
H	*Hispania* (USA)
LALR	*Latin American Literary Review*
LATR	*Latin American Theatre Review*
M	*El Mundo* (San Juan, PR)
MLN	*Modern Language Notes*
ND	*El Nuevo Día* (San Juan, PR)
P	*Postdata* (Río Piedras, PR)
PC	*Pensamiento Crítico* (San Juan, PR)
Pl	*Plural* (San Juan, PR)
RCR	*Revista Chicano-Riqueña* (Houston)
REHPR	*Revista de Estudios Hispánicos* (Río Piedras, PR)
RevIb	*Revista Iberoamericana*
RICP	*Revista del Instituto de Cultura Puertorriqueña*
S	*Sargasso* (San Juan, PR)
SJS	*San Juan Star*
SN	*Sin Nombre* (San Juan, PR)
T	*La Torre* (Nueva Época) (Río Piedras, PR)

INTRODUCTION

¡Desgraciado Almirante! Tu pobre América,
tu india virgen y hermosa de sangre cálida,
la perla de tus sueños, es una histérica
de convulsivos nervios y frente pálida.
[Ill-fated Admiral! Your poor America,
Your beautiful, hot-blooded Indian maiden,
the pearl of your dreams, is a hysteric
with shattered nerves and pallid brow.]

(Rubén Darío, "A Colón" [To Columbus], 1892)

THIS book is the most comprehensive study to date of Luis Rafael Sánchez's work, covering all the genres in which he has distinguished himself in his long and successful career as a short story writer, playwright, essayist, as well as celebrated author of the internationally acclaimed novel, *La guaracha del Macho Camacho* [Macho Camacho's Beat] (1976), and the generically hybrid novel-length text, *La importancia de llamarse Daniel Santos* [*The Importance of Being Daniel Santos*] (1988).

Sánchez's work follows in a great tradition of Pan-Caribbeanism represented so famously by figures such as Eugenio María de Hostos and José Martí. At the same time, it disallows any reductive appeal to Caribbean homogeneity by highlighting the fissures of the society and region in which and of which he writes. His is a disjunctive perspective that problematizes Pan-Caribbeanism.

His local prominence as the island's most important writer is further enhanced by his unprecedented international success as a novelist and as an author regarded by important figures such as Carlos Fuentes and Gabriel García Márquez as one of their peers. Widely traveled and currently living six months a year in New York, Sánchez's perspective is an unheroically cosmopolitan one, which contrasts with two strands of Puerto Rican intellectuality to which I shall refer throughout this study. On the one hand, with the exile perspective of a legendary nationalist such as Hostos and, on the other, with that of local critics of Puerto Rico's supposed backward insularity, such as Antonio S. Pedreira. Sánchez displaces any concept of self-sacrifice justified by the high ideals of a utopian political project and represented by Hostos's doomed struggle to forge a Pan-Caribbean Confederation.[1] He also refutes Pedreira's picture of isolation, the result of a classical education that made Pedreira keenly feel the distance that separated him, as a Puerto Rican, from what he felt were the glories of his European heritage.[2] Sánchez replaces abstraction and ideal with careful reflection on the possibilities of asserting concrete forms of Caribbean and Latin American identity in the face of continuing colonialism, modernization, diaspora, and the massification of culture.

Above all, Sánchez rejects the martyrdom and pessimism of both intellectual strands in favor of his depiction of a popular sense of Puerto Rican humor. Considering its prominence in his *œuvre*, it is only natural that I follow other readers in referring to Sánchez's pioneering consideration of a previously neglected popular culture as a vital element in a highly contested Puerto Rican identity. I would wish my major contribution to Sánchez scholarship to be a vigorous reflection on how, in a coarse vernacular laced with learned Spanish word play, Sánchez humorously explores the both the complexities of the vexing issue of Puerto Rican identity and the related difficulty of proposing any project of independence within a Puerto Rican context.

While the vehicle of his portrayal of conflictive nationality has been his own pungent brand of humor Sánchez's optimism is unmistakable and untypical. And yet I have had to endeavor throughout this book to address a curious blind-spot in most previous criticism. Though all of Sánchez's work deals with serious themes most studies fail to adequately convey and discuss the humor of his work. Luce López-Baralt is probably the first scholar to devote an entire article to humor in the writer's work, while Efraín Barradas and Carmen Vázquez Arce follow her in observing how humor is used by him as a subversive distancing strategy.[3] However, no critic has developed López-Baralt's juxtaposition of the narrator's critically humorous perspective in *La guaracha* with the characters' recourse

---

[1] A detailed account of Hostos's career is provided by Bosch.

[2] On Pedreira, see Flores ("The Insular").

[3] See López-Baralt ("La prosa;" 1985); Barradas (*Para leer* 65-79); Vázquez Arce (*Por la vereda* 17, 22, 25-27, 59-64, 71-72, 84-85, 119-21, 218). Also see Beauchamp, and Corral.

to humor as an escapist means of surviving the harsh conditions of
their lives. In fact, López-Baralt goes as far as to suggest that the
novel's critical perspective is blunted by often being indistinguishable from the characters' escapist humor. Though López-Baralt's
observation may be valid I suggest that the blurring of the narrative
and the characters' perspective is part of, as I indicate especially in
the fifth chapter on the essays, Sánchez's departure from the advantaged critical posture of traditional Puerto Rican writing.

Apart from the excellent work of the three scholars I have just
discussed it is surprising that much criticism still fails to seriously
appraise Sánchez's exceptionally enjoyable humor, which he con-
summately modulates between coarseness, subtle irony, wryness,
absurdity, and grotesqueness. It is surely this attractive quality, evident in all areas of his writing, that to a large extent attracts readers.
Sánchez's own pronouncements on humor in interviews and essays
should have been taken seriously long ago. For him, humor is a way
of critically confronting reality.[4] In his essay "Literatura puertorriqueña y realidad colonial" [Puerto Rican Literature and Colonial
Reality] (1974) he outlines the mission of his comedy by declaring
that Puerto Rican writers must attack the apathy, complacency, and
self-delusion of colonialism by "la utilización del humor que desin-
fla y hiere" [the use of a humor that deflates and wounds] (15). For
him, humor is an "arte corrosivo para demoler las mentiras" [a corrosive art for demolishing lies] (15).[5]

The fact that Sánchez's own self-definition as a humorous writer
has not been heeded has less to do with lack of a sense of humor on
the part of literary scholars and critics (though this is all too often
demonstrated) than with the literary tradition in which Sánchez is
writing. As Efraín Barradas astutely observes (*Para leer* 27):

> En nuestras letras como bien ha señalado Luce López Baralt no
> abundan los humoristas. Nuestros literatos tienden a tomarlo
> todo, a sí mismos inclusive, muy en serio. Es en nuestra literatura
> donde abundan, en cambio, la angustia, el pesimismo y la
> evasión al pasado. Dentro de ese contexto el humor de Sánchez
> resulta más chocante y agresivo.[6]

---

[4] See interviews with the following: Barradas ("El lenguaje" 105); Cordero
Ávila; Díaz Quiñones ("El oficio" 29).

[5] For further discussion of this strategy see interview with Barradas ("El lenguaje" 106); Corral (76-77).

[6] On this point, also see Vázquez Arce (*Por la vereda* 227).

[As Luce López Baralt has pointed out, there is not an abundance of humorists in our letters. Our literati tend to take everything, including themselves, very seriously. It is precisely in our literature, on the other hand, that there is an abundance of anguish, pessimism and evasion of the past. In this context Sánchez's humor seems even more shocking and aggressive.]

The earnest pessimism just described has much to do with the "catastrofismo" described by Irma Rivera Nieves (*El tema*). According to her there is a tendency in Puerto Rican intellectual and political life to reduce all issues to a fatalistic identification with the island's colonial status or a call to arms against colonial exploitation.[7] At several points in this study, I shall associate this fatalistic pessimism with a downturn in the fortunes of the class represented by most Puerto Rican writers and intellectuals.

Carmen Vázquez (*Por la vereda* 160-61) correctly concludes that one of Sánchez's most resonant achievements is to have opened the way for younger writers to write seriously through humor. In fact, so much so is this the case that the literary landscape Barradas sketched in monochrome in 1981 has now been colored by the arrival to full maturity of first-rate writers like Magali García Ramis, Edgardo Rodríguez Juliá, and Ana Lydia Vega, all of whose use and enjoyment of humor signals contemporary Puerto Rican literature's broader spectrum of expression.

Sánchez is nothing if not an innovator, so that the following chapters provide illustrations of Sánchez's importance as a pioneer of what may be a major preoccupation of recent Puerto Rican literature: that is, the rewriting of an authoritarian intellectual tradition (Gelpí, *Literatura* 17-44). Sánchez himself is consistently sensitive to Puerto Rican cultural identity's survival by dint of daily reworking the terms of a dependence further complicated by internal class, racial, and sexual conflicts. It is such sensitivity that questions the credibility of traditional intellectual debate, which has sought to define the essence of a unified "ser puertorriqueño" [Puerto Rican being] (Vázquez Arce, *Por la vereda* 164). The sociopolitical satire of modern Puerto Rico undertaken by Sánchez throughout his work is unmistakable. But, it is only by observing his dissociation from earlier Puerto Rican writers that one is able to appreciate the extent of

---

[7] See also Barradas ("La importancia" 194, 197).

the writer's innovative depiction of the incursion of mass culture as part of an uneven and rapid modernization, and he discards the nostalgia of previous Puerto Rican writing in favor of dispassionate irony.

Though the writers before Sánchez had also portrayed marginal figures in Puerto Rican society his protagonists–often blacks, homosexuals, mulattoes, women outcasts–do not take center stage as ciphers illustrating the presumed angst of modern man [sic]. They are not perceived as beings alienated from the apparently universal values of humanism by the evil dislocations of the modern world, but instead as anti-heroes of Puerto Rico's precipitous modernization. I trace Puerto Rican writers' moralizing to the political experiences of their traditionally identifying with the Puerto Rican landed classes, which suffered a rapid decline in their social and economic influence as a result of such modernization. In this respect, Sánchez's ironical exaltation of marginal figures emerges from a subtler rendering of social transformation on the part of writers who came of age during a period of accelerated intellectual and social upheaval in Puerto Rico, the Caribbean and Latin America, dating from the 1960s.

Sánchez irony is directed at Puerto Rican writers' nostalgia for a Hispanic past, represented by them as the fountain-head of virtuous Puerto Ricanness. It will become clear in my discussion of the works I have selected that such nostalgia reflects the class-privilege of a semi-feudal, slave-owning past under Spanish rule. And I will show that the emergence of new identities in Sánchez's work is historically justified by the emergence of previously silenced social groups as a result of American colonialism's transformation of Puerto Rico into a burgeoning industrial society. I will argue that Sánchez's discomfort with the patrician literary tradition of his country is closely linked to his mulatto, working-class background. His identification with non-elite groups is rooted in his being the product of the relatively more liberal colonialism of American rule. It was the social modernization constituted by this that allowed the consolidation of a new working and an incipient professional class, greater rights for blacks and women, as well the increasing social mobility that allowed Sánchez to rise from a humble background and occupy a privileged, if uncomfortable, place among the ranks of Puerto Rico's *criollo,* university-educated, middle-class intelligentsia.

Sánchez has been a pioneer and promises to continue being one. The search for new directions is foreshadowed by his ever more urgent pursuit of innovation through increasing experimentation and use of ambiguity. As a result of her examination of the writer's 1975 short story "Ojos de sosiego ajenos" [Calm Eyes Not my Own] and his unpublished 1979 play *Parábola del andarín* [Parable of the Walker] Vázquez (*Por la vereda* 203-13) identifies absurdist minimalism as a vehicle Sánchez might develop to further his already parodic representation of literary forms. This new approach would sacrifice plot in favor of establishing non-realist situations through which artistic convention and philosophical questions may be explored. Paradoxically, if Sánchez's work does follow the path of artistic abstraction, this would constitute a radical political provocation within the context of Puerto Rican literary tradition. For, as José Luis González has observed ("Sobre la literatura" 145-46), Puerto Rican writers risk censure or, even worse, indifference, if they deviate from the time-honored search for a meaningful Puerto Rican identity in the face of an alienating modernizing colonialism; the avowed purpose of all serious Puerto Rican literature. Even the attempts at literary experimentalism of the 1950s and 1960s by writers such as Francisco Arriví and René Marqués very obviously served as allegorical explorations of an overriding question of identity (Colón Zayas, *El teatro* 22-28). A move towards art for art's sake on the part of Sánchez would further distance him from the Puerto Rican intelligentsia's expression of a specifically class-based crisis of identity.

In terms of the contemporary development of Puerto Rican literature Sánchez should be considered a transitional figure between the paternalism of his country's literary tradition and the full-blown defiance of younger Puerto Rican writers. Edgardo Rodríguez Juliá joins him in his work as a catalyst by also rewriting history according to non-elite and Afro-Antillean identities (Gelpí, *Literatura* 17-60). In Rodríguez Juliá's novels, *La renuncia del héroe Baltasar* [The Resignation of the Hero Balthazar] (1974) and *La noche oscura del Niño Avilés* [The Dark Night of Niño Avilés] (1984), his imaginative reappraisal of literary tradition as ideologically determined artifice takes the form of a historicization of fiction. Inversely, in his "crónicas" the construction of Puerto Rican history and historical figures is highlighted by being fictionalized, as in *Las tribulaciones de Jonás* [The Tribulations of Jonah] (1981), *El entierro de Cortijo* [Cortijo's

Funeral] (1983), *Una noche con Iris Chacón* [A Night with Iris Chacón] (1986), *Puertorriqueños* [Puerto Ricans] (1988), *El cruce de la Bahía de Guánica* [The Crossing of Guánica Bay] (1989), and *Peloteros* [Ball Players] (1997).

If in the work of Luis Rafael Sánchez and Edgardo Rodríguez Juliá the voice of historical authority falters and is undone from within through subtle parody more recent writing is joyfully patricidal in the celebration of its own voices. Embracing their marginal subjectivity as a means of rejecting the pompous mantle of spokesman of the nation, anyway denied to them, women's voices ironically break the local bounds of literary propriety to explore social, sexual, and racial taboos, as in Rosario Ferré's *Papeles de Pandora* [The Youngest Doll] (1976). In a more lighthearted vein Ana Lydia Vega's work, as in *Encancaranublado y otros cuentos de naufragio* [Encancaranublado and Other Shipwreck Stories] (1982) and *Falsas crónicas del sur* [True and False Romances] (1991), satirizes gendered and racially specific stereotypes of national identity. She achieves this by rewriting literary genres and, like Sánchez, looking beyond Puerto Rico's supposed isolation to a broader Caribbean culture where high and popular culture are revised from a woman's perspective. Meanwhile, Vega's cosmopolitanism and untraditionally optimistic humor turns black in Manuel Ramos Otero's violently explicit exploration of homosexuality as a metaphor for Puerto Ricans' diasporic nationality, in *El cuento de la Mujer del Mar* [The Story of the Woman of the Sea] (1979). On the other hand, in Magali García Ramis's *Felices días, tío Sergio* [Happy Days, Uncle Sergio] (1986) the homosexual character of the title replaces the ubiquitous father-figures of Puerto Rican literature in an ironic rewriting of national and family relations. But, as if the homosexualization of paternalism were not enough, García Ramis further eschews authoritarianism in her feminist use of a child narrator whose dialogues with her uncle are the democratic counterpart of the supposedly edifying lessons of tradition (Gelpí, *Literatura* 94-100). Clearly indebted to Sánchez, by following his irreverent precedent, Puerto Rican writers are freer than ever before to pose their national identity as a continuing series of questions rather than an article of faith.

Sharing the same spirit of curiosity my work is informed by discussions taking place in Puerto Rico, the Caribbean, Latin America, and the metropolises. These discussions concern questions of feminist, psychoanalytic, postmodern, and postcolonial theory in relation to hysteria, abjection, the body and the nation, tradition and innovation, public and private politics, as well as the location of the intellectual. And, allied to my discussion of the available secondary literature I have engaged with several theoretical models. For example, in my first chapter on terms of identity in *Quíntuples* my choice of a theoretical model based on Julia Kristeva's psychoanalytical research into modernist literature is stimulated by recognition of the status of psychoanalysis as one of the cornerstones of metropolitan cultural theory and the uncanny displacement of the latter suggested by a Rubén Darío poem. His "A Colón," cited as an epigraph to this introduction, ostensibly bemoans the chaotic betrayal of Arcadian indigenous traditions and Utopian schemes of modernity by the vicissitudes of Latin American history. For Darío the betrayal of conquest and conflict unleashed by colonialism motivates his apparent elegy to a paradise lost and heroic enterprise. On the other hand, this poem, by a writer who sought to renovate Latin American literature through a creative rereading of tradition and fashion contains the seed of my entire discussion of *Quíntuples*, concerning the possibilities of hysteria as a creative liberation from colonial identities that manages to seduce metropolitan forms of knowledge.

Sánchez's work links the latter to the constant colonization and eventual capitalist incorporation of Puerto Rico. In his accounts the ironic agency Puerto Ricans win through their daily engagement with life in a modern colony is contingent on the antecedent roles permitted them by their dependancy. The Puerto Rican situation presents an extreme example of the decentering of humanist individuality undertaken by post-Saussurean linguistics, philosophy, and psychoanalysis. According to these, individuals only ever emerge through their positioning as subjects in language. How close Sánchez's work comes to the irreducible promise of postcolonial theory as expounded by critics such as Homi K. Bhabha, and the related if not identical field of postmodern theory as explored by Jean Baudrillard, whose relevance I discuss in greater detail in the conclusion to this book! A promise of unforeseen identity emerging from the ironic performance of roles demarcated under the totalitarian jurisdiction of colonialism and capitalism. On the other hand, if postmodernism is, in Jean-François Lyotard's sense, a mistrust of "master narratives," Sánchez's texts can only partially be called postmodern. For, though they question traditional Puerto Rican nationalism, they are still driven by the emancipatory project of championing Puerto Rican nationality, albeit in a more egalitarian and flexible form (Cruz-Malavé, "Repetition" 153-56). On the other hand, though *La guaracha* could be interpreted as a "master narrative" that attempts a global portrait of all strata of Puerto Rican society and its problems, Carlos J. Alonso has convincingly argued that the novel's self-reflective, polyrhythmic, multi-register, and multi-generic form counters any all-encompassing aim.

In the fourth chapter on Sánchez's novels, I explore the writer's disruption of binding masculine identities in the Caribbean and Latin America, by recourse to Freudian paradigms of repression. Though this is not a common approach to Sánchez's work, I am not the first to employ psychoanalytical models. For example, Joseph Chadwick juxtaposes Marxian commodity fetishism and Freudian sexual fetishism in his discussion of *La guaracha* and Agnes I. Lugo Ortiz examines the treatment of homosexuality in the short story "¡Jum!" with reference to Julia Kristeva's work on abjection. However, my study for the first time examines the writer's pointed disruption of European science's supposedly universal truths by means of their displacement to specifically colonial situations with their own history.

Beyond his local prominence and from an acknowledged position in the first rank of Spanish American and Hispanic Caribbean literature Sánchez has been associated rightly by his critics with writers such as Severo Sarduy, Manuel Puig, and Guillermo Cabrera Infante.[8] Such association largely emerges from a shared interest on the part of Sánchez, Sarduy, and Cabrera Infante in registering a Caribbean vernacular as part of the portrayal of urban culture undertaken by them and Puig. However, vernacular forms constitute only one level of the writer's repertoire, which also makes learned allusions to and reworks the texts of high culture. The multi-layered, exhaustive linguistic and conceptual elaboration of Sánchez's literary language has been likened, though with some reservations, with the "baroque," "neo-baroque," or mannerist style of the Latin American writers mentioned. A further dimension of the multiple layering of Sánchez's work is its formal and generic hybridity. This has lead to María Vaquero de Ramírez's (51) definition of *La guaracha* as "teatro novelado" [novelized theater], to the clas-

---

[8] Barradas interview ("El lenguaje" 105); Ben-Ur ("Myth Montage"); Feliciano Fabre (xx); Ortega ("Teoría" 31, 45); Parkinson Zamora; Rama.

sification of "La guagua aérea" [The Flying Bus] as both an essay and short story, and to the presentation of what could be considered a novelistic work, *La importancia de llamarse Daniel Santos*, as a piece of sociological research.[9]

Faced with a broad-ranging body of work and impressed like other critics with its culturally pregnant form, I have chosen to undertake a close reading of certain representative texts. Such an approach is not only able to provide a detailed examination of important themes by focusing on their significant discrete moments but also acknowledges the importance of language as the undisguised instrument Sánchez employs to parody the rhetoric of politics and culture. My close reading firstly highlights his awareness of Puerto Rican reality's mediation by his society's "texts." Secondly, by focusing on the textual reflexivity of Sánchez's work I underline his problematization of traditional claims to speak directly for the *pueblo* on the part not only of Puerto Rican intellectuals but also of scientific or emancipatory cultural projects such as bourgeois realism or Marxist polemic. Close attention to the textuality of Sánchez's work also foregrounds his faith, as an islander, in the Spanish language as the one unifying element through which all Puerto Ricans can express themselves, whatever the divisions of their highly fragmented society. And it is only a close reading that can draw attention to the porousness of his Spanish-language perspective. The constant linguistic reinvention of Spanish by Puerto Ricans, a capacity celebrated by Sánchez, merely serves as the point of departure for transnational identities rather than a pluralistic home where the huge range and multiple conflicts of Puerto Ricans' experiences may be reconciled in a united expression of nationality. Beyond this, Juan Flores has shown how US Puerto Ricans' predominant bilingualism allows them the freedom to express multiple cultural affiliations made possible by their navigation be-

---

[9] On Sánchez's literary language, see Barradas interview ("El lenguaje" 105-07); Ben-Ur ("Hacia" 215); Ortega interview ("Teoría" 30-33; "Luis Rafael Sánchez" 238-39); Vázquez Arce (*Por la vereda* 22). On the formal and generic hybridity discussed, see Aparicio ("Entre" 85); Corral (78-79); Cruz-Malavé ("Repetition" 44-45); Gelpí (*Literatura* 17-45). In his 1985 interview with Gregory Rabassa, Sánchez (177) refers to *La importancia* as "una especie de ensayo" [a sort of essay], while in his 1994 interview with Barradas, the writer again associates *La importancia* with his work as an essayist (108).

tween the dual poles of their nationality on the island and in the United States.[10]

The critical approach I have chosen allows me to locate the pragmatism of the writer's perspective in the form of his texts. Allied with Sánchez's playful *bricolage* of linguistic registers and literary forms is his knowing use of mass media techniques, such as montage, cross-cutting, advertising slogans, and the appeals to sentimentality of popular music. Arnaldo Cruz-Malavé ("Repetition" 38-39) rightly praises Sánchez's pioneering achievement: "No Puerto Rican writer before Sánchez's *La guaracha* had been able to frontally address the media, to speak its language, to assume its mode, to position himself *within* it in order to critique it." Referring to the research of Aníbal González ("To Write"), Cruz-Malavé sets Sánchez's achievement against Puerto Rican intellectuals' previous hostility towards the mass media's role in the industrialization of the island. According to Cruz-Malavé, these intellectuals felt threatened by the sort of literacy they believed was promoted by American colonialism and which, in their view, threatened to divert the potential public of high culture into becoming the exclusive consumers of the mass media. While Cruz-Malavé's account of the perceived threats posed by massification is accurate, in my fourth chapter on the novels I go further to show how Sánchez maps a contemporary Antillean culture where high culture and commercial art forms such as the guaracha and bolero intersect in a popular culture that excludes neither.

There is a sense of inevitability in Sánchez's displacement, not replacement, of tradition, with parody being perhaps inescapably the form he has exercised in all his writing. Parody's dynamic reiteration of a recognizable and hitherto respected past is a necessary part of its irreverence. Sánchez's irreverence necessarily is always aware that the language, identity, and concepts used by writers are always borrowed, especially in a Caribbean defined by colonialism. I choose to underline this point by using my first chapter to show how Caribbean writing is never written on the clean slate of a pristine imagination but involves the dual task of acknowledgment and effacement represented by the palimpsest. I shall argue there that the protagonists of the play *Quíntuples* exploit the possibilities of-

---

[10] Flores ("Puerto Rican Literature;" "Qué"), Flores, Attinasi, and Pedro Pedraza Jr.

fered by their membership of a show business troupe to exhaust their stereotypical roles in performance. Thus performance itself, especially in the genre of drama, questions the very terms of inherited identity and opens the way to unforeseen socio-political and national personae exceeding those offered by colonial history or metropolitan intellectual traditions such as Freudianism.

Tracing the dramatic metaphor further, I argue that such a history and intellectual traditions, including my own reading as a European scholar, are merely scripts on which Caribbean "actors" and writers may improvise unpredictably. My readings aim to show how, through parody, Sánchez's work draws attention to the interests behind traditional representations of national identity. In this respect the characters of *Quíntuples* are representative of Sánchez's writing strategy as a whole; another reason this is the first text I discuss. Like them, the writer does not reject tradition in the idealistic search for ivory-tower originality but ironically embraces its clichés as the subject of his work. Accordingly, throughout this study I constantly return to the four interwoven areas of sexuality, gender, class, and race, where he both finds new possibilities in old forms and shows how ideology is the very stuff of identity. So much is this the case, that, in the second chapter, which discusses a popular film adaptation of selected texts by Sánchez, the very desire of Puerto Ricans for liberating identities is questioned through an examination of the nostalgic attraction of traditional nationalism. In the third chapter, on the theme of race in three short stories, the question first arises of the extent to which the search for new identities may perpetuate as well as revise colonial dependence. Such ambiguities contribute to the perceptible tension of Sánchez's work.

No Puerto Rican writer can escape the history of his own literature or vocation. Both the already mentioned Puerto Rican intellectual, Antonio S. Pedreira, and his previously revered compatriot, the writer René Marqués, not only loom large over the argument of this study but also over all the intellectual debate, artistic practice, and political discourse on the island. Throughout this book I have engaged with the ideas of these two figures since it is clear that an ironic refutation of their patriarchal, patrician, racist, hispanophile, and psychologically determinist view of national identity is central to Sánchez's literary project. It is obvious that Pedreira's and Marqués's views represent the historical experience of a particular Puerto Rican elite, while Sánchez's work makes a point of registering the historical experiences of lowly sectors of society. Therefore, I have considered it of paramount importance continually to inform my discussion with reference to the work of general, social and cultural historians of the island who have in recent years attempted to rewrite the elitist historiographical counterpart of the literary tradition Sánchez questions. The desire for renovation is well expressed by Arcadio Díaz Quiñones's recognition of the need for a renewal defined as "metodológica y conceptual, y deseosa de marcar también la ruptura con el discurso patriarcal y paternalista" [methodological and conceptual, and also anxious of signaling a break with patriarchal, paternalistic discourse] ("Recordando" 18). Díaz Quiñones' project parallels Sánchez's and takes the form of a long-term study of the Spanish Caribbean's intellectual history.[11]

Joining Díaz Quiñones as key figures in the renovation he wishes are Juan Flores, José Luis González, and A. G. Quintero Rivera. In opposition to Pedreira's and Marqués's belief that modernization has constituted an emasculating alienation of Puerto Rican society from its Hispanic roots, the contemporary intellectuals I have mentioned see their society not as an essence to be defended but as a dynamic complex of class relations. For them, as for Sánchez, by accelerating the decline of the semi-feudal class represented by Pedreira and Marqués, American colonization and its accompanying industrialization gave voice to the previously silenced majority (Díaz Quiñones, "Tomás Blanco" 25, 34, 72-76).

In my chapter on Sánchez's novel-length texts I read the ideological conflict represented by radically heterogeneous interpretations of Puerto Rican history in the light of Roberto Fernández Retamar's interpretation of broader Latin American debates. These concern the terms of civilization or barbarism that should be applied to the region's incipient modernity. Fernández Retamar's Marxist assertion of marginal Caribbean identities is in harmony with the working-class sympathies of the intellectual iconoclasts discussed above. Both the Cuban critic and progressive Puerto Rican intellectuals embrace the social changes brought on by modernization as a step forward towards civilization and away from the tyrannical barbarism of a pre-industrial age, whose representatives, on the other hand, view modernity as the degeneration of civilized tradition into barbarism. It is by perfectly exhibiting a vibrant im-

---

[11] "Recordando;" "The Hispanic-Caribbean;" *La memoria;* "Pedro Henríquez."

provisatory dynamic that non-elite culture is able in the work of progressive intellectuals to be viewed as a positive paradigm of nationality. One of Sánchez's achievements is to have enlarged this new perspective by placing unprecedented emphasis, as I have already observed, on sexuality, gender, and race as decisive, often conflictive, factors in new Puerto Rican identities.

At one point in the fifth chapter on Sánchez's essays, my discussion of the writer's occasional alignment with traditionally sexist attitudes is illuminated by the feminist studies undertaken by Irma Rivera Nieves (*El tema*), Carlos Rojas Osorio, and Aurea María Sotomayor. Within the context of nineteenth-century ideas, their research examines those of Eugenio María de Hostos concerning Puerto Rican nationality and the role of women. These scholars show how, while Hostos's ideas emerged from the liberal desire for social justice in Latin America, his recourse to essentialist gender models served as a reinforcement of traditional women's roles. Though Hostos championed the education and equal status of women he clearly delimited masculine and feminine spheres of action. According to these, education for women would prepare them as instruments of patriotism whose predominantly emotional natures would be channeled into instilling pride in a Puerto Rican identity in their children and wards. Meanwhile, men would strive for national emancipation through their actions in public life. Informed by this research, I have been better able to explain Sánchez's paradoxical stance as a progressive advocate of radical change in Puerto Rican society who occasionally supports his arguments by recourse to regressive attitudes towards women. Against this should be set Sánchez's ironical portrayal of passive feminine roles that allow the possibility of surreptitious agency. As will be seen, this is certainly the case with the female characters of *Quíntuples* and the short story "Aleluya negra" [Black Halleluiah].

Though Sánchez has significantly innovated Puerto Rican literary tradition I do not ignore Juan G. Gelpí's qualification of the idea of Sánchez's break with that tradition. For Gelpí (*Literatura* 41), Sánchez's work constitutes "ni ruptura violenta ni homenaje incondicional . . . más bien, una escritura híbrida" [neither a violent break nor an unconditional homage . . . rather a hybrid form of writing]. This statement is based on Gelpí's belief that while Sánchez parodies highbrow intellectual tradition he often has recourse to its critical authoritarianism. In a study of *La guaracha*,

Carlos J. Alonso challenges Gelpí's assertion in terms with which my study of *Quíntuples* fully agrees. Alonso studies what he defines as the "Dionysian" and "Apollonian" counterpoint that propels *La guaracha*'s structure. According to him, this counterpoint operates at the level of a narrative poised uncertainly between self-conscious "Apollonian" textuality and a disruptively "Dionysian" musicality. Such playful counterpoint preempts the absolutist authoritarianism to which Gelpí refers. In my discussion of *Quíntuples* I transpose Alonso's use of the classical terms "Dionysian" and "Apollonian," into the modern psychoanalytic register of Julia Kristeva's discussion of the "symbolic" and "semiotic" dimensions of literary language.

My first chapter, tracing Sánchez's controlled counterpoint in *Quíntuples*, forms a counterpoint itself with my chapter on the essays. There, I discuss the virtually unexplored area of the writer's intriguing lapses into an authoritarian orthodoxy that produces troubling ambivalences founded on the hybridity Gelpí identifies. This should be traced to Sánchez's precarious position between his origins as a working-class mulatto and his privileged location within a patrician national literature. Nevertheless, in spite of the fact that parody itself is reliant on established antecedents, not only can ambivalence, by definition, not be absolutist but I claim that the dangerous navigation of passionately contested nationalist traditions makes the increasing detachment of Sánchez's most recent work the result of a deep engagement with his culture and rescues it from cold flawlessness.

It is clear that any critical contextualization of a writer's portrayal of his own society should take some account of that writer's ideological situation in the very society he observes. However, there has been insufficient attention paid to the ambiguities resulting from a position of presumed critical objectivity sometimes adopted by Sánchez, and to his interested location in the society he discusses. This is in stark contrast, only partially explained by the greater critical detachment afforded by historical distance, to the increasing number of studies concerning the ideological hue of older Puerto Rican writers, particularly sacred monsters such as José de Diego, René Marqués, Antonio S. Pedreira, and Manuel Zeno Gandía. [12] In

---

[12] Barradas ("El machismo"), Díaz Quiñones ("Recordando"), Flores ("The Insular Vision;" "Refiguring"); Flores and Campos, Gelpí (*Literatura*), J. L. González ("El país;" "Literatura e identidad").

an effort to encourage research in an underdeveloped area of Sánchez studies, the longest chapter of this thesis deals with Sánchez's essays and the writer's role as a social commentator.[13] The complex treatment in the essays of questions relating to a colonial Caribbean culture illuminates Sánchez's maturity as a writer of narrative and drama. Indeed, the essays reveal Sánchez's very difficult struggle to reconcile his sincere political commitment to an independent future for Puerto Rico with his growing reflections on the inevitable cultural mediation involved in any act of social observation, as well as the compromised location of any social observer. With regard to this location Sánchez has come to discard the possibility of an Archimedean vantage point outside it. The overall delay between developments in his essay work and his precocious earlier non-essay work marks the paradoxical detachment with which, through the more openly mediated nature of fiction and drama, Sánchez has been able to reflect on the class and cultural compromises that shape his more ideologically determined work as an essayist.

The rhetorical context of the essayist's political stance cannot be avoided. I juxtapose the thundering declaration of Sánchez's national and class affiliations with the development of an original literary voice. At this point, Partha Chaterjee's thoughts on nationalist rhetoric, cited by Arcadio Díaz Quiñones ("The Hispanic Caribbean" 116), come to mind: "elitism becomes inescapable . . . because the act of cultural synthesis can, in fact, be performed only by a supremely cultivated and refined intellect. It is a project of national-cultural regeneration in which the intelligentsia leads and the nation follows." However, in the context of the Puerto Rican intelligentsia's traditionally exclusive authoritarianism, Sánchez's silences suggest that there remains much to be said on the question of a galvanizing Puerto Ricanness but that perhaps it is not appropriate for Puerto Rican intellectuals to take the authority to say it for granted.

---

[13] Carmen Vázquez Arce is exceptional amongst scholars for having devoted much attention to studying the historical and cultural context of Sánchez's essays, which she considers an integral part of his work as a writer. Sánchez's essays are the object of study of not only her unpublished 1984 thesis, "Salsa y control: el discurso expositivo de Luis Rafael Sánchez" [Salsa and Control: The Expositive Discourse of Luis Rafael Sánchez] but also a forthcoming book.

CHAPTER 1

"¡EL CUENTO NO ES EL CUENTO! ¡EL CUENTO ES QUIEN LO CUENTA!": TERMS OF IDENTITY IN *QUÍNTUPLES* (1985)

> I am part of Being to the degree that I go beyond it.
>
> (Fanon, *Black Skin* 229)

QUÍNTUPLES [Quintuplets] marks Luis Rafael Sánchez's most definitive disruption of the traditional form of Puerto Rican theater to date. This tradition emerged out of a reaction against the unsettling social changes brought about after the Second World War by Puerto Rico's precipitous, American sponsored industrialization, a process I shall describe in greater detail in the next chapter and to which I shall constantly refer throughout this book. The major playwrights who were formed during this period, figures such as René Marqués and Francisco Arriví, helped establish what has become a conventionally dark rendition of Puerto Rican life under American tutelage. Realist in their intention, these playwrights chose as their subject matter the sorrows of emigration and unemployment, as well as the upheavals that emerged out of the island's rapid transition from a rural to an urban society. The violence of the colonial subjection they portrayed also offered them the opportunity to criticize First World modernization through their intense characterizations of protagonists riven by the existential angst of city life. Notwithstanding its presentation as a realist rendering of an alienated society, the work of these playwrights often resorts to lyrical, ironical, or forcefully dramatic symbolism. The resulting sense of tragedy and pessimism or, more hopefully, transcendent spirituality tends, through sublimating catharsis, to undermine the authors' presumable aim to sufficiently provoke their audiences' patriotic outrage so that they will break the shackles of their colonization in a groundswell of independentist fervor.

Quíntuples certainly offers a startling contrast to the tradition I have just discussed. The play is the culmination of Sánchez's dramatic work in comedy, farce, parody, and anti-realism, work initiated with his *Cuento de Cucarachita Viudita* [Tale of Doñita Widowbug] (1959) and *La farsa del amor compradito* [The Farce of True Love's Bargain] (1960), and explores comic forms hitherto underdeveloped on the island for fear of trivializing the serious sociopolitical questions exercising the minds of intellectuals. By rejecting the fatalistic didacticism of his predecessors and most of his contemporaries, Sánchez has been able to avoid humanist sentimentalism by diverting the allegorical pull of Puerto Rican drama onto more unpredictable individual characters, whose everyday decisions he optimistically allows to have surprisingly profound political repercussions.[1]

Sánchez's two-act play presents a series of monologues delivered by the six members of the fictional Puerto Rican show business troupe, The Morrison Quintuplets. Their performance supposedly takes place in front of the delegates at a Conference on Family Affairs. Each of the quintuplets presents an improvised speech about his or her experiences of life as a member of the Morrison family. Being the master performer and head of the family, Papá Morrison is the last to speak, as a would-be representative of the consistent paternalism of Puerto Rican culture. Ultimately, the Morrison family comes to represent the Puerto Rican nation, in another manifestation of a metaphor central to Puerto Rican cultural discourse: the presentation of Puerto Rico as a family.[2]

Only two actors play all the Morrisons. On the back cover of the Ediciones del Norte edition of the play the reader is informed that each Morrison "vodevilescamente 'improvisa'" ["improvises" in vaudevillian manner]. In a stage direction (xv), the play itself is described as vaudeville, "una aventura de la imaginación" [an adventure of the imagination], and a parody of "una comedia de sus-

---

[1] To place *Quíntuples* within the trajectory of Sánchez's theatrical career and in relation to a specific theatrical tradition, I would recommend the following studies of his work and examinations of Puerto Rican drama: Barradas (*Para leer* 11-47), Colón Zayas (*El teatro*), Márquez, Meléndez ("El espejo"), Morales Faedo, J. E. González ("La literatura dramática"), Morfi, Perivolaris, Suárez Radillo, Waldman, Woodyard. On *Quíntuples* itself, see Huertas, Meléndez ("Lo uno"), Morell (*"Quíntuples"*).

[2] On paternalism in the context of Puerto Rican culture, see Gelpí (*Literatura*). On the use of family as a metaphor, see Gelpí (*Literatura* 1-60, 65, 84-85, 158).

penso" [a play of suspense]. These descriptions indicate the installation of established models, in the form of stereotypes, which are imaginatively purloined in the Morrisons' improvisations by means of the histrionic intensity of melodrama, the mock-heroism of parody, or the frivolously playful tone of the popular theatrical form, the "sainete" (xv).[3]

The foregrounding of performance and inauthenticity raises the following question: How can the Morrisons be said to represent Puerto Rican identity when its integrity is threatened by processes associated with hysteria and the abjection discussed by Julia Kristeva in her *Powers of Horror: An Essay on Abjection*? Such a problematic form of identity inevitably affects the reception of the play as political allegory, especially since sociopolitical contradictions are observed in terms of the portrayal of individual characters rather than discussed in generalized abstractions. In tracing the Morrisons' improvised appropriation a major paradox arises at the levels of both characterization and the play's very dynamic. On the one hand, there is highlighted a fluid process of open-ended change, in preference to established models. Meanwhile, on the other, change still relies on acknowledgment and identification according to those models. Keeping the above complexities in mind I have considered both Kristeva's "subject in process," or "open system" of identity, as well as her examination of abjection, of major importance in this study of the play's problematic search for a Puerto Rican identity.[4] Naturally, in adapting Kristeva's ideas–first applied to iconoclastic and bleak European writers of the past, such as Lautréamont, Mallarmé, Céline–to an accessible, contemporary Latin American writer of comic works differences of tone, perspective, and approach accompany distinct historico-cultural situations and coincide with separate modes of dependence and appropriation.

When reflecting on the possibility of Caribbean identity, the problems of any recourse to psychoanalysis as a privileged form of analysis are particularly acute. Being a metropolitan science, psychoanalysis universalizes men's and women's "problems" according to psychic structures that transcend as well as conveniently undervalue the geographical and political locations of individuality. The

---

[3] As a popular Hispanic theatrical form the *sainete*, like vaudeville, relies on satire and the parody of society's mores.

[4] On the "subject in process," see Kristeva (*Revolution* ix, 22, 58, 233). On her "open system" of identity, see Lechte (72, 101, 114, 139, 183-84).

politico-economic space of Caribbean individualities might be subsumed by authoritarian psychoanalytic truths that would speak for
all men and preempt the threat of deviant identities through the order of science. However, if psychoanalysis is at best only tentatively
a science, in the Caribbean it joins other spaces of knowledge, such
as History, Tradition, and Politics, whose orderly textuality dis-
solves into fluidity when these become scripts against which
Caribbeans may readily improvise.[5] This is certainly the case with
the Morrisons, whose performances undermine the detailed and
lengthy stage directions provided by Sánchez (xiii-xiv, 1) and af-
fording him the opportunity ironically to assume the traditional authoritarianism of European science and the paternalism expected of
Puerto Rican intellectuals; a position that, as a Puerto Rican intellectual himself, he is often obliged to assume and which I shall examine extensively in my chapter on his essays. In *Quíntuples*, the
author's directions dictatorially delimit the performers' freedom to
stray from his instructions, a challenge which, as will be demonstrated, no self-respecting actor or Puerto Rican can fail to accept.

1. HYSTERIA

    Freudian psychoanalysis has identified hysteria as a condition
where predominantly female subjects pathologically struggle and
unconsciously reject the feminine identities assigned to them by patriarchal cultures. Jacques Lacan ("Bisexualité") has subsequently
highlighted hysteria as the inevitable abnormality inherent in the attempt to reduce both women and men to gendered identities.
These repeatedly fracture under the pressure of inevitably having to
reenact the Oedipal crisis on the rickety stage of the primary Oedipal structure: language (Lacan, *Encore*).
    Hysteria, in its popular or stricter psychoanalytical senses, char-
acterizes the tone and all the performances in *Quíntuples* and
reaches a crescendo with Papá Morrison's improvisation, "un
crescendo formidable, tan histérico como la música de Wagner" [a
formidable crescendo, as hysterical as the music of Wagner] (71).

---

    [5] In one of the most advanced discussions of Caribbean culture to date, Antonio
Benítez Rojo identifies such a "polyrhythmic" form of improvisation as the defining
process that unites the region's seemingly irreconcilable cultural diversity.

Papá's hysteria is the culmination of that of all the Morrisons, also perhaps the expression of a displaced, distorted, and ill-represented identity. The frustrations and dangers of a hysterical identity may be illustrated by examining Dafne's and Bianca's performances, where Dafne takes the valiant risk of being overtaken by hysteria for the sake of her insubordinate pose as a sex symbol, while Bianca presents a classic case of the hysteric.

The first Morrison to perform is Dafne Morrison. Film stars from Catherine Deneuve to María Félix, are cited in describing her (1). Outdoing them all, Dafne is a "cruce mejoradísimo" [ultra-improved cross] (1) of these sex symbols. The audience is forewarned that an ironic tone is being established when role models with a camp appeal and gay following are cited, such as Bette Midler (1). Campness is reinforced by a reference to the queenly image of Diana Ross (1). Thus, a precedent is set for Sánchez's characters to create their personae by poaching from an international repertoire of popular icons incorporated into Puerto Rican culture. The Morrisons' poaching involves a camp revision of these icons.

Dafne wears the alluring red dress of the scarlet woman, the *femme fatale*, the torch singer and the Latin bombshell in the style of Iris Chacón, the outrageous Puerto Rican singer, dancer, and television superstar known as *La Vedette* and, in an example of Puerto Rican *Spanglish*, *El volcano puertorriqueño*. Dafne's name is that of a flower with no true petals but whose sepals resemble petals; the implication being that all identity is a matter of the performance and projection of credible, if illusory, images. Dafne is a self-creation who cannot be fixed to an essence. Artifice nullifies the importance of her unadorned physical appearance: "Si Dafne Morrison no fuera tan bella–más bella que nadie–no importaría demasiado. Porque la menor imperfección física habría sido, astutamente, combatida por los esplendores del maquillaje que luce" [if Dafne Morrison were not so beautiful–more beautiful than anybody–it would not matter too much. Because the slightest physical flaw would have been cunningly combated by the splendors of the make-up she displays] (2).

Dafne's performance implies a masquerade, whose rejection of the notion of an essential femininity involves the assumption of a mask of femininity (Apter; Doane 25-26). Indeed, Dafne's smile is described as "teatro inolvidable" [unforgettable theater] (2), while she is "falsamente adorable" [falsely adorable] (9). Furthermore, after comparison of her with a whole host of famous actresses and singers, her flirtation with the audience is described as follows (2):

> Dafne Morrison sonríe, uno por uno, a los trescientos espectadores o congresistas. Después, con los manierismos peculiares de las estrellas de cine mudo y las bailarinas flamencas, se vuelve coqueta, juguetona, provocadora.

> [Dafne Morrison smiles, one by one, to the three-hundred spectators or delegates. Afterwards, with the mannerisms peculiar to a silent movie star or a flamenco dancer, she becomes flirtatious, playful, provocative.]

On the other hand, the "histeria terminal" [terminal hysteria] (2) of Dafne's performance is linked to her anxious desire for the definitive image, openly asserted by her statement that "¡Soy aspirante a mito!" [I aspire to myth] (5). By becoming a myth, she would attain a privileged position in relation to semiotic systems, for mythology is a privileged symbolic structure of shared beliefs which defines cultures and peoples. If this is so, then Dafne may aspire to the stability of myth with the intention of counteracting the potentially destabilizing nature of masquerade. Masquerade may threaten female identity because it obliges the masquerading woman to alternate between the active and passive positions of spectator (of her own image) and spectacle (the fetishized female).

Masquerade, in the form of Dafne's improvisation, disrupts fixed positions of gender. As Dafne disingenuously declares, "la improvisación corre el peligro de la dispersión" [improvisation runs the risk of dispersion] (6). The dispersion to which she refers may equate with the dissolution of a fixed subject-object dichotomy, according to which woman, as the fetishized female body or film image, is subjected to the voyeurism of the masculine spectator. Through her improvised masquerade, Dafne is able to project herself as a deliberate fetish pre-viewed by herself as an empowered spectator, though she does so only through a reversal not a remodeling of the semiotic systems on which she depends.

The masquerader's vacillation between the supposedly masculine and feminine positions of spectator and spectacle may be compared to the hysteric's dilemma. The hysteric appears unable to be contained by a totalized concept of gender (Ragland-Sullivan,

"Hysteria"). It is true that Dafne differs from the hysteric in one important respect: hers is the knowing, controlled vacillation of the masquerader. This allows her the confidence to refer to herself as "loca de atarme" [raving mad] (10). Still, the phrase "la improvisación corre el peligro de la dispersión" also refers to the risk the masquerader may run. She treads a fine line between spectacle and spectator, dependence on her masculine audience and autonomy. Firstly, there is the risk of losing control and becoming indistinguishable from the passive object, the fetishized female. Indeed, the success of masquerade depends on the reinforcement of fetishized femininity through the latter's projection. And, by riding the blurred boundary between fetishism and masquerade, the masquerader's assumed proximity to hysteria constantly threatens her with dispersion or disappearance as a subject (Ragland-Sullivan, "Hysteria"). For the masquerader's risk of fragmentation is implicit in any simultaneous occupation of multiple positions in relation to systems of knowledge and sexuality. Bianca Morrison's subsequent performance (31-41) serves to illustrate the potential dangers of hysterical fragmentation.

Bianca personifies the inappropriateness of gendered identity. From the outset of her improvisation, she is sexually ambiguous, "quisquillosamente femenina a través de su vestimenta masculina" [fussily feminine under her masculine attire] (31). Like the hysterics Breuer and Freud treated, she is unable to reconcile her experience as a woman with the pre-established cultural determinism of sexual roles. Like Freud's Dora, Bianca closely identifies with masculinity.[6] But she is denied access to the privileges of masculinity by the gender culturally assigned to her (Ragland-Sullivan, "Dora"). Bianca's desire for masculinity is manifested through her wearing of a man's suit and her masculinization. Because dynamic, coherent communication through language is associated with a masculine position in language she steps into her role power-dressed as a man. In her masculine guise, "dueña aparente de todas las situaciones . . . . se dirige exactamente al facistol" [apparent mistress of all situations . . . . she heads straight for the lectern] (31). She also adopts a manner of speaking that is "de oración corta, algo tajante" [terse in its expression, somewhat forceful] (32), identified with the masculine-gen-

---

[6] On Breuer's and Freud's work and on Freud's subsequent individual work in the area of hysteria, see Freud & Breuer, and Freud ("Fragment").

dered strong, silent type, the tough guy. This masculinized position, however, also cannot contain her though she desperately clings to it in "un impulso artificial y hasta peligroso" [a man-made, somewhat unstable impulse] (35). Her failure is evidenced by attacks of hysteria, the breakdown of masculine self-composure. What cannot be communicated in language is expressed in uncontrollable corporeal symptoms–anxiety, addiction, fits–and loss of linguistic control (Freudian slips).

Bianca's powerlessness arises from the elusive nature of her models. Lacking Dafne's detachment, she is unable to take possession of her prototypes. Sliding between the multiplicity of the models assigned to her (32)–Bianca Jagger, Shakespeare's two Bianca's– her vertigo does not allow her a sufficiently stable basis for appropriation. Instead, she remains dependent, a mirror in which others are reflected. As a non-person, she is thus constantly eclipsed, a fact proved by the vehemence of her denial: "no me llamo Dafne" [my name is not Dafne] (33).

Bianca's very name suggests the whiteness of an empty, unwritten page. Unable to fill the page of identity, she remains unexpressed, without a language of her own. Consequently, polylingualism, the recourse to more than one language, is manifested in the use of the Italian Bianca instead of the Spanish Blanca (32, 35). The multiplicity of polylingualism may be compared to the vacillating sexuality of the psychoanalytically defined hysteric. [7] Moreover, Bianca's polylingualism may be translated into the conflictive, multicultural history of Puerto Rico, which, for the most part, is not directly alluded to in Quíntuples. Exceptionally, the conflictive nature of this history is touched upon by Bianca, in an undisguised political reference to the shooting, in 1954, of US congressmen by Puerto Rican nationalists (36) (Scarano 778-79).

Initially alienated from her assigned gender, Bianca dangerously overidentifies with masculinity and pays the price for entrusting herself to totalizing models. Meanwhile, Dafne detaches herself from the torment of inappropriate models of femininity by manipulating iconic representations of women in a masquerade. Ultimately

---

[7] Hysterical polylingualism was recorded in the case of Anna O. Anna O's polylingualism revealed itself as an inability to understand or communicate in her native German and a tendency to speak in one or more foreign tongues, in sequence or, at times of extreme anxiety, in an unintelligible mixture (Freud & Breuer 25).

however, the complexities of Dafne's course of action are hard to bear. Dafne creatively appropriates established female stereotypes through her made-to-measure masquerade. But the dangers of masquerade oblige her to seek the stability of enduring myth. Ironically, enduring myths are nowhere to be found. Instead, there is myth as the fetish of mass culture. Film stars embody this type of myth. Far from enduring they are shown to be eminently recyclable commodities.

Bianca's symptoms form part of a pathology revealed by all the Morrisons' excessive, even freakish, behavior in performance. The extreme nature of the Morrisons' performance signals constant and transcendental struggle for constantly disputed identities subject to the scrutiny of authority, represented by what I presume to be a specialist audience of experts at the "Congreso de Asuntos de la Familia" [Conference on Family Affairs] (xiv). [8] For Puerto Rico, at a border between the First and Third Worlds, authority is constantly disputed at the level of language and culture, which are always implicated in the economic and political power relations that determine Puerto Rico's dependence in relation to an authority that has never wholly been its own.

The constant hysteria of the play may point to the failure of established discourses unable to contain or sustain specific Puerto Rican men and women who struggle with their identities in both the spheres of gender and nationality. In psychoanalytic terms, hysteria may result from the irresolution of the Oedipal phase. In specific cultural terms, this irresolution may be translated into the instability of Puerto Rico's position between two languages, several cultures

---

[8] All the Morrisons adopt names other than their given ones (32). The baptism of the three male Morrisons as Ifigenio evidences the instability of their identity, in an inversion of the hysterical bisexuality I have traced in female hysterics. The fore-grounded theatricality of *Quíntuples*, suggests that the male characters have been named after the tragic Greek heroine Iphigenia: "Tres distintas personas y un solo nombre verdadero: Ifigenio. No es cómico. Es trágico" [Three different people and only one real name between them: Ifigenio. This is not comic. It is tragic] (32). The bisexual transformation of a woman's name into a man's makes evident the weakness of rigid gender positions and undermines the male Morrisons' masculinity.

The adoption of new names implies liberating reinvention. In fact, this reinvention involves dependence since it constitutes an improvisation within a theatrical tradition (classical Greek theatre). Finally, the game of improvisation is a serious one ("no es cómico. Es trágico") since it challenges identities established as a result of conflict within a network of economic, social, political, and cultural contexts.

and cultural strata, the First and the Third Worlds.[9] Paradoxically, in addition to being a symptom of displacement hysteria translates into a possible condition of survival. As well as indicating unease and disorientation hysteria provides the margin with a means of response and appropriation. As an unsettling dissipation, it may function in terms of Paul Julian Smith's exhaustive undoing by overdoing (*Laws* 26), or even as a precondition of progress, since it may be perceived as a dissatisfaction with current delimitations.

Such a view seems to be supported by the important role played by the first psychoanalytically defined hysterics in furthering social causes such as feminism, unionism, and psychoanalysis itself (Appignanesi & Forrester). Nevertheless, hysteria may function positively only as a precondition for transition into a more integrated social role, not as an end in itself. For instance, in Bianca's case confinement to her role as a suitable case for treatment by an audience of experts would reinforce her marginalization. If such were the case, Bianca would be imprisoned by her "histérica pasión" [hysterical passion] (41). But this is not the case. As an intense performer, she compels, providing "una porfiada liberación" [a tenacious liberation] (41) through the pleasure of entertainment. This provides the means to proceed beyond the neuroses of individual characters, who merely provide ephemeral roles for the performer.

2. ABJECTION

Paralleling hysteria, abjection provides another manifestation of the disintegration of unsatisfactory identities. Two of the Morrisons, Baby and Carlota, display symptoms that compare to Kristevan abjection.

According to Kristeva (*Powers* 12-13), the basis of abjection can be traced to a point just prior to the resolution of the Oedipus Complex and to the child's separation from the pre-Oedipal mother. This intermediate stage supposedly anticipates the establishment of the delimited speaking subject and involves the physical expulsion of defiled body products preceding the establishment of a

---

[9] For the contextualization, in Puerto Rican cultural discourse, of hysteria as one manifestation of the constant theme of colonial dependence as disease, see Gelpí (*Literatura*, esp. 54-55).

clean body (inside) in opposition to a defiled outside (69-72). The process of expulsion and delimitation is held to anticipate, as its physical equivalent, the rejection in the Oedipal phase of the mother in favor of the father, whose law is assumed to govern family, social, and cultural being (73-75).

Abject nausea emerges from the failure definitively to complete the process of expulsion and separation and is evidenced by the instability of inside and outside boundaries, resulting in the disruption of identity (13-15). Consequently, certain corporeal elements are considered disorderly and disruptive since they are perceived as occupying an ambiguous space both inside and outside and so horrifyingly blur the subject's boundaries. The physical elements referred to may all be associated with menstrual blood and bodily waste (e.g. cut hair, nail parings, sweat). By being products of bodily functions these elements are manifestations of nature, the threatening counterpart of culture. As such, they are evidence of the natural cycle of birth and death which may be associated with a fecund mother who inspires dread through the incest she may provoke (69-89).

In many cultures these elements have been shown to be subject to ritual acts of cleansing aimed at purifying the body, reinforcing the boundaries between the body and its polluting outside (Douglas), as well as preventing a regressive dissolution of identity. According to the same terms, disease also threatens boundaries by involving the contamination of a clean body by an outside agent that becomes part of that body (Kristeva, *Powers* 93, 101-03, 127). Meanwhile, in all cultures, the corpse, as ambiguous object both human and non-human, impure because of its transformation into rotting material, hence excrement, is subject to ritual funerary acts. These are aimed at clearly marking the boundaries of life and death and preventing the contamination of the living by the dead (108-10).

The dissolution of self implied by abjection and its corporeal symptoms relates to Baby's mute shock and anger when his brother, Mandrake Morrison, refers to Baby's soiling himself as a child (Sánchez, *Quíntuples* 24). Further abject symptoms are Baby's copious sweating (24-25), and obsessive shaving (19). Baby seems to occupy a liminal space at the threshold of identity, further confirmed by his speaking to himself (19-20). With one foot in the symbolic arena of language, he is able to speak, but has not fully taken up a clear position in relation to dialogic relationships. Baby speaks, but not as an integrated subject to equals. He speaks to himself and when he does address the audience he is full of uncertainty (20, 25, 29).

Already marked as an immature subject by his name, Baby is similarly made conspicuous by his weak eyesight and thick glasses (19). The clean detachment of the spectator from the object of his gaze may be viewed as a consequent manifestation of the dialogic distinction between self and other arising from a resolution of the Oedipal phase and the entry into language. On the other hand, Baby's visual inadequacy merely suggests another manifestation of his failure to achieve the prerequisite detachment of the culturally integrated subject/viewer.

In contrast to Dafne's skillful masquerade and manipulation of language, Baby is a failed postmodernist. He is unable to achieve detachment and is therefore "tierno y cursi" [mushy and sentimental] (23) when he takes Papá Morrison's clichés of utopian domestic bliss at face value. Baby is a slave to these clichés rather than able to invest them with new meaning and intent by distancing himself sufficiently to employ strategies such as parody, irony, or camp. By these means he would have been able to remake to his own requirements his terms of reference and the language that defines him, reinvent his family history and identity. The transgressive dissipation of Baby's infantile tantrums temporarily enables him to assert himself (24), perhaps the only way he is able to do so. Subsequently, however, Baby's standing as a subject is always threatened and undermined since he is generally only able to conform to rather than rework the given terms of his existence.

Baby's liminality as an abject, tenuously acculturated subject may be signaled by several elements suggesting blurred boundaries. These elements are: 1) Baby's grey suit (19). Grey is a neutral color between black and white. [10] 2) Baby's mixed emotions: "Se ríe hacia dentro–como si la risa lo entretuviera a la par que lo avergonzara" [He laughs inwardly–as if laughter both amused and embarrassed him] (p. 21). 3) Baby's inward laughter in the same scene. All of these indications point to Baby's characterization as a borderline case. If this is so, then the empty wire cage he carries symbolizes his

---

[10] Grey also predominates as the key colour in the attire of the similarly liminal character, Carlota (55-56).

haunting and marginalized confinement by a position in language and culture he cannot occupy. Similarly, Carlota Morrison's improvisation constitutes a further exploration of pathological liminality.

While Baby is characterized as a wimp, Carlota is defined according to the stereotypes of the good wife, who is overly solicitous towards her husband, and the responsible teacher; in short, by her "ordinariez decente" [decent mediocrity] (55). As a woman, Carlota is not fully integrated or represented in the social sphere determining her social roles and her "compromisos profesionales" [professional commitments] (56). As a caricature of the virtuous wife she perhaps attempts to compensate for her alienation from the traditionally male-dominated sphere of public life through a reinforcement of the woman's traditional privilege in the domestic arena. Her complex displacement underscores the often conflicting nature of individual, sexual, social, and national interests. By stating that "soy maestra de español aunque no ejerzo" [I am a teacher of Spanish even though I don't practice] (57) Carlota expresses her inability to teach a language that cannot represent her socially as a woman, even though, as a Puerto Rican, she may have struggled, as many have, to establish Spanish as her national language. [11]

Uncomfortable in the social domain mediated by language, Carlota finds her place in society through illness and a usurpation of identity undertaken from its unsettling margin. The inscription of her supposed illnesses into language is made possible by the mediation of a tradition of medical discourse, specifically that of symptom reading (semiology/σημειολογία), dating back to the medical practice of ancient Greece. By means of her status as a patient Carlota, like Bianca, enters language and, though she is unable to function in society as a fully integrated subject ("aunque no ejerzo"), as the object of medical practice she finds a voice through the hypochondriac performance of or allusion to significant symptoms. That we are dealing with a problematic coming into being, through

---

[11] Between 1902 and 1949, the U.S. colonial government imposed English as the language of instruction in education establishments on the island, an unpopular and ineffectual measure which was resisted by students and teachers, who staged strikes and protests. Finally, in 1949, under Muñoz Marín's incumbency as Governor legislation was introduced to reestablish Spanish as the language of instruction in schools, anticipating the PPD's 1991 legislation recognizing Spanish as the official language of Puerto Rico.

a mediating discourse, is evidenced by the fact that Carlota's symptoms seem to have no basis in actual illness. Later, Papá refers to "enfermedades que los médicos no descubrían" [illnesses that the doctors failed to discover] (69). With no basis in an actual pathology, Carlota's symptoms are conjured into significant language by a hypochondriac well read in mass-circulation health publications. As such, she employs the signifiers of an established popular discourse to reestablish her authority as a "maestra que va a dictar cátedra" [teacher who is going to deliver a lecture] (56). Nevertheless, the fact that Carlota is forced to such extreme measures implies torment as well as legitimation. She is obliged to suffer her manufactured ailments as if they were real, "enfermedades . . . verdaderamente suyas porque las padece" [illnesses . . . truly hers because she suffers them] (56). Carlota's ailments constitute the symptoms of her painful marginalization as a woman.

By occupying a liminal position in relation to identity Carlota is exceedingly vulnerable to abjection, which in her case takes four main forms. Food and drink, disease, death, and smells disrupt the boundary separating the subject's inside and outside. A preoccupation with all four forms surfaces in Carlota's phobic attitude to food, her hypochondria, morbidity, and sensitivity to what she perceives as offensive smells. If narcissism indicates a desire for the detachment and well defined ego of identity, then Carlota is constantly threatened. However, her constant articulation of the illnesses that threaten to assail her preempt their threat. Hence, the statement "Qué bien estás Carlota Morrison" [How well you look Carlota Morrison] (49) is resented by her since the integrity of a healthy woman suggests the body's potential vulnerability. Ultimately, a compliment makes Carlota feel "herida en su amor propio" [wounded in her self-esteem] (49).

In a negative example of identity's prerequisite expulsion of disorderly agents Carlota unsuccessfully disavows the body and its needs. Her desire for a detached, well defined identity as a woman and a Puerto Rican partly takes the form of a phobia in relation to food (59) and drink (57), both possible agents of abjection (Kristeva, *Powers* 75-77, 93, 95-99, 119). As oral objects, food and drink suggest abjection because they highlight the border between the natural and cultural. The mouth's ingestion of nourishment is the natural counterpart of its production of speech, as well as pointing back to the infant's breast-feeding and thus threatening a regression from the adult use of language, by means of which s/he functions as a socially integrated subject. May the height of abjection not be to talk with one's mouth full of food? In any case, Carlota's disavowal can never be successful, however strict her diet. The body's inevitable demands for food and drink exacerbate what has become Carlota's obsession.

Disease, associated with encroaching waste and decay, provokes Carlota's hypochondria by representing the threat of being engulfed and made impure by infection from an autonomous outside agent: "los microbios nos asedian" (56). Meanwhile, Kristeva's assertion (*Powers* 3-4) that death is the ultimate form of abjection is confirmed by Carlota's awareness of the imminence of death: "total, dentro de cien años todos seremos calvos, todos seremos cadáveres indiferenciados" [in short, within a hundred years all that will remain of us will be our skulls, our indistinguishable corpses] (56).

Carlota feels similarly endangered by smells that threaten to engulf her. The blurring of the boundary between clean and impure increases due to the fact that the smell that offends Carlota is cologne. The wearing of perfume is usually a sign of civilized, clean living. Here, perfume offends through a typically abject process. Beneath its guise as an accessory of social(izing) sophistication lies the threat of the irrepressibly impure. And, it is impurity which perfume seeks to suppress, the bodily processes from which body odor results. It is because of this very struggle to stave off imminent corruption that Carlota exclaims: "¡Qué perfume más polémico!" [What a questionable scent!] (57).

In addition to the already mentioned agents of abjection should be added pregnancy, as a state that imitates abjection's disruption of borders. Elizabeth Grosz (95) suggests that, in pregnancy, the mother surrenders her autonomy to bodily processes that supersede conscious control; pregnancy "'happens to' women." Therefore, as mothers, women's fragile identity within language and culture is undermined in favor of their status as natural, or "hinge between nature and culture" (96). Their weakening as subjects is reinforced by the blurring of the boundary separating inside and outside as a result of the confusion brought about by the pregnant woman's carrying of a baby which is of but also separate from her and by the intimate maternal nurturance of the infant. However, as well as possibly threatening her integrity, pregnancy also empowers Carlota. By asserting a feminine consciousness centered in the female body and tenuously bound to ego boundaries, Carlota is able to undermine the boundaries between subject and object. At the same time, by holding fast to her social role as mother, the assurance of the community's future, Carlota's cultural role is guaranteed. By negotiating the territory between nature and culture Carlota reshapes the mold of identity and gains in stature. This is achieved by transforming her threatening bodily status as a mother into a social welfare concern for the coordinated network of helpers she enlists (64) from the audience, two members of which climb onto the stage to assist her, under her instructions, when she suddenly goes into labor; such enlistment disrupting established and gendered dialogic relationships through the collapse of the traditional distance between actor and audience. [12] This distance has already been minimized by the role assigned to the audience as participants of the Conference (xiii) and the previous Morrisons' direct addresses to that audience "en diálogos para una voz" [in dialogues for one voice] (xiv).

Carlota's empowerment does not limit itself to her new found authority as a character: "la firmeza de una autoritaria y firme maestra de español" [the mastery of an authoritarian and masterful teacher of Spanish] (58). The fact that she is enabled to issue confident orders which are obeyed by the audience is proof of her effectiveness as a performer. Carlota reaches her apotheosis with a consummate recital of poetry, perfectly synchronized with her exit in full labor (65). Similarly and even more radically, though Baby's (assumed) character is pitiful his ill-executed delivery of a purportedly humorous anecdote concerning a Russian ballerina (21) and his abject fantasies concerning his feline friend Gallo Pelón, "el gato más perro que existe" [the most dogged cat in existence] (27), provide (perhaps perverse) pleasure, through which performance itself eclipses the greyness of theory and the clinical depiction of pathological individuals.

3. ACKNOWLEDGMENT

By way of "diálogos para una voz" the Morrisons depend on their audience for acknowledgment of their identities by projecting approved stereotypes, while aspiring to autonomy through appro-

---

[12] On the actor-audience relationship in Sánchez's theatre, see Morales Faedo.

priative strategies. Such conflictive tension, manifested by the specular form of the Morrisons' relationship with the audience, is central to the play's fascination. As Dafne states, the Morrisons' improvisations "corre[n] el peligro de la dispersión" since they vacillate
precariously between the privileged center stage of the improvising
performer and dispersion as a consequence of constantly desiring
the approval of others, intense desire of which is marked by the
relentlessly operatic tone of the Morrisons' performances, their
"irreprimible urgencia" [irrepressible urgency] (xv). At the same
time, the intersubjectivity of such desire is indicated by its being
"cercano a la danza frenética" [close to frenetic dancing] (xv). The
quotation used in the title of this chapter highlights the intimate coexistence of the conflictive processes at work in the Morrisons'
performances, underscoring the privilege of liberating innovation,
dependence on the "cuento" [story], or identity, dictated to the
subject, and the value invested in the "cuento" by the Morrisons. A
reconciliation of the tension produced is provided by moments of
performative pleasure. Mandrake Morrison manfully illustrates and
navigates the limitations and pitfalls of the specular relationship of
the Quintuplets with their audience.

The exuberant assurance of Mandrake's improvisation as "un
hombre irremediablemente bello" [an incurably handsome man]
(43) is rooted in his conviction concerning the artificiality and inauthentic nature of culture. The cultural commodities on which Mandrake models his improvisation are, like Dafne's, firstly those of
mass culture and show business, in particular cinema, and, secondly, foreign. His role models are Cinecittà's Steve Reeves (43) and
"los grandes gesticuladores del cine italiano" [the great gesticula-
tors of Italian cinema] (44). Similarly his gestures are those of "el
mejor estilo charro del cine mejicano" [the best *charro* style of Mexican cinema] (50).[13] Mandrake is enabled to make these stereotypical models his own by the specificity of the Puerto Rican context in
which his performance takes place. Puerto Ricanization is in fact a
major process of all the Morrisons' performances and is inherent in
their accents, turns of phrase, and idiomatic usages; elements more
pronounced when viewing the play than when reading it. In Mandrake's performance specificity is asserted through the translation
of foreign role models, such as Vittorio Gassman, into the Puerto

---

[13] The *charro* is a stereotypically Mexican cowboy figure.

Rican dandy Mandrake represents (43-44). Furthermore, the "des-garrada intensidad que proponen los seis personajes" [unrestrained intensity projected by the six characters] and the "wagnerización de las anécdotas" [the Wagnerization of their anecdotes] (xiii) permit Mandrake to distance himself from the stereotypes that define him through exaggeration and caricature.

A cinematic context also enables Mandrake's reconstruction of the Biblical story of the Flood in a narrative that invokes Fellini (47), is recounted in "una larga secuencia que los asistentes al Congreso de Asuntos de la Familia deben cinematizar" [a long sequence that the delegates to the Conference on Family Affairs have to imagine as cinema] (47), and is reduced to a screenplay for a film similar to another script of the "final del mundo" [end of the world] (48) already sold to American television. Thus, the screenplay of the story of the Flood becomes a negotiable commodity exchanged within a network of economic, ideological, political, and cultural relations. It is implied that the myths at the center of civilizations are profitable super-productions serving the interests of Catholicism and Capitalism.

To accept that culture is based on the exchange of manufactured commodities rather than on eternal truths is to accept that the rights to these commodities may be negotiated, purchased, or pirated. It is to this entitlement that Mandrake appeals when he affirms that "¡El cuento no es el cuento! ¡El cuento es quien lo cuenta!" [The story is not the story itself! The story is in the telling!] (50, 53), asserting his faith in the power of the individual performance to resituate, renew, and expropriate pre-established cultural products. At the same time, Mandrake's desire to participate as an insider in his society's cultural discourse, or "cuento" is underscored by the exclamatory ("¡!") tone of his assertion. Such desire is determined by his stated sense of social dependence in the lines: "es prestada mi belleza irremediable. No sé si préstamo es la palabra que me vale" [my incurable handsomeness is on loan. I don't know if the very speech that serves me is also a loan] (52). Mandrake alludes to the economic, political, and ideological dimensions of creative survival in society by suggesting that the materials (language, persona) of his performance are "lent" to him by the culture in whose processes he participates as a performer who interacts with other members (the audience) of a common public space. In return for the privilege accorded him Mandrake is obliged to abide by his society's laws.

Mandrake tells the audience that the props for his improvisation are loaned to him by a Puerto Rican street tramp, "El Diablo," and that in exchange for these he has made a Faustian pact with the tramp. Mandrake's association with El Diablo is made possible by the potentially transgressive nature of improvisation, which brings him close to the outcast status of the "Devil." His uneasy relationship with El Diablo is revealed by his fear ("palidece" [he turns pale]) of ominous knocks at the door (53). His fear is simultaneously that of meeting again and being associated with El Diablo, the outsider, and of punishment at the hands of some sort of totalitarian police acting on behalf of his host society. It is on this society, represented by the authority of the conference's specialist audience, that Mandrake depends for the liberty that allows his improvisation. Survival as a relatively free individual depends on a careful juggling of the restrictions placed on the individual by his host society. Since Mandrake is a consummate cultural acrobat, cunningly balancing between dependence and innovation, he is finally able to laugh off any restrictions: "Falsamente asustado huye, se persigna. Después, sonríe, carcajea" [Faking terror he flees, crosses himself. Afterwards, he smiles, roars with laughter] (53). At the same time, the audience is given licence to laugh with him since their identification with his performance does not involve transgression but only a tantalizing dipping of their toe into the fanciful and tenuously reflective waters of improvisation. By adhering to society's restrictions Mandrake acknowledges that society potentially threatens to call back the loan of his culturally dependent persona and cancel the freedom of speech he exercises. Well aware that his speech can never be wholly his own but is hired out under social contract Mandrake highlights his contingent position as a speaking subject and performer.

Mandrake's brilliant negotiation of his dependence makes possible his renaming as "Mandrake el Mago" [Mandrake the Magician], a show business conjurer of "maña graciosa de mago"[amusing magical resourcefulness] (51) and "alevosía" [deceit] (44), the latter quality consisting in his refurbishment of what he depends on through an exhaustive adherence and dedicated (all too dedicated) mimicry. He cannot be faulted or punished as a transgressor since imitative performance allows him and his audience an alibi, another approved place: the legitimate space of his stereotypical models. Imitation simultaneously wins him acknowledgment through the recognition of established stereotypes as well as diverting attention and blame from the renewable area of liberatingly unlegislated possibilities he opens up through extravagant entertainment.

In terms of Puerto Rico's uneasy relationship with the United States, the Morrisons' specular relationship with their audience implies nationalism's simultaneous impulses towards both autonomy and legitimation. The latter is sought by appeal to the privileged power from which the dependency demands acknowledgment and against which the dependency struggles. In fact, the dependency, in struggling for autonomy or independence seeks recognition of the self it seeks to govern. The Morrisons' disparate struggle for identity in relation to a relatively stable other (their audience) implies Puerto Rico's struggle to achieve coherent nationhood in relation to other established nations, especially the United States.

4. AFFILIATION

For Dafne he is an idealized role model, for Baby an impossible act to follow, for Bianca a tyrannical patriarch, for Mandrake a male rival to be outdone, for Carlota a dependable parent in whom one confides, and for all a standard against which to be judged.[14] Papá Morisson not only hovers as a constant presence in all his children's recollections but also provides an ironic model for the quintuplets' cultural empowerment, founded on their affiliation to him.

---

[14] DAFNE. Un gran tipo Papá Morrison, mundanal, liviano, fiestea, mujerea, a pesar de su impedimento fiestea y mujerea, lleva las finanzas de los Quíntuples Morrison, escribe los libretos que habitualmente representamos. [Papá Morrison is a great character, a man of the world, a swinger, he parties, womanizes, indeed he parties and womanizes in spite of his handicap, he manages the Morrison Quintuplets finances, and writes the scripts we routinely perform] (p. 6).

BABY. Papá fue el embelequero [Papá was the fraudster] (p. 23).

BIANCA. Papá Morrison dijo el que no trabaja no come [Papá Morrison said that whoever doesn't work doesn't eat] (pp. 37-38).

MANDRAKE. Ifigenio Dos está prohibido sustantivarme. Un desliz de Papá Morisson que hace rato perdoné. [It is forbidden to use the name Ifigenio Two when referring to me. One of Papá Morrison's slips I excused some while ago] (p. 46).

CARLOTA. Sólo a Papá Morrison repito. Ningún otro de los restantes quíntuples debe enterarse [I repeat: only Papá Morrison. None of the other quintuplets should find out] (61)

Papá is an ironic paragon of the supposedly disempowered Puerto Rican portrayed by nationalist intellectuals such as Antonio S. Pedreira and René Marqués. Though disempowerment is indicated by his confinement to a wheelchair, Papá overcomes disability/disempowerment through masterful improvisation. In effect, his example is the most cogently liberating since, through cultural hybridization, comic deflation, and exaggeration he appropriates and undoes the archetype of the Oedipal father, the patriarch; perhaps the most binding stereotype in the context of the Puerto Rican paternalism explored by critics such as Juan G. Gelpí (*Literatura*). Furthermore, the irreverence his offspring dutifully inherit from him parodies the respectful maintenance of tradition dictated by paternalism.

To a large extent, Papá improvises on European, particularly Spanish, models. Romanticism is suggested by association with Gustavo Adolfo Bécquer (70) and the host of popular musical forms (71) influenced by that movement's liberal social criticism (Zavala *Culture* 204). Other forms appropriated by Papá are romantic fiction (71) and a repertoire of overblown gestures belonging to opera and making possible his "afectación de divo operístico" [opera star's affectation] (70). The mixture of popular and high cultural models in Papá's improvisation indicates a *bricolage* inherent in the chosen models themselves. The composers of boleros, such as the cited Agustín Lara (71) or Daniel Santos (74), like those of the tango and earlier danza, reworked both the canonic poetry of high culture and popular idioms (Zavala *Culture* 156-59, 161, 164-67). In addition to Papá's choice of the above figures, the cited (71) Juan Morel Campos's cultural flexibility in both setting music to accompany Bécquer's lyrical lieder and composing jingles to advertise sherries and cognacs should also be mentioned (Zavala *Culture* 165). The choice of all the above figures points not only to the borrowing of European models but also the mixing and matching that characterizes Papá's and all the Morrisons' performances.

On one level Romanticism is an appropriate reference point for Papá's improvisation. Papá's grand gestures resonate with the excessive rhetorical flourishes of Romanticism and deliver the coup de grâce on his models. Papá's adoptive reworking of Romanticism is anticipated by the choice of Bécquer as his major role model. Bécquer should actually be classified as a post-Romantic poet who distilled Romanticism's excesses into a sparer, more intimate style.

Therefore, Papá's appropriated model is not strictly speaking Romanticism but Bécquer's precedent of reelaborating exhausted antecedents. Such a precedent was later followed by the composers of danzas, boleros and tangos. The licence of such reelaboration allows Papá's performance to materialize as a highly bombastic contrast to Bécquer. Also, in the same way that Agustín Lara and Daniel Santos reworked high culture for popular performance, literature is appropriated in Papá's performance of a cabaret. And, just as Papá sportively customizes the wheelchair, making his handicap more bearable (67), his improvisation provides some freedom from his models.

The reworking of antecedents, however, can never be definitive but implies a constant process of renewal. The Don Juan figure Papá cuts in his younger days (75-77) is a Puerto Rican version of José Zorrilla's Romantic Don Juan Tenorio (1844), who, in his turn, remodels Tirso de Molina's Don Juan, in his *El burlador de Sevilla* [The Trickster of Seville] (1630). On the other hand, Papá's statement that "de Gustavo Adolfo Bécquer me cuido" [Gustavo Adolfo Bécquer is my thing] (70) is significantly inflected by Papá's later mention of figures such as Morel Campos and materializes in Papá's performance. In the same way that high culture merges with the popular in the bolero and in figures such as Morel Campos, literature is modified in Papá's performance of a cabaret to highlight the way all performances of plays (and all readers of books) undertake such remodeling.

Improvisation also allows the actor playing Papá provisionally to renounce his role through an exhaustion of his models in a final frenzy of ham acting and overblown passion (77). But, release is not absolute since it is incorporated as a dramatic device, propelling the play into a wider exploration of the interplay between dependence and renewal. As the culmination of Papá's performance, the two actors who have portrayed the Morrisons ostensibly relinquish their roles. Onstage and out of character, as it were, they deliver their thoughts on the nature of theater as a manifest artifice set up between consenting interlocutors (78-79). They also reflect on the nature of theatrical improvisation as the balanced interaction of a given script, in their words "premeditación" [premeditation], and individual performance, or "alevosía" [deceit] (78-79). Through this brilliant theatrical coup the improvisatory processes examined by the play ironically transcend the theatrical space to implicate the historical world beyond.

5. CONCLUSION

> La locura instalada en la cordura.
> [Madness as part of sanity]
>
> (xiii)

The creative reworking of individual and political identity is founded on the very form of *Quíntuples*, with the humorous hollowing out of stereotype effected by the burlesque tone of the play, suggesting new possibilities beyond convention and the depiction of individual neuroses.

The tantalizing counterpoint of established representation and performative release ("locura") results in moments of rapture that transcend improvisation's tension between innovation and acknowledgment. At these moments, music, rhythm, pose, poetry, humor, and seduction predominate over the denotative aspects of the performance, constituting a disruption since the narrative is not furthered by such moments but merely provides the pretext for pleasurable spectacle that, in effect, arrests the progression of that narrative into euphoria. In the same way music interrupts the narrative flow of the *sainete*. The resulting suspense of narrative is enhanced by frequently timing these peaks of performance at the interstices between the Morrisons' individual narratives, the gaps in their storytelling, the apotheoses of Dafne, Bianca, Mandrake, Carlota, and Papá taking place on their entrances and exits from the stage. [15]

Theater provides an exemplary model of appropriation by means of its grandstand demonstration of an "open system" of identity, with the activity of the artist functioning as the perfect "open system," made possible by the loosening of stereotypes through the latter's carnivalization in performance. Through performance stereotypes are employed in a masquerade as elements open to playful reworking rather than as inevitable reflections of essential truths (Zavala *Culture* 61-62). In his excellent study of Julia Kristeva's work, John Lechte illustrates this creative process of negotiation by referring to Jackson Pollock's painting, *Blue Poles* (1952).

---

[15] Baby's performance is the exception, its pleasure residing in his very failure to achieve any kind of exaltation.

Lechte highlights the typically postmodern installation of established, codified forms, in this case straight lines, which are then "attacked" by overlaying the lines with improvisatory forms and "explosive" colors that create a tension between the rhythms that arise in the process and materiality of painting, and symbolically significant forms. As Lechte writes (140-41), the artist's attack represents an "expenditure" that:

> produces stasis, or "un arrêt éphémère" (an ephemeral stop). Expenditure thus presupposes stasis–the breaks in *Blue Poles*, the "explosiveness" of yellow, etc.–which, in Pollock's work, or the work of any artist, is semioticized and becomes "art" as it emerges in the social sphere. In this way the destructiveness of the drive (it attacks the symbolic) is made to serve creative ends. Through rhythm Pollock provides an analytic insight into the basis (the materiality) of painting, and possibly into the basis of art itself.

It may be assumed that the "ephemeral stops" mentioned above parallel the moments of rapture to which I refer earlier, these "stops" constituting sites and moments where the materiality of performance intersects with and exceeds the stereotypes on which the Morrisons' improvisations are based. In their turn, and as symbolic manifestations, these stereotypes dialectically interact with the pleasure of performance, providing it with "the means of entering into a set of social and subjective relations" (145).

By orchestrating the process of production Lechte describes the artist acts as a channel of disruptive drives, which are translated into a socially recognized entity: art. Consequently, art marks the dependence, difference, and heterogeneity of the relationship between representational precedent and its unprecedented diversion. The artist, like the hysteric, or the abject, seems simultaneously to occupy both sides of this disjunction. But the artist's hysteria must be a controlled flirtation with hysteria if artistic practice is to remain anchored in the symbolic dimension of culture rather than the bodily drives. This is necessarily so if the artist is to communicate within and through a cultural discourse. Therefore, as artists, the Morrisons cannot be viewed as hysterical victims. They are able to distance themselves sufficiently from their inherent hysteria, albeit to varying degrees, so as to participate creatively in their specific culture by harnessing their anxiety with established forms in the service of unbinding cultural restrictions. By testing the limits of identity the artist, as a "subject in process," constantly pulverizes and pluralizes the unitary subject represented by the stereotype.

The multiple roles of the two actors dissolve unsatisfactory models of identity into hysteria and abjection, in a series of creative, funny, liberating, but also tormenting, dependent, and precarious performances. The constant search for identity, represented by the above symptoms and frenetic switching of roles on the part of the two actors, leads to the problematization of supposedly stable models of identity, whose provisionality is highlighted by improvisation and crisis.

In the fifth scene of the play crisis takes the form of cyclical repetition with Carlota's pregnancy and imminent birth of quintuplets, whose historical legacy under colonialism might be to relive the crisis of Puerto Rican identity experienced by their forebears. A historical continuity/contiguity is suggested by an incestuous blurring of generations and relationships on the part of Carlota. Her instructions are that it is Papá who is to be informed first of her incipient labour (61). He takes priority over, even substitutes, her husband, who is treated more like a child by being pampered (62). Carlota comes to occupy the place of her own mother and in pregnancy retrogressively repeats her own as well as all the quintuplets' births, suggesting the possible perpetuation of Puerto Rico's historico-political situation. But, as the play's only constancy, repetition also takes the form of the quintupled repetition on the part of the characters of aspiration, in the form of wishful thinking, dynamic assertion, and fantasy. Dafne dreams of stardom (5), Baby of life as a lion tamer (28), Bianca yearns for a strong persona (31, 34), Mandrake exudes a self-confidence based on his conviction that the individual may predominate over socio-cultural restrictions (50), Carlota labors for authority (58), and Papá fantasizes about Casanovan conquests (76-77). In addition, there is repetition in the moments of release to which I have referred, the sharing of hackneyed catchphrases (a standard language inviting renewal) by different characters (e.g. 2, 16, 68; 4, 68) or their repeated use by the same character (50, 53), all the above repetitions taking place in the context of constraining, historically contingent identities.

The actors' repeated release through pleasure translates into the urgent return of unfulfilled dreams, which perhaps relate to and, more importantly, rework the terms of any projected independence, nationality, or freedom. Faced with the traumatic dependence that underlies daily life in a colony, such release supersedes the personal histories recounted, supersedes the history of Puerto Rico. The dependence of the island is overtaken by the body's agency and dreams beyond accountability to a fixed historical form of hegemonist nationhood, the "cuento" that weighs heavily and insistently on Puerto Ricans, in the form of colonialism or dogmatic nationalism. These historical discourses become a burden if their traditional terms remain unchallenged, if they constitute the only "cuento" available. If that is the case, then invocation of the latter through franchisement, or even emancipatory revolution, only constitutes a partial victory on unsatisfactory terms. In *Quíntuples*, this is not the case. Instead, the possibility of profoundly new configurations is suggested at the individual, socio-political, and national levels. On all levels the characters are ephemerally empowered by a renovative self-representation that seduces the audience into acknowledging exorbitant spaces beyond established forms. The search for new and liberating spaces motivates such a relationship with the past. It is the very pursuit of creative redefinition, at the level of the individual man and woman, society and nation, that propels Luis Rafael Sánchez's *Quíntuples*.

CHAPTER 2

LA GUAGUA AÉREA: MOVING PICTURES OF PUERTO RICAN NATIONALITY AT THIRTY-ONE THOUSAND FEET

> – ¿De dónde ere?
> – Pues mira, eso e lo que quisiera saber.
> ["Where you from?"
> "That's exactly what I'd like to know."]
> (Dialogue from 1993 film version of Luis
> Rafael Sánchez's "La guagua aérea")

OCTOBER 1993 saw the opening, in San Juan of Luis Molina Casanova's film *La guagua aérea* [The Flying Bus]. In the form of flashbacks, it includes adaptations of two short stories by Luis Rafael Sánchez, "La maroma" [The Con Trick] and "Tiene la noche una raíz" [The Night Has its Reasons], both of which form part of the Puerto Rican writer's first collection of short stories, *En cuerpo de camisa* [Shirt Sleeves Unbuttoned] (1966). Like Sánchez's essay of the same title, the plot of the film concerns the events of one flight on the cheap shuttle service between San Juan and New York. This chapter will deal with the redirecting of Sánchez's dissenting work into easily recognizable mainstream entertainment and how this is achieved by recourse to certain discourses of Puerto Rican intellectual history relating to an image of the nation as a family. I shall claim that this traditional image contrasts with Sánchez's depiction of a kaleidoscopic nationality emerging from a sense of dispersal and belonging rooted in the Puerto Rican diaspora.[1] Moreover, in my view, Molina's film is merely the most recent example of persistent and vain attempts, mostly by Puerto Rican cultural elites, to contain the social differences accentuated by Sánchez's texts. It will become clear in this chapter how such conservatism approximates the traditional authoritarianism of main-

---

[1] On air migration as feature of Puerto Rican literature since the 1950s, see Sandoval Sánchez.

stream culture and politics on the island. Typically, these have incorporated the belief in Puerto Rico's chronic decomposition as a means to legitimate their programs of national salvation.

1. FAMILY UNITY

> – Para eso somos los boricuas: para ayudarnos.
> [That's what we Puerto Ricans are for: helping each other.]
>
> (Character in film version of *La guagua aérea*)

The dedication in the opening credits to the director's mother, wife, and daughter anticipates what is to come through its masculine perception of family relations. In the opening airport scene, the importance of family values is underlined with tearful farewells between passengers and their families. These scenes anticipate the flashback of what is presented–through meaningful looks and gushing music–as a heart-rending farewell between a departing son and his father who is now, some time later, flying to New York to see him. The father, Don Faustino, is given a central role throughout the film as well as providing the framing device. It is through his memories, introduced and concluded by his voice-over, of the flight of *La guagua aérea*, on 20 December 1960, that the story is presented. In this chapter I shall show how, as a patriarch and key narrative device, Don Faustino is crucial to the film's themes and perspective.

From the beginning, a cheap and cheerful tone is struck; from the worried passenger who asks at the ticket desk whether the plane has a full tank of petrol to the woman who is desperate to go to the toilet (a running joke throughout the film), to the opening credits consisting of a cartoon of the flight of the *guagua*. Sentimentality is established through the voice-over of Don Faustino's nostalgic reminiscence about the flight many years ago, and subsequently followed up by the story of the middle-aged man with six months to live who becomes reconciled with the wife from whom he has drifted apart, the story of the prostitute who shows her maternal instincts for the first time, and the story of a Puerto Rican taxi driver down on his luck. Hence the tone of the film continues, veering rather haphazardly between broad humor and pathos that take as their rather distant starting point the work of Luis Rafael Sánchez.

2. NATIONALITY IN TRANSIT: *EN CUERPO DE CAMISA,* "LA GUAGUA AÉREA"

¿Qué somos y cómo somos?
[What are we and how are we?]

Since the first edition of *En cuerpo de camisa,* in 1966, Sánchez's work has challenged the above question of Puerto Rican identity asked by Antonio S. Pedreira in his editorial for the second issue of the journal *Índice* [Index] in 1929 and which has been the focus of Puerto Rican intellectual debate to this day.[2] Parallel to this challenge, the publication of this short story collection marked his separation from most of the post-1930s literary canon and particularly his direct literary elders; writers like René Marqués and Abelardo Díaz Alfaro.[3] Their work is characterized by an idealization of Puerto Rico's Spanish heritage, harsh criticism of corrupt modern urban life as opposed to a harmonious, traditional rural life, political didacticism, the portrayal of heroic sacrifice, and a refined, literary style of Spanish.[4]

Though Sánchez's earliest works, such as "El trapito" [Beloved Rag] (1957), "Destierro" [Exile] (1959), and "Espuelas" [Spurs] (1960), follow the literary model set by his predecessors, with the publication of *En cuerpo de camisa* he challenged every constituent of that model.[5] To a large extent, Spanish culture succumbs to the

---

[2] See Flores (Insular Vision, 17-19; *Refiguring* 92-93), Gelpí (*Literatura* 7-8, 19, 28), and Scarano (683-85).

[3] It must be stressed that Sánchez's estrangement from his predecessors is selective rather than absolute (cf. Interview with Barradas, "El lenguaje" 105). For instance, as Carmen Vázquez Arce has observed (*Por la vereda* 21-22, 32, 44-45, 60, 110, 119, 151, 165), the influence of Emilio S. Belaval is perceptible in *En cuerpo de camisa* (also see Barradas, "La importancia" 194). Sánchez's affinity with Belaval is felt in his sense of the grotesque as well as his unromanticized portrayal of the violence of rural life. Vitalina Alfonso (23-24), also finds similarities between characters and motifs in *La guaracha* and Belaval's short story "María Teresa monta en calesa" [María Teresa Rides in a Buggy].

[4] Vázquez Arce (*Por la vereda* 42).

[5] Important critics of Sánchez's short stories have been Barradas (*Para leer* 49-79; "Cuerpo"), Cachán, Gelpí ("La cuentística"), J. E. González ("El primer libro"), Lugo-Ortiz, Morell ("El paraíso"), and Vázquez Arce (*Por la vereda*). On "La maroma" and "Tiene la noche una raíz," see Vázquez Arce (*Por la vereda* 110-18). Nevertheless, since *En cuerpo de camisa* has been virtually ignored by most critics, it would repay closer attention.

threat and seduction of Afro-Antillean culture in "Aleluya negra" [Black Halleluiah], the modernity of the city is no longer tragically threatening but is treated parodically, in "Que sabe a paraíso" [The Taste of Paradise] and "Etc," while the paradise lost of rural life becomes an intolerant, murderous hell for the homosexual mulatto and classless pariah who is the protagonist of "¡Jum!" Didacticism is replaced by paradox and satire, heroic sacrifice by the marginalized anti-hero(ine)'s pragmatic endurance. Meanwhile, formal Peninsular Spanish is replaced by a stylized, coarsely humorous, vernacular Puerto Rican and a recuperation of Golden Age literature (Cervantes) as a model, or the grotesquely detailed exaggeration of a Quevedo or a Valle Inclán.[6]

What are we and how are we?: in this collection, Sánchez is wary of the question asked by all Puerto Rican intellectuals since, in its search for a Puerto Rican identity, it has tended to disguise the different positions from which it is asked or been permitted to be asked. It is the very diversity of this identity that he is still exploring in his essay, "La guagua aérea."

What are we and how are we? Though the question will not go away, some sixty years later it can, somewhat pointedly, be rephrased by one of Sánchez's equally ironic compatriots. Edgardo Rodríguez Juliá asks (El entierro 90): "¿Familia puertorriqueña o país de muchas tribus?" [Puerto Rican family or country of many tribes?]. The same question finds very different responses in Sánchez's essay and Molina's film.

In Sánchez's "La guagua aérea," as in Molina's, an airplane provides the space where its passengers, as representatives of an only recently industrialized Puerto Rico, tussle with American modernity.[7] The writer traces their "automática convergencia" [spontaneous solidarity] (12) to their experiences of the Puerto Rican diaspora and their simultaneous occupation of diverse locations in a modern, largely urbanized world. The irreclaimable fragmentation of this world reaches an extreme with the Puerto Rican nation's concur-

---

[6] For example: "la nariz de Tisbe es anchota en vuelta de tirabuzón, cómoda por dentro y por fuera" [Thisbe's nose follows the trajectory of a corkscrew, amply comfortable both inside and outside] ("Tiene la noche" 78).

[7] Sánchez's constant revision of his work means that the 1997 version of "La guagua" differs in several significant ways from the 1983 original, though without contradicting the original's overall perspective. Therefore, I shall read both as part of an evolving text and, at several points, compare one against the other.

rent occupation of these spaces in a mainly dual urban context constituted by San Juan and New York.[8] The passengers' accounts of their lives draw the multiple boundaries of the nation by charting a disparate topography ranging from the island's forests and beaches, provincial towns, Bachelor and Bocaccio (San Juan gay and lesbian bars), to the South Bronx, "el fucking job," a Jewish pawnshop, and a project in New Jersey. Though flung apart by the centrifugal forces of modernization and only brought together again in the quintessentially modern space of the airplane, the Puerto Rican passengers display open familiarity. This is rooted in the physical proximity and residual communality of a pre-industrial world still vividly remembered by some and very much alive in many cultural practices.[9] Immersed in these, Sánchez is able to refer to the "remanente de la comunidad tribal" [remnants of tribal communality] ("La guagua," 1983, 10) that sparks the fiery solidarity of the passengers, described as "la solidaridad de los isleños que es pura flama" [A solidarity amongst the islanders that is a pure flame] (10). A pure flame of communality that emigrates with and solders together Puerto Ricans so that, when the narrator asks his "vecina" [neighbor] ("La guagua," 1994, 20) in the seat next to him which village or country town ("pueblo") she is from, New York is her reply (21). Thus, Uncle Sam's poor relatives collectively, as a *pueblo*, make their home away from home in the modern metropolis. Such communality is a strength if one takes the cohesion expressed therein as the emigrants' solidarity in the face of adversity. At the same time, as a tribal remnant, this cohesion is problematic since it plays into the hands of American colonialism's paternalistic mission to civilize or punish its tribal neighbors and ethnic minorities.[10] It is perhaps awareness of this problem that has lead Sánchez to excise his tribalist terminology from the revised version of the essay which appears in his 1994 collection of essays, *La guagua aérea*.

Thrown together from different backgrounds, the passengers share the physical pleasure of storytelling and laughter. Being close to the orality of a pre-industrial culture, they celebrate diversity by creatively recounting the full range of Puerto Rican experience:

---

[8] Puerto Rico's fragmentation as a nation whose center is neither here nor there is, I would suggest, perfectly represented by the metaphor of passengers on an airplane. On this point, also see Sandoval Sánchez (194-202).

[9] Cf. Santiago Valles (*"Subject People"* 31, 38-39, 42-43).

[10] Santiago Valles (*"Subject People"* 25-27, 30).

"Anécdotas, por millar, de boricuas que viajan, a diario, entre el eliseo desacreditado que ha pasado a ser Nueva York y el edén inhabitable que se ha vuelto Puerto Rico" [Tales by the thousands, of Puerto Ricans who travel daily between the discredited Elysium New York has come to be and the uninhabitable Eden that Puerto Rico has become] (15). Their anecdotes are told with varying purpose and effect by a rich cast of characters who share the common experience of emigration, as well as subsequent anti-spik discrimination, in a roomy language open to all-comers.[11] But this bindingly fertile orality introduces a disruptive element into the ordered but pregnable space represented by the aircraft, whose modernity presupposes different rules to the dangerous volubility it carries in the form of the passengers' "risería sediciosa" [seditious merriment] ("La guagua," 1983, 9).[12]

Perhaps the airplane is the last refuge of displaced Enlightenment ideals of totality, progress, and unity, which have lost their gravity as certainties. Almost perfectly self-sufficient, airplanes advance to their preordained destinations on the technological wings of indisputable scientific reason. With perfect containment and purpose, aviation transcends the precipitous fragmentation of our age. If this is so, conflict is inevitable, since this airplane's Puerto Rican passengers challenge containment with their simultaneously unifying but also plural pre-modernity. It is hardly surprising, then, that Sánchez reports that they feel literally imprisoned in their seats ("La guagua," 1994, 13). Meanwhile, the untenability of any homogenizing order of modernity is betrayed by its defensively totalitarian reaction to disobedience.

The perceived threat posed by the Puerto Rican passengers is illustrated in pathological terms and by exaggeration: "la carcajada *contagia* los *cientos* de pasajeros" [laughter *infects* the *hundreds* of passengers] (12, my emphasis). While their creativity produces contagious laughter, such laughter jeopardizes the safety of the aircraft

---

[11] On the racial prejudice suffered by Puerto Ricans, see Scarano (775), Flores ("Puerto Rican" 146), Flores, Attinasi, and Pedro Pedraza Jr. (168), and Flores and Campos (133-37).

[12] The exclusion of the adjectives "sediciosa" and "peligroso" [dangerous] from the revised version does not disguise the conflicts at play in the original. These remain foregrounded in terms of "la resistencia a las afrentas, a los prejuicios a cara pelá" [resistance to affronts, to the bare-faced prejudice] ("La guagua," 1994, 15), and "anécdotas desgraciadas de puertorriqueños, colonizados hasta el meollo" [wretched tales of Puerto Ricans colonized to their marrow] (15).

with undermining infection. At first contamination is merely a cause of apprehension for the gringo crew, since we read that it is immune to laughter (12). But as the situation on board gradually becomes more carnivalesque with the escape of Don Faustino's crabs, an incident recounted in the film, the air hostess's anxiety spreads to the rest of the crew and becomes disciplinarian action. With what Sánchez likens to the hysterical vehemence of a spoof Hitler (13), the captain apprehends the owner of the cancerous crabs that threaten the health of the aircraft whose immune system, the security system (13), fails to detect the pernicious crustaceans, which are described in the text as "la materia infanda" [the noxious matter] (13). The reader learns that the crabs are a couple (12) and a solitary hoot of laughter is reproduced by the rest of the passengers to such a pitch that the cabin is threatened with depressurization (12). On the one hand a pre-modern culture based on multiple yet communal relationships is portrayed as fertile and full of pleasurable possibilities while, here, fecundity signifies the threat to metropolitan modernity posed by the proliferating, overwhelming malady supposedly represented by the Third World. Accordingly, when one considers that the same Latin word, *cancer*, signifies both crab and cancer, then one can envisage the escape of a couple of crabs, male and female, as both a positive image of creative rurality and the threatening spread of a cancer.

In contrast to the Puerto Ricans, who are united by their expansive orality, the *gringos* are also united in their own spontaneous solidarity but on a different scale of development, such a distinction being more extensively explored in the original version of the essay. Theirs may be considered a technologically mediated familiarity, exemplified by the common cultural language of cinema, which, to a certain extent, accommodates difference through the multiplicity of its subject matter and genres. The physicality of the American characters is cinematographic. The narrator compares the sex appeal of a blonde air hostess to that of the actress Fay Wray (11). Meanwhile, the crew demand the troublesome crab owner's identification in a manner reminiscent of a cross between German Expression and the slapstick comedy of Buster Keaton or Charlie Chaplin ("La guagua," 1983, 7).[13]

---

[13] These cinematic references are excluded from the revised version.

In a further confrontation between the American crew and the Puerto Rican passengers, technology is wielded by the former as a weapon against the inventive, perhaps threatening orality the latter. On the announcement by the captain of the projection of a Richard Pryor film, a wit on board notes: "El Capitán quiere matarnos la nota poniéndonos a ver una película del moreno que se achicharró por andar arrebatao" [The Captain wants to poop our party by making us watch a movie of the darkie who got burnt for running around after a good time] ("La guagua," 1994, 16). In this way perhaps a strategic move is made to arrest the seditious merriment of the Third-Worlders on board by its recontextualization in terms of the cautionary cinematic humor represented by an African American's sobering experiences. [14] However, such tactics are constantly countered. For instance, a move is made by the narrator to associate cinematic space with a form of Hispanic melodrama recognizable to Puerto Ricans who, with their country's industrialization, became cinema goers, particularly of Mexican films. [15] While in both versions of the essay the narrator informs his readers that when Puerto Ricans weep it is worthy of Mexican cinema (18), in the original version of the essay cinematic space is literally taken over by the crab owner, who blocks the screen onto which the Richard Pryor film is being projected ("La guagua," 1983, 9). His "sombra chinesca" [Chinese shadow] (9) eclipses the film images. The use of an Oriental adjective perhaps implies the undermining of the West's great twentieth-century invention by a threatening difference and an anterior stage of technological development is evoked by the play of shadows reminiscent of magic lantern shows. [16] More specifically, the cultural assertion of this scene is reinforced by its association with one of the founding texts of Puerto Rican literature and cultural nationalism: Manuel A. Alonso's *El jíbaro* (1849-83). One chapter of this collection of essays, poems, and *costumbrista* vignettes concerning Puerto Rican culture, education, folklore, and customs describes the author's visit to a magic lantern show (164-67).

The multiple distinctions between Puerto Ricans and Americans, as well as those within the two nationalities, are never clear-

---

[14] The sub-text here is Richard Pryor's well-known brush with death as a result of smoking crack cocaine.

[15] See Vázquez Arce (*Por la vereda* 187).

[16] For this observation, I owe thanks to Professor Paul Julian Smith.

cut. For instance, class cuts through the "raya invisible" [invisible line] ("La guagua," 1994, 13) between *gringos* and *boricuas*. As in the film, there are the Americanized Puerto Ricans, or "yankizados" (17), represented here by the passengers ensconced in First Class. But, unlike the film, unequal relations of power are telling. Though, between sips of Californian champagne, the assimilated Puerto Ricans, "boricuas gringaos" (17), are able to review and pass acid comments, in English, on those who "will never make it because they are trash" (17) [originally in English], they cannot be confronted because they occupy a separate section of the plane. In the film, however, the equivalent to these characters, a mulatto businessman, occupies a seat in the same section as all the other passengers, becoming one of the family or a problem to be confronted within the context of the family, rather than an example of the divisive resentments within a centrifugal conception of Puerto Rican nationhood. Visually marked by his skin color and a business suit, he optimistically represents both the potential for social advancement and the possibility of eventual reconciliation between classes and racial groupings.

As for the essay's narrative perspective, it occupies a privileged though not detached position. Though the narrator is able to observe both the tourist class and first-class passengers, as well as the American crew, he is seated with the tourist class passengers, to whom he sympathetically refers as "vecinos," or neighbors (16). For instance, the crab owner's enumeration of what he carries along on his frequent trips to New York elicit the following favorable comments (18):

> Cuando los ve el corazón miope y el juicio deformado, parecen chapucería costumbrista, mediocre color local, folklore liviano. Hasta síndrome del lelolai.
>
> Pero que, cuando se los trata con justicia, avienen a pulcras expresiones de un temperamento que, día a día, establece la diferencia y asegura la permanencia.

> [When they are observed by a short-sighted heart and distorted judgment, they seem picturesque trash, mediocre local color, lightweight folklore. Even part of a hula hoop and voodoo complex.
>
> But when they are dealt with fairly, they come together in gorgeous expressions of a temperament which, day to day, establishes its difference and assures its permanence.]

A capacity for survival, or "temperamento," facilitates survival ("permanencia") by a quotidian self-assertion that is able to constantly renew itself ("establece la diferencia"). Such fluidity is perhaps not able to be contained by colonial modernity, described in the original version as a "devastadora yankización" [devastating Yankification] ("La gaugua," 1983, 9). Difficult to define in any colonial language, including Spanish, Puerto Ricanness takes place as a form of unclassifiable performance (9): "A pesar de y no obstante que y tal vez si y aunque tampoco y desde luego y quizás un y acaso por y demás tartamudeces dialécticas o recursos de inauguración enunciativa" [In spite of and nevertheless because and perhaps if and nor even though and naturally and maybe so and perchance because and other dialectic stammerings or resourses of encunciative commencement].

Incompletion and hesitance points here to the contingent needs of the moment which are constantly overtaken and renewed. The performance of Puerto Ricans is vibrant because it is always fired by an awareness of their immediate situation within the unequal relationship between Puerto Rico and the United States described by Sánchez as a "gramática catastrofista que se emperra en conjugar nuestra inexorable y devastadora yankización" [grammar of catastrophe that insists on conjugating our inexorable and devastating Yankification] (9). In this sense language articulates resistance with a sense of history, according to a flexible grammar imbued with a memory of colonial violence and a stubborn sense of survival.

I have shown how Sánchez presents Puerto Rican nationality as that which cannot be reduced to an essence, since its diversity increases as the story progresses and it has daily to negotiate internal and external differences. Instead, Puerto Rican culture provides a common space where multiple relationships are acted out and expressed through an "idioma vasto y basto" [huge rough and ready language] ("La guagua," 1994, 15). Puerto Rican culture is shown simultaneously to represent constancy and constant self-invention, even though Sánchez's profound faith in Puerto Rican Spanish is clearly that of an islander and underplays the complex bilingualism of US Puerto Ricans. [17] I shall show how the cultural fluidity portrayed by Sánchez is ignored by the one-dimensional communality

---

[17] On the question of bilingualism, see Flores ("'Bumbún';" "Cortijo's Revenge;" "Puerto Rican"), and Negrón-Muntaner.

depicted in the film version and involves a dual process of memory and invention whose constant transformations evade definitive incorporation into grand historical, paternalistic, or political discourses: "Es la historia que no se aprovecha en los libros de Historia" [It is the history which is untapped by history books] (21). Moreover, the pre-modern coincides with the postmodern in its disruption of rigid cultural models through unruly and pleasurable individual performance. At the same time, might not such contingency merely constitute the permissible outer limits of Puerto Rico's historically established colonial status as an Associated Commonwealth whose freedom is delimited by the terms of its Free Associated Statehood? [18]

3. FAMILY VALUES

> – Esto es lo malo de este país: no hay privacidad.
> [That's what's bad about this country: there's no privacy.]
>
> (Character in Molina's *La guagua aérea*)

If Sánchez wittily problematizes the question of national identity, Molina uses it as a vehicle of knockabout entertainment. By doing so, he might be blamed of gross simplification. But it would be wrong to use a critical comparison between Sánchez's and Molina's work simply to reaffirm the old binary opposition that sanctions the assumed superiority of serious literature by contrasting its complexity with the supposed frivolity of popular entertainment. To a certain extent it is true that the popularity of such entertainment rests on its reassuring appeal to popularly held assumptions which, while often unquestioned, are the historical result of ideological struggles at the heart of cultures. [19] Moreover, in Molina's case at least, the preoccupations these assumptions serve to conceal or pacify have also been shared by serious cultural criticism, literature, and politics in Puerto Rico. Hence, I shall claim that Molina revisits the ap-

---

[18] The following authors deal with the extremely complex and controversial subject of colonialism in relation to modern Puerto Rico: Flores, J. L. González, Maldonado-Denis, Meléndez and Meléndez, and Rodríguez Beruff.

[19] On entertainment as part of society's "common sense" and on the under-theorized distinction between art and entertainment, see Dyer (1-15).

parent transparency shared by a certain type of cultural conservatism on the island and participates in its defensiveness against what are perceived as the threatening divisions of society.

Although it would undoubtedly be interesting to take a broad view and trace this conservative form of reading through an examination of the reception of Sánchez's plays and novels, I shall restrict myself to a revealing example of the reception of his short stories on the island as this is directly relevant to this chapter and provides an illuminating context to Molina's narrative.

In its reading of the collection, Loreina Santos Silva's 1981 article *"En cuerpo de camisa o los malamañosos"* [*En cuerpo de camisa* or the Grifters] consistently appeals to the family values most forcefully promoted by Luis Muñoz Marín, the populist leader of the Partido Popular Democrático [Popular Democratic Party], which he founded in 1938.[20] He was the prime modernizer in Puerto Rico's development from an agricultural to industrial economy and a collaborator with the United States in founding the Free Associated State (1952), which he lead as Puerto Rico's first elected Governor (1948-64). The constitutional designation above sanctioned the island's status as a semi-autonomous dependency of the United States.[21] Muñoz Marín's well recorded populism was anticipated by the messianic texts of the so-called Generation of 1930. Its leading light, Antonio S. Pedreira, purports to trace Puerto Rico's colonial isolation, apathy, and historical directionlessness in an essay, *Insularismo* [Insularism] (1934), that is the prime example of his generation's dominant ideology.[22] According to this, all classes and interests were to be merged under the paternalistic leadership of an enlightened, charismatic visionary often identified with Pedreira himself and subsequently with Muñoz Marín. Such a visionary would guide, unite, and cure the presently ailing but potentially great Puerto Rican family out of its isolated fragmentation and dependence into a healthy new age of autonomous progress.

Santos's conventionalism with regard to family values is evident in her ready labeling of Sánchez's marginal anti-heroes as "anor-

---

[20] In outlining Santos' critical approach to *En cuerpo de camisa*, I have found Vázquez Arce's account of Santos's article helpful (*Por la vereda* 76-78).

[21] See Morales Carrión (277-82).

[22] On the Generation of 1930 and Pedreira, See Díaz Quiñones ("La vida inclemente"), Flores ("The Insular Vision" 18-19), Gelpí (*Literatura* 9-12, 20-25), J. L. González ("Sobre la literatura" 148), Pedreira, and Scarano (710-16, 775-77).

males" [abnormal] (21). Moreover, Santos duplicates a traditional ply of Puerto Rican nationalism by raising the specter of disorder to justify her promotion of conservative values and established authority. The move to incorporate the social conflict inherent in Sánchez's portrayal of Puerto Rican society is unmistakable in Santos's appraisal of his story "Tiene la noche una raíz." She writes (24, my emphasis): "*A pesar de que* sabemos que Gurdelia es una prostituta, aprendemos a coparticipar de su frustración y a reconocer en la madre hipotética un recodo de pureza" [*In spite of the fact* that we know that Gurdelia (the protagonist) is a prostitute, we learn to join her in her frustration and to recognize an inkling of purity in this hypothetical mother]. Santos's criticism then goes on to take a further disturbing turn when her condescending recuperation of "abnormality" becomes a sinister plea for "tolerance" towards the "disease of homosexuality," in her analysis of "¡Jum!," a story concerning the lynching of a mulatto homosexual. She writes (27): "Si la homosexualidad es sicológica, lo que requiere es tratamiento apropiado y sobre todo comprensión de parte de familiares y allegados. Si es de tipo fisiológico, por lo tanto, incurable, requiere aún más tolerancia" [If homosexuality is psychological, what it requires is the appropriate treatment and above all understanding on the part of the nearest and dearest. If it is physiological in character, therefore incurable, it requires even more tolerance]. The road to Santos's approach is more directly laid by the treatment of outsider-protagonists in the work of the canonical writers from whom, as I have already acknowledged in this chapter and my introduction, Sánchez distances himself. Their depiction of alienation inevitably points to a supposed degradation of social values, which are conspicuous by their overbearing absence. Similarly, much Puerto Rican criticism of Sánchez's work discusses the so-called alienation of his characters as a way of invoking an "authentic" Puerto Ricanness through its supposed decadence.[23]

Alienation has been a concept and term used too readily by Puerto Rican writers and critics. It implies separation from an original essence. It is difficult to apply to Sánchez's mature work since this consistently suggests the inaccessibility of a supposedly pure identity. Identity in his work is always, has always been, mediated

---

[23] For example, see Arrillaga, González Maldonado, Martínez López, Padua, Umpierre.

by culture, language, and history. If there is alienation it is inherent
to living in any society. A concept used negatively by critics and
writers, and expressing their wishful nostalgia for lost origins, conversely, for Sánchez, alienation is the possibility offered to individuals of performing and reinventing the multiple social roles available
to them. Meanwhile, the bourgeois background of most Puerto Rican intellectuals is evidenced by the fact that the nostalgia I have
described–in contrast to Sánchez's vehement anti-nostalgia–has
been shared indiscriminately by critics and writers from widely divergent positions along the political spectrum.[24]

In the context of Puerto Rican critical tradition, Santos's prejudices involve not only the content but also a reaction to the form of
Sánchez's texts here. As Juan G. Gelpí (*Literatura* 11-12) has convincingly argued, most Puerto Rican criticism, almost exclusively
patrician in outlook, has tended to counter the ideological and social fissures produced by the island's rapid modernization under US
colonialism by privileging certain literary forms over others, with
poetry and the short story, whose forms are necessarily fragmentary,
being undervalued in favor of the extended essay and novel. For
these critics, the dominance of the latter forms rested on what they
considered their all-embracing depiction of reality in the service of
establishing a unified, if hierarchical, national identity. Under this
institutionalized orthodoxy, the overarching themes of nationalism
and social order preceded, were presented as truth through realism,
and projected as political aims through what served as discursive
forms of literature.

As a more comprehensive study of the writer's work confirms,
even if Santos were to examine Sánchez's novels she would not find
what she seems to be looking for. On the contrary, the extension of
novelistic form only helps to unrelentingly throw into doubt the
unifying totality of form and content promoted by orthodox Puerto
Rican criticism, and concisely ironized in Sánchez's short stories.
For example, *La guaracha del Macho Camacho* tells the story of dys-
functional families in the form of a fragmented, non-consecutive
narrative. According to Bakhtinian terms, then, the critical tradition

---

[24] On Sánchez's importance in initiating a new wave of Puerto Rican literature
that challenges "the drive towards a synthetic formulation of culture and nationality" characterizing traditional Puerto Rican cultural criticism, see Carlos J. Alonso's
excellent work (Quotation above, 350).

Santos represents may be described as "monologic." That is, it is based on a defensively static concept of the subject, social roles, and nationality. Alternatively, Sánchez's work represents a "dialogic" mode of representation; dialogic in the sense of promising change through ambiguity and the confrontation of distinct and contradictory views. The irony, intertextuality, and parody of his work offer exemplary means of challenging monologism's simplifying resolutions.[25] Even the conventionally monologic form of the Puerto Rican essay, written in the authoritarian voice of a master intellectual, gives way to the polyphony of "La guagua aérea," where the narrator's voice is one amongst many, and where he literally enters into dialogue with his co-passengers. Polyphony is aided by such extensive recourse to the verbal pyrotechnics of his fiction and the theatrically compelling characterization of his dramatic work, that "La guagua aérea" often veers as close to Sánchez's own short story work as to any tradition of Puerto Rican or Latin American essay writing.[26]

Another critic, Eliseo Colón Zayas, has followed in Santos's footsteps by dialectically asserting the primacy of a yearned-for Puerto Rican soul. In a 1981 article significantly entitled, "La problemática del ser puertorriqueño en los cuentos de Luis Rafael Sánchez" [The Problems of Puerto Rican Being in the Short Stories of Luis Rafael Sánchez], he writes (23-24):

> La sociedad puertorriqueña ha sido una de las formas de vida que más ha sufrido debido a la dependencia cultural con respecto a la cultura norteamericana. Aunque esta contaminación de la

---

[25] On the conception of "monologic" and "dialogic" forms of representation, see Bakhtin (*Problems*). Gozo has given an incisive Bakhtinian account of irony and carnivalization in *La guaracha*.

[26] I have used the term essay tentatively to classify Sánchez's text. Even though, as dramatic anecdote, it can almost as easily be read as a short story, because of its factuality, sociological observation, undisguised presence of the writer as narrator, autobiographical references and concluding interview format ("La guagua," 1994, 21), I favour its classification as non-fiction. Besides, "La guagua aérea" is the title text of a 1994 collection of essays by Sánchez. However, the text's simultaneous inclusion in collections of essays (Rodríguez de Laguna 17-25) and classification as "cuento" ("La guagua," 1983, 6) or "tale" (Flores, "Cortijo's" 104) has increased confusion. Useful in this context is Aníbal González's 1995 review of *La guagua aérea*. He shows how "La guagua aérea" is a postmodern reworking of dominant motifs and themes in Puerto Rican and Latin American essay writing, revolving around the journey as a process of self-discovery and the supposed isolation of Puerto Rican culture.

cultura puertorriqueña es cada día mayor, no podemos relegar a menor importancia esa sociedad que se desarrolla en Puerto Rico con anterioridad a la intervención norteamericana y que gozaba de mayor integración en las zonas rurales de la isla.

[Puerto Rican society has been one of the ways of life that has suffered most owing to its cultural dependence with regard to American culture. Even though this contamination of Puerto Rican culture increases daily, we cannot undervalue that form of society which developed in Puerto Rico prior to American intervention and which enjoyed its most integrated form in the rural areas of the island.]

Like Sánchez's direct literary predecessors, Colón sets an Arcadian Puerto Ricanness against its assumed alienation by the modernizing urbanization of American colonialism. On the other hand, his defensiveness against foreign "contamination" recalls the Generation of 1930's abject fear of cultural contamination of what they considered original cultural unity by the virus of multiplying change. For its part, the crab scene of Sánchez's essay is imbued with Puerto Rican cultural history by transforming its dominant imagery. In this instance, the threat of contamination is filled with dialogic possibilities, in a reversal where popular culture's unruly prevalence over modernity is only one possibility. Concurrent with a reading from this point of view is Sánchez's dispassionate exploration of a possible defense mechanism against the abject fear traditionally expressed by Puerto Rican intellectuals, in his illustration of a process of projection onto the colonizer of what has been a particularly Puerto Rican apprehension.[27]

Though Colón's sharing of this apprehension is not exceptional, he surprisingly admits the oppressive historical context of the Puerto Rican culture he defends (24):

Pero hay que ver que estos valores que se han mantenido en muchos centros rurales de la isla y que han pasado, algunos de ellos, a formar parte del inconsciente puertorriqueño, representan el legado de la dominación española en la isla. La ideología colo-

---

[27] I use the term projection in its properly psychoanalytic sense of an operation where "the subject attributes tendencies, desires, [fears], etc., to others that he refuses to recognise in himself" (Laplanche and Pontalis 351).

nialista y patriarcal española está presente en la isla en sus más reaccionarias instituciones como son la familia, la moral religiosa, el machismo, el paternalismo, etc.

[But it must be realized that those values which have been maintained in many of the island's rural centers and which, at least partially, have come to form part of the Puerto Rican unconscious, represent the legacy of the Spanish domination of the island. Spain's colonialist, patriarchal ideology lives on in the island in its most reactionary institutions, such as the family, religious morality, machismo, paternalism, etc.]

Colón then expresses the view that Sánchez's short stories set out to criticize the stifling ideology of Puerto Rico's Hispanic legacy and its institutions. While I would agree with this assertion, I cannot agree with the claim expounded throughout Colón's article that Sánchez's criticism involves a dystopic depiction of modern Puerto Rican life. Nor can I concur with his familiar reduction of Sánchez's literary world to the one-track preoccupation with a hackneyed dark night of the Puerto Rican soul: "Lo que encontramos *En cuerpo de camisa* es un lenguaje metafórico (y aún alegórico) del alma puertorriqueña contemporánea, de su dolor, de su frustración, de su posibilidad" [what we find in *En cuerpo de camisa* is a metaphorical language (even an allegorical one) of the contemporary Puerto Rican soul, of its pain, its frustration, its potential] (Colón 25). [28]

Colón's and Santos's approach could almost be a blueprint for Molina's: faced with "abnormality" or "illness," an appeal to family unity and family values saves the day as a means of promoting a unifying national identity. Nostalgia for a supposed integrity informs the treatment of the two main stories recounted in Molina's film. The first of these is "La maroma," which is presented in the

[28] Ostensibly more progressive criticism also often reacts defensively to Sánchez's work. In her feminist discussion of *La guaracha*'s female characters, María del Rosario Marín ignores or is perhaps disturbed by the liberatingly parodic possibilities of previously repressive gender identities, already discussed in my previous chapter on *Quíntuples* and again to be examined in my chapter on the novels. Instead, she invokes a singular and, for her, authentic femininity: "¿Permitirá nuestra época raspar el barniz incrustado desde hace tantos siglos e incesantemente acumulado hasta conseguir que los auténticos rasgos del rostro femenino puedan aparecer a la luz del día?" [Will our day and age allow us to scrape off the encrusted coating accumulated incessantly over so many centuries so that we manage to permit the true features of the female to come to light?] (20).

form of a flashback experienced by the story's protagonist, a beggar who by feigning blindness manages to live off the charity of his community. He is so successful that a collection is made to fund an operation to restore his sight. The story ends with an affirmation of this charitable deed carried out in favor of "este santo y manso y buen hombre" [this saintly, gentle, and good man] ("La maroma," 15). The pre-positioning of the adjective in "buen hombre," which in Spanish may mean "harmless/simple man" or even "fool" (Butt and Benjamin 69), ironically signals that the last laugh is had at the expense of the *pícaro*, or rogue.

The film takes up where the short story ends and foresakes the story's ironic twist in favor of a wholesome resolution. This has the blindman flying to New York with his parish priest, who is accompanying him to the hospital where the eye operation is to be carried out. On a particularly bumpy stretch of the flight the blindman fears for his life and confesses his "maroma," or con trick, in an act of good faith toward his religious father and his community. Thus, the literary *pícaro*'s conventionally loose ties to family life are here tightened in mitigation of Sánchez's unsentimental depiction of social life.

In the short story, if the protagonist initially uses society for his benefit then, ultimately, society also uses him. Towards the end of the story the community celebrates its act of charity with grotesque exhibitionism (15):

> Una vieja tragacristos lo abraza fuertemente mientras masculla corderos degollados . . . Otro, menos piadoso, exclama que a todo cerdo le llega su San Martín, la vieja tragacristos lo empuja para que se arrodille y salude el día grande . . . Ve, éste, a través de su ceguera, la berruga que muerde el labio de la decrépita, berruga que inicia la rimbombante jaculatoria en que se agradece al Altísimo la cosecha de vides.

> [An old godglutton crushes him in her arms whilst she gurgles like a flock of decapitaded lambs . . . Another, less pious member of the mob, exclaims that eventually every pig has to go to its slaughter, the old godglutton forces him to his knees to pray thanks for this day of plenty . . . and, though blind, he manages to see the mole that is eating away the lip of the hag, the mole that begins the resoundingly fervent prayer in which the Lord on High is thanked for the harvest of vines.]

The violent language and actions of this spectacle overwhelm the blindman, as a bestial mob gathers in a true display of power relations between society and a marginalized individual (15). And, at the head of this day of reckoning is the priest, who pompously intones his parish's deed (15). It seems that the blindman's bluff is called and surpassed by what is portrayed as a community of self-serving religious hypocrites.

In Molina's film, the unsympathetic character of the old hag appears only momentarily. Her prominence in the short story is replaced by a scene showing a kindly neighbor who takes it upon herself to feed the fraudulent blindman on her porch with no one to witness her charity. The threatening portrayal of a mob is replaced by the slapstick pursuit of the fleeing fraudster by a town which wants to celebrate his imminent cure. The fast pace and rapid editing of the chase, as well as accompanying circus music, are used for a comic effect that plays down the ominous dimension of the short story. Discarded are the references to San Martín, when pigs are traditionally slaughtered in Hispanic countries, and, subsequently, Innocents' Day (15), when the collection was begun. The reference to the latter religious celebration and its traditional association with practical jokes underlines the fraudster's hoisting on his own petard, as well as the opportunistic nature of society. Instead, the film version moves away from satire to concentrate on an individual's anti-social behavior, which is in the end reformed.

Absent from the film version is the positive dimension of anti-social behavior. Though the protagonist's display of a quality valued by mainstream society, resourcefulness, leads to his downfall, the character's unmistakable enterprise offers hope. Though the protagonist of "La maroma" may have chosen his way of life from a limited range of possibilities, the ironic effectiveness of his initiative suggests the possibility of renewal. The sense of this is reinforced by the role of humor, which implies transgression and reworking the established through irony, deflation, and a multiplication of meanings.

The other main story used in the film is "Tiene la noche una raíz," which deals with the maternal feelings that are for the first time aroused in a veteran prostitute, Gurdelia Grifitos, when she meets a young boy of ten, Cuco. The potential sentimentality of such a story lends itself to the overall tone of the film. However, this ignores the intolerance, hypocrisy, and violence Gurdelia encounters in Sánchez's deceptively simple tale. The sympathy aroused by the character of Gurdelia precludes the distance or ambiguity required for the type of humor exercised in "La maroma." In "Tiene la noche una raíz" sympathetic humor is mainly generated by the ironic contrasts set up between a prostitute and the supposed pillars of her community.

The story begins with three pious ladies who, after attending mass (19):

> Iban deprisita . . . con la sana esperanza de acabar de prisita el rosario para regresar al beaterío y echar, ¡ya libres de pecados!, el ojo por las rendijas y saber quién alquilaba esa noche el colchón de la Gurdelia . . . . ¡La vergüenza de los vergonzosos, el pecado del pueblo todo!

> [They were hurrying along . . . with the wholesome expectation of neatly finishing off their rosaries so that they could return to the sanctimoniousness of casting an eye–free of sin thank God!–through the cracks and finding out who was hiring Gurdelia's mattress that night . . . . The most shameful of the shameful, and the unredeemed sin of all the town!]

As in "La maroma," the protagonist is confronted with a piety whose exhibitionism is affirmed, perhaps in the public voice of the community, by the exclamatory remarks of the above passage, as well as by the empty ritual of rosaries, and whose hypocrisy is revealed in the final lines by the unveiling of prurient spite.

Gurdelia's marginalized position as a prostitute is reinforced perhaps by her probable racial categorization. Hence a distance may be established between the respectable women of her community, whose whiteness does not have to be mentioned since it forms a zero degree of racial order, and Gurdelia Grifitos, whose racial mixture is signaled by her surname. *Grifo* in Puerto Rican Spanish refers to someone born to a black father and a mulatto mother. While *grifos* are usually darker than mulattoes, the diminutive suffix may suggest that Gurdelia's is paler than might be expected. Later she is described as a "negrita" (20), using the diminutive in possibly a similar way. The subsequent use against Gurdelia of black magic spells, or "fufús" (20), normally associated with Afro-Antillean culture, by the female members of a white, Christian community ironically confirms the central role of Afro-Caribbean traditions even in the practices of those sectors of Puerto Rican society that have traditionally discriminated against the most visible heirs of that heritage. In Molina's film, the racial discrimination faced by the protagonist is avoided by the convenient ambiguity of cinematic representation. Not once is the character named in the film, while the other verbal indicators I have indicated are also absent. Therefore, the pointedness of verbal representation is diluted by the more open nature of visual art, perfectly exemplified by the uncertain racial identity of Idalia Pérez Garay, the actress who takes on the role of the prostitute. Pérez Garay's skin is dark enough for her to be taken for a pale *mulata*, yet pale enough to be southern European.

The hypocrisy, spite, and harassment of her by the respectable members of the community are set against the Gurdelia's subsequent transformation into a paragon of upstanding behavior when confronted with Cuco at her door: "Gurdelia puso cara de vecina y se llevó las manos a la cintura como cualquier mujer honrada" [Gurdelia put on her housewife's face and rested her hands on her waist like any honorable woman] (21). In an ironic twist, Gurdelia is obliged to assume such a role by an ostensibly decent Catholic society's hypocritical encouragement of an assertive masculinity urged through sexual relations with a prostitute who, on the one hand, is condemned but on the other is desired, who carries the burden of female sexuality so that other women in the community might be identified as pious and respectable. In a humorous play on the piety established earlier Cuco is motivated to visit her by overhearing his father, in conversation with a friend, describing the pleasure of his visits to Gurdelia as heavenly ("devino" [sic]) (21).

In the face of such hypocrisy, Gurdelia is presented as an honorable character provoked to righteous anger by the corrupt values of legitimate society and the roles it demands of its members. Significantly, her anger is motivated by a maternal concern that takes her beyond her assigned role as a prostitute and the corrupt values of her society (22):

> El vientre le dio un sacudón y las palabras le salieron.
> – Usté e un niño. Eso son mala costumbre.

> [Her womb tightened as the words came out. "You're a child. These're bad habits."]

This assertion is countered by Cuco's embryonic mimicry of over-bearing masculinity. "Yo soy un hombre" [I am a man] (20) he repeats with dejection. Such are the pressures to be a man that Cuco is not allowed to be what he is, a child. The tension between social values and the individual are further manifested by Cuco's childlike behavior when, between the first and subsequent assertions of his manhood, he starts to cry: "Cuco puso la boca apucherada, como para llorar hasta mañana y entre puchero y gemido decía–que soy un hombre" [Cuco pouted, as if he were going to cry until dawn and between pouts and whimpers kept saying–but I am a man] (23). Gurdelia's intimation of her latent physical potentialities as a woman and her unprecedented relationship with Cuco suggest other possibilities beyond her role as a prostitute. Thus, she chooses to close her house to customers that night (23) as a woman able, in a limited sense, to choose her way of life in a restrictive society.

The complexity and extent of the tensions between individual and society just described are minimized by Molina's film, which limits the social context of the story to scenes where Gurdelia finds a black magic talisman on her doorstep, spots her neighbor spying on her through drawn curtains, walks past an admiring group of men playing cards, among whom is Cuco, and then past a couple of gossiping women in the street. However, through the use of up-tempo music interspersed with incidental music more suitable for a mock suspense thriller, and flowing montage interspersed with ominous asides, these scenes are reduced to comic moments of local color and unfulfilled grand guignol. Meanwhile, the mellow colors and low-key lighting of the meeting between Gurdelia and Cuco emphasize the sentimentality of her scenes with him. This sentimentality–anticipated by a poignant bolero that accompanies the interior scenes–reaches its climax with the shot where Gurdelia holds the dozing Cuco in her arms while she sings a lullaby. The framing and chiaroscuro of this medium shot is reminiscent of a painting of the Madonna and child.

Finally, social conflict is entirely ignored as Gurdelia is presented as just another passenger, of modestly elegant attire, who dreams of a better life in America. Indeed, as she prepares to disembark at the end of the film she receives the good wishes of an avuncular fellow passenger, who unwittingly overlooks Gurdelia's specific marginality as a prostitute by including her in the implied general economic marginality of Puerto Rico, a country where, according to him, basically decent people are forced to get by any way they can, or "buscárselas." His comment to her that everyone has to find a way of bringing home the bacon ("hay que ganarse las habichuelas") is acknowledged by Gurdelia's laughter which, though knowing, becomes subsumed as sign of recognition and solidarity in the overall sentimentalism of the film. In this, Gurdelia, an anonymous free agent is able to shut up shop for good and leave for America, like any ambitious Puerto Rican.

The trouble is that Sánchez's marginal characters are not any Puerto Ricans but specific subjects with apparently little in common apart from their marginality. If such is the case, then what do Puerto Ricans share which might provide an alternative to Molina's view of Puerto Ricans as members of the same family who find themselves together in the same boat or, in this case, plane? Perhaps it is a common but pluralistic linguistic space, formed by Puerto Rican experience on the island and in the United States, a space allowing for the coexistence and conflict of various expressions of different experiences. The latter are inflected variously, from the drug slang of "Que sabe a paraíso" to the black Puerto Rican of "Aleluya negra." The impossibility of finding a universal expression of Puerto Rican nationality is further conveyed by the sheer variety of literary languages employed in the stories. "Memoria de un eclipse" [Memory of an Eclipse] is written in the language of popular romantic fiction. On the other hand, in "Ejemplo del muerto que se murió sin avisar que moría" [Exemplum of the Dead Man Who Died Suddenly without Telling Anybody], Sánchez has recourse to medieval *exemplum*-collections, while, in "La maroma," "Etc," and "Tiene la noche una raíz" he indulges in learned, Golden Age word play. Molina's film either excludes these stories or reformulates their respective vernaculars and literary languages in favor of a standardized *puertorriqueño* spoken by all the characters. Such a contrast in terms of language between Sánchez's and Molina's works reflects two disparate perspectives on family life. In the film, there is the "enforced resolution of contradiction" (P. J. Smith, "Letter") while, in Sánchez's texts, the Puerto Rican family is the site for the constant reinvention of conflicting and unevenly privileged identities.

Stories that are beyond enlistment to the nostalgic yearning for well-worn discourses are excluded from the film. These stories concern disturbing marginalities, the profound social splits in which they are involved, as well as their distortion of officially promoted values. Certainly, the setting of the film in the past (1960) is instrumental in promoting a nostalgia which was acknowledged by several older members of the audiences with whom I sat. They reminisced loudly about the conditions on the *guagua* and the reasons why they had traveled. Such nostalgia is avoided by Sánchez's essay, whose recent historical setting can be ascertained by references to President Reagan and Richard Pryor ("La guagua," 1994, 16-17).

Ultimately, all the stories in *En cuerpo de camisa* present problematic situations. But it would have been extremely difficult to lighten the overall tone of several stories. "¡Jum!," as I have mentioned, involves a homosexual protagonist who is viciously persecuted to death. "Que sabe a paraíso" grotesquely parodies capitalist values such as consumerism and entrepreneurship by setting these in an urban underworld of drug trafficking and prostitution. "Aleluya negra" involves class and racial discrimination between whites and blacks, as well as between blacks themselves, and depicts a violent sexuality which has been characterized as misogynist (Fernández Olmos). In another instance, already mentioned, the film's story of the reconciliation between the middle-aged couple is completely eclipsed by "La parentela" [Relations], a story where greed and hatred lead a married couple to kill each other. Through exclusion the difficult stories mentioned above are remarginalized by Molina's film in favor of a paradoxical form of traditional family values that takes into account both the failures as well as persistence of Puerto Rican patriarchy. Shown to be vulnerable, these values are reinforced by a nationalistic enlistment of the audience's longstanding political discontent and a redirection of Puerto Rican society's internal frictions towards an outside enemy: the United States.

Anti-American feeling takes several forms in the film. Firstly, there is the justified resentment expressed at the anti-spik prejudice experienced by the embittered taxi driver and a young mulatto mother, who disabuses a first-time emigrant of any illusions he might have concerning life in America. Secondly, there is the unsympathetic portrayal of intolerant and disdainful Americans, represented by the air hostesses of the film's "Trans-International" airplane, and an FBI agent. The hostesses respond histrionically, with tantrums, tears, rage, to their Puerto Rican passengers' unruly behavior, while the FBI agent refuses a friendly offer of Puerto Rican food by one of the passengers. The disciplinarian nature of the authority represented by the American characters is signaled by the hostesses' severe uniforms and the virtual uniform of the FBI man's suit and fedora, which he does not remove even in the plane. Furthermore, he accompanies a Puerto Rican man, who is handcuffed to him. The stiff authoritarianism represented by the American characters is constantly undermined by the fun-loving spirit of the Puerto Rican passengers. Thwarted, authoritarianism turns to exasperation or spite. An example of the latter presents itself when, upon arrival at La Guardia Airport, one of the hostesses gloatingly announces the icy temperature in New York, an announcement which ends with the following malicious aside: "Freeze!" The disharmony of US-Puerto Rican relations is definitively indicated by the presence of the handcuffed Puerto Rican, who may be associated with the minoritarian but prominent independence movement. One of the most violent displays of the discontent expressed in the film and represented by this group was the 1954 shooting, at the House of Representatives, of five US congressmen by three Puerto Rican nationalists (Scarano 778-79).

As I shall show, the film's anti-Americanism may certainly be attributed to historical experience. But its contextualization within a totalizing metaphor of a Puerto Rican family links such sentiment to the intellectual and political expressions of the paternalistic nationalism promoted by the Generation of 1930. On the other hand, anti-Americanism is certainly not an essential attribute of Puerto Rican paternalism, as the case of Muñoz Marín's political transformation clearly shows. He moved from his early advocacy of vehement nationalism won through revolutionary socialism, in the 1920s, to his promotion, largely by sheer dint of his charismatic personality as father of the Free Associated State, of a policy of accommodation towards US-Puerto Rican relations. As part of this change, a concerted diversion of nationalism into a defense of a Puerto Rican cultural heritage and Spanish as the national language was undertaken by his party and will be further discussed below.[29]

Sánchez's own anti-Americanism is evident in some of his early stories, such as "Espuelas" or "Destierro," and the portrayal of Americanized characters, such as Benny, in his novel, *La guaracha del Macho Camacho*. However, by the time of Sánchez's "La guagua

---

[29] On Muñoz and his sublimation of nationalism into a cultural issue, see Díaz Quiñones ("La vida" 64-65; "Los años" 122); Flores and Campos (128-33); Morales Carrión (224-25, 71-72).

aérea," the anti-Americanism of his earlier works is replaced, as I
have shown, by a more complex, differentiated, and ironically ob-
servant perspective.

The film itself portrays the reintegration of marginal characters
into the fold of a united Puerto Rican family recognizable to a local
audience brought up on the family values promoted by the political
and intellectual leaders discussed earlier.[30] The blindman confesses
to the father-figure of the priest, the prostitute becomes, albeit temporarily, a mother. Therefore, it is possible to conclude that, while
Sánchez's work is shot through with ironic, satirical humor, Molina's film is comic only in the sense that everything is geared towards
a happy ending where all differences are reconciled. Meanwhile,
the reintegration of stray sheep reinforces the film's central theme
of the importance of sticking together as a family. This theme is established from the outset and its patriarchal message is upheld by
the father figure, Don Faustino, who against the wishes of his wife
and other members of his family insists on going to New York to
consult his son and heir before agreeing to sell the family home,
and by the story of the reconciliation of the middle-aged couple
who have drifted apart. Furthermore, the opening credits send a
clear message. They state that the film has been made by Puerto Rican artists and technicians, and with the financial as well as techni-
cal help of Puerto Rican cultural institutions such as the Fundación
Puertorriqueña de las Humanidades and the Universidad del Sagra-
do Corazón. Moreover, in a short promotional film projected before the feature film itself, José Luis "Chavito" Marrero, the actor
who plays Don Faustino, wearing granddad spectacles and beard
that make him look even more patriarchal than in the film, endorses
the latter as "el verdadero sentir de nuestro pueblo" [the true feeling of our people].

Even so, Molina's film cannot sustain its integrity as a glorified
home movie. Though the reassuring snugness of a cinema may be
associated with the intimacy of a darkened living room where family members gather to watch father's projection of sunny Super 8
films of his family, or even with a wish to return to the womb, traumatic family memories are too recent to forget in Puerto Rico. Even

---

[30] Family values dominated by a local patriarchy in its turn subsumed by the paternalism of America's self-styled Manifest Destiny as a colonial power (Scarano
538-39, 567-71).

while patriotically celebrating Puerto Rican culture Molina has to go some way to acknowledging the reasons for the national divisions explored by Sánchez.

Within the action of the film, "cultural nationalism" (Dávila, "Contending;" *Sponsored*) is further expressed when a group of passengers take out instruments and start singing and dancing together and, subsequently, when the passengers, disgusted with the food provided by the American airline, produce their own home-cooked Puerto Rican delicacies which are generously shared around. Meanwhile, characters who deny their Puerto Ricanness, like the boastful businessman who constantly sings the praises of the American Dream and pointedly refuses to accept the food being shared, are treated unfavorably since theirs is a betrayal of the family. The businessman is made to feel ridiculous by the hard working Puerto Rican taxi driver who recounts his harsh experience of the American Nightmare. The disloyal businessman is further used as a pretext to express the frictions felt by Puerto Rico's incomplete transition from agrarian pre-modernity to industrialized modernity. When the sackful of crabs escapes, part of Don Faustino's home-based crab farming business, the patriarch is confronted by the turncoat businessman, who is backed up by two American air hostesses. He reproves Don Faustino for his bumpkin's ways and expresses the belief that it is just such incidents that cause Puerto Ricans to be America's laughing stock. Highly indignant, Don Faustino asserts his right to breed crabs or any damn thing he likes regardless of what the businessman, Luis Muñoz Marín, and the President of the United States think.

It is interesting that Don Faustino's indignation is directed against both the businessman and the Governor of Puerto Rico. The businessman's perceived disloyalty may be seen as a product of the Governor's policies. In their turn, the Governor's links with several American presidents provide the historical background to Don Faustino's anger and the film's hostility to American culture.

In his capacity as a forger of closer ties with The United States, Luis Muñoz Marín, the Governor of Puerto Rico at the time of the film's action, was able to champion Operation Bootstrap. The latter, initiated in 1947 as an extension of Roosevelt's New Deal, involved collaboration with the American government aimed at rocketing Puerto Rico into the future as a fully industrialized nation. Though Operation Bootstrap was partially successful with it came chronic unemployment, inflation, continued dependence on the American economy, as well as massive emigration and an unsettling transfer of population from rural areas to cities. In addition, there was the importation of First World aspirations unable to be met by the majority of the population and by what was and is only the appendage of a First World economy. The resulting decline of Muñoz Marín's popularity, in combination with factional in-fighting within his party, lead to the downfall, in 1968, of his Partido Popular Democrático, which had dominated Puerto Rican Politics since Muñoz Marín's rise to power as Puerto Rico's first elected Governor, in 1948.[31]

The hostility towards Americans and American culture evidenced in the film must partly be based not only on the harshness of the Puerto Rican experience in America and also the disappointments resulting from Muñoz Marín's dreams of progress in association with a colonial superpower. Dreams whose failure lead to a massive diaspora and disappointments which have left Puerto Ricans feeling like second-class citizens to their First World neighbors. A feeling which, perhaps paradoxically, has lead a proportion of Puerto Ricans to believe that only full rights as the fifty-first United State will lead them to the fulfilment of the promises made to them by Muñoz Marín so long ago. But, such enmity is also typically compensatory for the economic and political dependence of Puerto Rico, as has been shown by Arlene Dávila (*Sponsored*, esp. 24-59), who has traced the increasingly vehement cultural assertion of a Puerto Rican identity at all levels of Puerto Rican society, even on the part of political parties espousing ever closer association with the United States.

---

[31] On Muñoz Marín's involvement with Operation Bootstrap, its successes and failures, and Muñoz's downfall, see Cachán (182), Flores and Campos (133-37), Morales Carrión (269, 273, 286, 295, 312-13), Rodríguez Juliá (*Puertorriqueños* 146-47), Scarano (722-23, 743-47, 749-64, 768-72, 789-94, 806-09, 817, 819-25), Vázquez Arce ("Salsa" 31-34).

4. CONCLUSION

> –Yo no tengo familia para dejarle nada.
> [I don't have any family to leave anything to.]
>
> (Gurdelia Grifitos, in Molina's *La guagua aérea*)

The divisions portrayed by Sánchez's essay are rigidly ordered under the conventional paternalism of the film version, whose conservatism might be based on an anachronistic reaction against the increasing problematization of authenticating views of national identity on the part of Puerto Rican cultural practices. In this sense, Molina is defensive of a certain view of Puerto Rican culture promoted by the Partido Popular Democrático during Luis Muñoz Marín's heyday.

According to the 1952 Commonwealth Constitution, approved by the US Congress, the new categorization of the colonial relationship, "would not change Puerto Rico's fundamental political, social, and economic relationship to the United States" (Fernández, Méndez Méndez, and Cueto 143). The business-as-usual attitude of the State Department is clear from the outset. Writing to the State Department in 1952, Governor Muñoz Marín asserted that Puerto Rico had now ceased to be a territory of the US, making way for a new relationship founded on a "compact" that could be changed only by the mutual agreement of the US and Puerto Rican governments. The State Department responded in the following terms, informing him that "the flat statement that Puerto Rican laws cannot be repealed or modified by external authority, and that Puerto Rico's status and terms of its association with the United States cannot be changed without Puerto Rico's full agreement has been modified to indicate that this is Puerto Rico's view" (143).

With the political avenues closed off by the colonizer's veto, Muñoz Marín's PPD channeled thwarted nationalist aspirations, which had led to armed conflict between the militantly independentist Nationalist Party and the authorities in 1950, into the cultural sphere, through major sponsorship of newly founded cultural institutions such as the Institute of Puerto Rican Culture (ICP) and the Division of Community Education (DIVEDCO), as well as programs under the auspices of these and other related institutions to promote the creation and diffusion of Spanish-language educational programs, Puerto Rican scholarship, letters, theater, film, and the visual arts. As Arlene Dávila points out ("Contending" 232-33), official cultural policy served a "foundational" purpose, where the divisions of Puerto Rican society were reconciled by the presentation of a "folklorized view of the nation whose main manifestations were the rapidly disappearing agrarian society with its customs and folklore." Such a view attempted to elide social divisions on the island, as well as those separating islanders and migrants, by constructing a binding "puertorriqueñidad" with which all Puerto Ricans might identify. The PPD compensated for the island's continuing political insufficiency and increased economic dependency under Free Associated Statehood by setting itself up as the proud defender of Puerto Rican cultural identity, while at the same time taking advantage of Cold War paranoia to enforce McCarthyist censorship legislation, allied with intensified repression and violent confrontation, to finally defeat the militant Puerto Rican Nationalist Party.

The new, post-Muñoz, corporate rather than state-sponsored climate and its possibilities, discussed by Arlene Dávila ("Contending;" *Sponsored* 169-207) are confirmed after the recognition in the opening credits of the Puerto Ricans and Puerto Rican institutions involved in the making of the film, when several of the major sponsors listed, in a film costing only $800,000 (Routte-Gómez 5), are North American or European multinationals such as Coca Cola, SmithKline Beecham, Johnson and Johnson, AT&T, Roche Pharmaceutical, and Kodak. Dávila acknowledges ("Contending" 234) that, in their attempt to attract consumption from all sectors of Puerto Rican society, "corporate sponsors appear to be serving as unwitting catalysts for the promotion of aspects of contemporary popular life that are rejected by official standards of national identity, thus adding a new dimension to Puerto Rico's cultural politics," and in the process highlighting the diverse constituencies, but also discrimination and contentiousness, of Puerto Rican cultural identity.[32] However, Molina's film also confirms Dávila's assertion ("Contending" 238-39) that sponsoring corporations not only subsidize cultural activities, such as this film, expressing the "true spirit" of Puerto Rico and supported by state or semi-state institutions but also "mass advertising campaigns [where] companies often reinforce images and ideas that have been institutionalized as represen-

---

[32] Also see Dávila (*Sponsored* 181-207).

tative by the government cultural institutions." They do so by identifying their products with "authentic" Puerto Rican culture and the *pueblo* (Dávila, *Sponsored* 181-207). To illustrate this point, the film is continually punctuated by blatant verbal or visual placement of products made by the film's sponsors, and provides an authenticating cinematic context for products presented in this setting as indispensable for "real" Puerto Ricans, such as Palo Viejo rum.

As to the question of identity, the inconclusive referendum on 14 November 1993, which narrowly favored Puerto Rico's continuing status as a Free Associated State, against full American Statehood or independent nationhood, has highlighted Puerto Rico's traditional problem in relation to whose family it belongs. Under the inescapable colonial, at best neocolonial, patronage of the United States as regional godfather, is this family to be nuclear (Associated), single parent (US state or Independent), or extended, as in the Caribbean federation proposed by intellectuals such as José Martí and his Puerto Rican counterparts, Ramón Emeterio Betances (1827-1898) and Eugenio María de Hostos (1839-1903)? Up until the last stages of the 1993 referendum opinion polls showed the popularity of statehood running neck and neck with that of a continuation of Puerto Rico's present Commonwealth status. In the end, the votes counted were as follows: 48.4% for a continuation of Commonwealth status, 46.2% for Statehood, and 4.4% for Independence. Therefore, a narrow majority of 2.2% opted for a continuation of Commonwealth status (*ND* 15 Nov. 1993: 1). However, if one takes into account the 4.4 % who voted for independence then we conclude that a majority (50.6%), if only a narrow majority, of the electorate were in one way or another in favor of a change of status. The increasing disenchantment with Commonwealth status becomes evident when one compares these results with those of the 1967 referendum, when 60.5% of the electorate voted for a continuation of Commonwealth status (Scarano 789). The referendum of 13 December 1998 produced similarly inconclusive results. However, the perceived desire for a change in status recorded in the previous referendum, more precisely a change in the way the status question is defined lead to the inclusion of an additional option, "ninguna de las anteriores" [none of the above (options)], which received 50.2% of the vote. Such uncertainty points to the fact that Puerto Ricans are disillusioned with the failures of modernization under the limited autonomy of Free Association, fearful of absorption as second-class citizens under Statehood within a country where hardship and discrimination have marked the experience of Puerto Rican migrants, who occupy an even lower rung of society than African Americans, and aware of the futile history of neocolonial "independence" in the Caribbean, particularly the traumatic events marking their neighbors supposed post-colonialism: that is, for example, brutal puppet regimes and occasional Monroe Doctrine intervention in both countries of Hispaniola, as well as invasion of Grenada, not to mention the hardships endured by Cubans under 40 years of a US-imposed embargo. Perhaps more importantly, for large sectors of the population, particularly younger Puerto Ricans, political identity in terms of nationality and voting citizenship are matters of indifference in the context of diaspora, the globalized marketplace, and internationalized images of cultural reference, where individual and group identity bypass nationality by being defined according to consumption (Santos).

Hence, to a large extent, the wholehearted laughter of the Puerto Rican audiences with whom I sat during four well-attended performances of *La guagua aérea*, in October and November of 1993, may have constituted more than a wishful nervous release from the difficulties of Puerto Rican national identity. Rather, it may confirm the audience's greater investment in a predominant "cultural nationalism" ever less dependent on government institutions in the context of transnational, market-driven, and hence necessarily more plural, corporate sponsorship. Puerto Ricans' ethnic identification according to cultural rather than formal political criteria or those related to an imagined nation-state perhaps points to the fact that cultural and ethnic criteria are more valid participatory forms of representation with regard to a transnational capitalist colony with no voting representation in an overseeing US Congress and between 43.5% and 75% of whose population lives beyond its shores in the United States.[33]

---

[33] The first figure is cited by Dávila (*Sponsored* 5), while the second is cited by Trías Monge (2).

CHAPTER 3

FAMILY VIOLENCE, PUERTO RICAN BLACKNESS,
AND THE CARIBBEAN CONTEXT OF THREE
SHORT STORIES

A LL Puerto Ricans have to live with the violent contradictions of
colonialism. However, Afro-Puerto Ricans have had in addition to survive slavery, denial, and distorted representations, largely
at the hands of their *criollo* compatriots. Perhaps with this history
in mind, Sánchez explores not only the resilience of black Puerto
Rican culture under colonialism but also its suffering. Within the
context of the *criollo* sector's long-term denial of the Afro-Antillean
element of Puerto Rican culture, Sánchez is perhaps only the second major Puerto Rican writer, after the poet Luis Palés Matos
(1898-1959), to attempt to represent his culture and society Afro-
centrically. Nevertheless, here and in the next chapter, I will show
how Sánchez's black writing breaks with Palés's reductively idealized *negrismo*, even though the latter's radicalism is undeniable in
the context of the 1930s, the height of *criollo* denial, when Palés poetry had its most controversial impact.[1] Still, instead of Palés's celebration of a black essence, locked in a binary opposition with the
supposed racial purity of mainstream *criollo* culture, Sánchez portrays blackness as the particular working through of a series of
complex, historical power relationships. Boldly, the writer's portrayal of cultural conflict, as well as a merely tenuous communality
and loyalty to authority in the first two stories examined, contra-
dicts the creole elite's traditionally wishful representation of Puerto

---

[1] See Díaz Quiñones ("Tomás Blanco" 31-32, 66-77, 81) and Luce López Baralt's introduction to her 1993 edition of Palés's most famous collection, *Tuntún de
pasa y grifería* (9-68).

Rican national identity.[2] According to this self-serving version, discussed in the previous chapter, Puerto Rico is a large family whose harmonious unity depends on the benign leadership of strong but enlightened creole father figures.

While it is true that Sánchez breaks with Palés's approach, it should be acknowledged that the ground for Sánchez's work is prepared by the courageously dissenting refutation of a "gran familia puertorriqueña" [great Puerto Rican family], already initiated not only by Palés but also by sociologists of the 1930s, such as José Colombán Rosario and Justina Carrión. Their scientific work complements and justifies Palés's by presenting a picture of a Puerto Rico divided by racism.[3] The groundbreaking work of the figures I have just mentioned has been updated in Isabelo Zenón Cruz's exhaustive two-volume work on racism and black themes in Puerto Rican literature, *Narciso descubre su trasero* [Narcissus Discovers his Backside] (1974-75). Meanwhile, José Luis González's indispensable 1979 essays, "El país de cuatro pisos" [The Four-Storeyed Country] and "Literatura e identidad nacional en Puerto Rico" [Literature and National Identity in Puerto Rico], revise official versions of sociocultural history. According to him, they do so by recognizing the traditional repression of Puerto Rico's fundamental Afro-Antilleanism.

Finally, I shall show how Sánchez eventually attempts to reconcile his problematization of national identity. In the first two stories I discuss, "Aleluya negra" [Black Halleluiah] and "¡Jum!" [Huh!], Sánchez fragments the concept of the unified national identity proposed by creole elites. On the other hand, in "Los negros pararon el caballo" [The Blacks Don't Get Taken for a Ride], he attempts to

---

[2] See Luce López Baralt's 1993 introduction to *Tuntún de pasa y grifería* (17-18, 36, 40, 73) and Santiago-Valles ("Puerto Rico" 141).

[3] On the work of these sociologists and for an introduction to the racial conflicts of "la gran familia" before and after the Thirties, see Díaz Quiñones ("Tomás Blanco" 32-34, 53-55, 63-67). Díaz Quiñones's discussion serves as an introduction to the most recent edition of Tomás Blanco's important 1938 essay, *El prejuicio racial en Puerto* [Racial Prejudice in Puerto Rico], which, though admitting discrimination, attempts to be conciliatory by recourse to the figure of the "Great Puerto Rican Family." For a discussion of Puerto Rican race relations on the island and in the United States, see Rodríguez, Torres, and *Centro*. For a discussion of Puerto Rican race relations within the context of wider Afro-Latin American culture, see Minority Rights Group (139-61). For a useful historical contextualization of racial prejudice, see Kinsbruner.

bring these fragments together in a new regional configuration.[4] Thus, roles are reversed and he himself defends unity against *criollo* discourses of fragmentation. For instance, an intellectual like Antonio S. Pedreira believed that Puerto Rican nationality was founded on a *mestiza* "guerra civil biológica" [biological civil war], where European blood had to constantly keep the threatening blood of an African "raza inferior" [inferior race] at bay (Díaz Quiñones "Tomás Blanco" 30). On the other hand, for Sánchez the historical experience of the "negros," referred to by the last story I discuss, provides the centre of gravity for a new paradigm of Caribbean unity. Just how valid is Sánchez's proposed synthesis?

1. "ALELUYA NEGRA:" PROMISCUOUS VIOLENCE AND CARIBBEAN WOMEN'S IDENTITY

Like his predecessor Palés Matos, Sánchez refutes the concept of nationalistic family unity. But his portrayal of conflict not only follows the fray across several levels of Puerto Rican society but also identifies conflict as the paradoxical mainstay of Caribbean identity. In the Caribbean of this story, unity can only take the form of dubious loyalties and surreptitious alliances, with the opportunities for these only arising through outbreaks of rebelliousness and violence. Rebelliousness is kindled in the protagonist, a young mulatto woman, by her attraction to celebrations being held on the sea front of the Puerto Rican town of Loíza Aldea by some "negros de orilla" [coastal blacks]. The place and time of the action are suggested by an allusion to "vejigantes" (28), demons represented by masked men from the Puerto Rican town of Loíza Aldea during the feast of Santiago. Ignoring her grandmother's warning that she runs grave risks if she attends, Caridad joins in and, as a consequence, is violently deflowered.[5]

Grandmother's chief objection to Caridad's wish to join the celebrations is that Caridad is a "negrita de solar" [household negrita]

    [4] A welcome study by Rafael Falcón incorporates brief reference (51-55) to the stories I discuss here in his investigation of the role of Afro-Antilleanism in the Puerto Rican short story.

    [5] In these sections on "Aleluya negra," I have found Carmen Vázquez Arce's excellent commentary on the story (*Por la vereda* 86-94) very helpful in developing my argument.

(27), whereas those celebrating are "negro [sic] de orillas que no se cepillan el trasero" [beach niggers who doesn't wipe their bum] (27). The grandmother's distinction between "negros de solar" and "negros de orilla" dates back to the days of slavery and sharply divided blacks, much in the same way as ante-bellum slave rebellions in America were often betrayed by black house servants who identified with their masters. Similarly, domestic slaves in Puerto Rico had greater contact with the cultural world of their masters and hence became partially assimilated into that world, while the "negros de orilla," as laboring field slaves, were more able to maintain their African traditions and religion. Also, most cases of slave unrest were initiated and lead by the rural blacks, who largely worked in the pre-industrialized sugar estates before their expansion as the focus for ever more centralized corporate municipalities where a labor force could be concentrated more easily. These rural blacks were more vulnerable than their domestic counterparts in the towns to the hardships resulting from recessionary periods in the sugar industry. Zenon Cruz observes (1: 257) that the high concentration of blacks in the coastal sugar estates led to an insult used among white Puerto Ricans during the period of the late eighteenth-century and based on the phrase "tener parientes en la Costa" (to have relatives on the Coast). It is precisely from this social stigma that the Grandmother wishes to dissociate herself and Caridad.[6]

Sánchez's story is concerned, therefore, with the historically determined confrontation between the grandmother's apparently as-

---

[6] On the differences between household blacks and coastal blacks, see Barradas (*Para leer* 60). On cases of slave unrest, see Baralt (163-64). On the establishment of corporate municipalities in Puerto Rico, see Quintero Rivera (*Conflictos de clase y política en el Puerto Rico del siglo* XIX 73, 113-14). Carmen Vázquez Arce (*Por la vereda* 90) updates Barradas's assertion of a historical, differentiated integration of black Puerto Ricans. She does so by referring to the marginalization of the poorest black groups during Puerto Rico's transformation from an agricultural to an industrial economy. According to her, in the concomitant shift of rural populations to San Juan many poor blacks came to occupy the outlying, especially seaboard, districts, "de manera que, gente de orilla se refiere a los marginados" [in such a way, that people of the coast refers to those marginalized]. Even more recently, Kelvin A. Santiago-Valles (*"Subject People"* 41-48) has examined this distinction in relation to an established black class of urban artisans, whose higher skills and education threatened the employment prospects of rural mulatto and white newcomers to the mostly coastal cities. Hence, the paler newcomers set themselves up as a supposedly white Iberian peasantry against the "'dark' [African] coastal laborers who were *in* but not *of* the Island" (Santiago-Valles, *"Subject People"* 44).

similated Christian, *criollo* world and the African world of the coastal blacks.[7] Confrontation between creolized blacks and the un-integrated coastal blacks is established by the grandmother's repri-mand, already cited at the beginning of this section. However, this reprimand is qualified by a humorous tone and imagery that per-haps conveys familiarity with a prohibited sector of Puerto Rican society. The grandmother's claim to intimate knowledge of the coastal blacks' toilet habits verges on the affectionate, with such an intimacy underlined by the grandmother's specific condemnation of a Carmelo whom she not only makes sure to discriminate against as a "negro prieto" or full black, but whom she also addresses by his first name. Furthermore, *criollo* culture is perhaps most palpable as a zero degree of social behavior and morality that obliges the grand-mother to disguise her true sympathies (cf. Santiago Valles, *"Subject People"* 44-46).

Other critics have already noted the coarse black humor with which Sánchez parodies Palés Matos's discourse of African sexuali-ty, undermining that model's lyrical vision of Afro-Antillean culture and its essentialist association of blackness with fervent sexuality.[8] Consequently, parody affords Sánchez the possibility of avoiding the lure of exalting eternal black values, in favor of stubbornly con-textualizing the eroticism of the coastal blacks within colonial pro-hibitions. These are ironically highlighted by Sánchez in his por-trayal of the grandmother, whose speech is so colorfully black that

---

[7] Purposely reflecting the racist appropriation in the Spanish Caribbean of a neutral term originally synonymous with "Antillean" (Zenón Cruz 1: 251), I use *creole* to refer to white Puerto Ricans of European descent. As Puerto Rico has a large, maybe predominant, mixed-race population, *criollo* is an ideologically loaded con-ception of racial purity rather than a distinction always self-evident in Puerto Rico's ethnicity. The ideology of *criollismo* has, in its first stage, evinced the Spanish colo-nizer's desire to mold an official national identity (white, European, feudal). Such a culture has served the colonizer's interests through those of his local intermediaries (J. L. González, "El país" 18). In a second stage, such a culture has been defended by the traditionally landowning, self-identified *criollo* elite whose power was under-mined by the social transformations caused by American colonialism ("El país" 17, 26-37; 1989c: 73). *Criollismo*'s distortion and weakness take the form of a disguised balance of colonial power relations as well as a devalorization of Afro-Caribbean popular traditions and ethnicity, while a mirage of cultural homogeneity is present-ed ("El país" 26-29, 35-39; 1989c: 74-76). Also, the promotion of outdated Euro-pean values is invalidated by Puerto Rico's dependence on America ("El país" 39; García).

[8] Arnaldo Cruz-Malavé ("Toward" 35, 46n3) and Vázquez Arce (*Por la vereda* 88-89).

it makes a striking contrast with her prejudice against full blacks. As denotation, the grandmother's speech may signal her conformity and subjection to a dominant system of racism and class discrimination (Vázquez Arce, *Por la vereda* 89). However, her extravagantly humorous use of language to insult the coastal blacks and the erotic devil within them verges on a pleasurable celebration of the forbidden. As in the rest of the story, the ironies presented by the speech, characterization, and attitudes of the grandmother rest on Sánchez's parody of the *negrista* literary tradition with which Palés is closely identified. In this instance, the parodied intertext would seem to be a poem by one of Palés' contemporaries, Fortunato Vizcarrondo, whose 1942 poem "¿Y tu agüela a'onde ejtá?" has "achieved [for him] what poets envy: a condition of anonymity" (Giusti Cordero 61). The title and especially one line from the poem are among the most used Puerto Rican proverbs, while Juan A. Giusti Cordero (60, 61 n30) informs us that "¿Y tu agüela a'onde ejtá?" became an "anthemic" song first interpreted by the legendary mulatto singer Ruth Fernández and eventually becoming the catchphrase of a popular white television comedian in blackface. The grandmother's inescapable blackness is anticipated by several aspects of Vizcarrondo's poem. Firstly, its title, which parallels the anglophone Caribbean saying "go home and look at your grandmother" (Giusti Cordero 74 n29), is used by Puerto Ricans to mock those who would deny the inherent mulatto or black background of themselves and most Caribbean people (cf. Kutzinski 66). [9] Secondly, the proverbial line from Vizcarrondo's poem, "el que no tiene dinga, tiene mandinga," frequently heard in everyday conversation in Puerto Rico and literally meaning "he who does not have Dinka blood has Mandinga blood," is again used as a negative or positive reminder of Puerto Ricans' racial and cultural heritage.

Thus, parody also seems to underline Sánchez's overdetermined use of the grandmother figure in "Aleluya negra" to assert her pervasive and undeniable blackness. This is further confirmed by the

---

[9] In her timely, but disappointing study, *La mujer negra en la literatura puertorriqueña*, Marie Ramos Rosado refers (7-8, 16-17) to the appearance of the theme of the grandmother hidden in the kitchen because of her blackness in Eleuterio Derkes' 1883 play, *Tío Fele* [Uncle Fele], Matías González García's short story, "La gloria de don Ramiro" [The Glory of don Ramiro] (c. 1935), and Francisco Arriví's 1958 play, *Vejigantes* [Carnival Demons].

grandmother's repeated references to the devil inside the coastal blacks, since Giusti Cordero reminds us (72 n8) that the proverbial line from Vizcarrondo's poem has a further connotation, based on the sense that was given to the term *mandinga* in the Spanish colonial era, as "the devil." Thus, this further translation might read: "he who does not have Africa in him, has the devil." According to such a binary opposition, if Carmelo and the other "prietos" have the devil inside, then the grandmother has Africa in her. The more vehemently she discriminates against the "prietos," the blacker she becomes.

On the other hand, the world of the "negros de orilla," though disavowed, takes possession of Caridad. She joins the celebrations, "viroteando las niñas; dando melao y suspiros, remeneando el nalgaje" [rolling her eyeballs; giving syrupy moans and sighing, waggling her tail-feather], and is "¡tan fogosa que los cocos no se atreven caer!" [burning so hot that the coconuts are hiding safely away from her, high up in their trees] (28). Moreover, the ironies of the ending emerge from the definitive eclipse (and exposure) of the grandmother's social pretense by the coastal blacks' possession of Caridad. After her deflowering, instead of going to a Catholic priest or a doctor, she visits a folk herbalist, whose "casucha" (31) suggests the shack of a black inhabitant of the former Puerto Rican shanty towns. The herbalist first makes the sign of the cross over Caridad but then administers a contraceptive potion, whose effect is so violent that the girl has to part her legs and allow the devil Carmelo has implanted in her to take leave of her body (32). The reader is unmistakably taken into the world of spiritualism and *santería*, prominent elements of Puerto Rican popular culture. [10] Finally, Caridad falls asleep to the drumbeat of the continuing celebrations and dreams under the star of the African deity, Bacumbé (32).

Caridad's disloyalty to the restrictions of pre-ordained identity is typical of many of Sánchez's characters–*Quíntuples* supplies a whole cast of examples played by just two actors–and, according to Antonio Benítez Rojo (*The Repeating Island* 1992, 242-61), of all Caribbean people. Made up of the splintered remnants of several incongruous cultures, they belong to all of them and none of them.

---

[10] On this incident, Vázquez Arce (*Por la vereda* 93) considers that Caridad is ostensibly able to exorcise the "diablo" of prohibited black eroticism, in the form of Carmelo's sperm, while still enjoying her new status as an initiate.

Never comfortable as only African, European, Chinese, or Asian, Christian, Jewish, Muslim, or Hindu, or any of the infinite variety of ethnic and cultural identities that have been sucked into the Caribbean, its inhabitants are constantly fleeing each of their identities, since none of them represents them wholly. Meanwhile, a sweet-and-sour reconciliation between the ingredients of Caribbeanness is impossible, since these are fundamentally incongruous. For instance, how to reconcile the linear European sense of modern Progress with the Afro-Antillean circularity of ritual performance? Or, the exclusive virtue and vice of Christian morality with the shady dealings of the *orishas*, whose power is abundantly amoral? [11] The violence of colonialism and slavery forced together the disparate elements of Caribbean identity, and violence has continued to scar their alliances and enmities ever since. Qualified enmity and alliance not only colors the grandmother's and Caridad's hostility and attraction to the "negros de orilla," but also the possible readings of Caridad's experiences with them.

Nativist folklore might have provided a satisfying resolution to Sánchez's tale. Typically, however, the Africanism of Bacumbé, moonlit dreams, and drums is dangerously loaded and resonates with ironic possibilities. The lyrical ending initially appears to reinforce positively the view of blackness as a liberating Dionysian power that prevails over the sexual prohibitions of bourgeois *criollo* values. One could with at least equal validity criticize the misogyny involved in Caridad's apparently violent deflowering. Indeed, after she is pursued through a palm grove by Carmelo, he smothers her scream with his hand and promises that "te voy a dar lo tuyo" [I'm going to give you what's coming to you] (28). Finally, he pushes her to the ground, where "las bocas revientan en sangre, las barrigas se friccionan" [blood wells from their mouths, their bellies grind] (31), and Caridad "siente la flor despuntando y solloza compases de tum triste" [feels the slow gash of her maidenhead and sobs to the rhythm of a sad drum] (31). The assertion of black culture seems to depend on an act of violence against a woman, an act of violence confirming the racist view of black masculinity represented by the image of the lascivious black rapist. The possible misogyny of the story is made worse by the fact that Caridad is shown, in the words

---

[11] On this amorality, see Barradas (*Para leer* 59-61), Benítez Rojo (*The Repeating Island* 1992: 169).

of many a rapist, to be asking for it by longing to join in forbidden black festivities. In this respect, the sexualized portrayal of Caridad is as deep-seated and institutionalized as that of Carmelo. The research of Miriam Jiménez Román (13) into race and identity illustrates my assertion by stating that, with regard to nineteenth-century race legislation on the island, and within the context of a rigid patriarchal morality prescribed by the Catholic Church and enforced legislatively by the State, *pardas* [mixed race women] were particularly vulnerable, being regarded as naturally lacking in moral rectitude, and therefore as the instigator, rather than the victim, of (white and black) male and (white) female aggression (and desire). To compound Caridad's vulnerability as a mixed race object of aggression, it is also worth recalling the long history of both black and white hostility, or at least ambivalence, in the Caribbean toward mulattoes, who, by definition, disrupt stable categories of racial identity (López Cantos 262-80; Kutzinski 172). Such hostile objectification of the *mulata* parallels the portrayal of her as a dangerously immoral, socially transgressive, and lascivious seductress (Kutzinski 17-42, 59-80, 191; Moreno Fraginals 21).

From yet another position, one might argue that Caridad enters knowingly into the coastal blacks' bacchanal, and undergoes a ritual of initiation into womanhood and Afro-Antillean culture. This reading would be supported by the fact that she is finally allowed to attend by her grandmother, who might be considered to tantalize her by denying her forbidden fruit. Such enticement might very well be mutual since, against the background of a seductive drumbeat, the granddaughter's first words are a plea for her grandmother to listen (27). Ostensibly asking for permission, she also appeals to the older woman's secret attraction to what she hears. Meanwhile, during the prolonged portrayal of Caridad's deflowering, what may be condemned as rape may instead involve an ambiguous manipulation of prohibition, paralleling her grandmother's use of language, that permits delight in forbidden pleasure and marking the intensified assertiveness of Puerto Rican women across the generations, from Spanish colonialism to the present day. In the following lines, the grandmother's gloatingly ambiguous condemnation is juxtaposed with the explicit physicality of Caridad's sexual encounter (31): "Oye la voz de la Güela–eso negro tienen el diablo por dentro–. Oye la respiración de Carmelo el Retinto pisoteándole la nuca" [she hears the voice of Granma, "them niggers got the devil inside 'em." She hears Carmelo the Raven's breath galloping over the back of her neck.].

I would argue that the surreptitious alliance that emerges from the relationship between Caridad and her grandmother is not without literary precedent. Beyond an acknowledgment of the prevalence of the extended over the nuclear family in the Caribbean, Evelyn O'Callaghan has observed (56, 67 n5) that, in a number of Caribbean texts by women, mothers are portrayed as carriers of a conservative, colonial ethos and instruments of repressive socialization for their daughters, who resent them because of this, while grandmothers represent Caribbean women's subversive potential based on their knowledge and skills beyond those identified with women's roles as wives and mothers under patriarchy. Thus, perhaps it is hinted that the grandmother's hidden desire is fulfilled in Caridad's violent, but painfully liberating, experience. Moreover, Caridad appears to have planned what she would do after her supposed initiation, by not hesitating in deciding to visit the folk healer, Colasa (31-32).

Caridad's coming-of-age is certainly disturbing in its portrayal of female assertion arising out of a woman's submission to violence. Though brutally deflowered, or raped, Caridad seems to assert herself by transcending the restrictions of her grandmother's world. But I would argue that Sánchez's consciously literary portrayal is a parodic illustration and pragmatic release from the restrictions placed on women in mainstream Caribbean nationalist culture and, in this instance, its Afro-Caribbeanist counterpart, both of which, as Vera M. Kutzinski has observed (163-97), have objectified women and smothered their voices. According to Kutzinski, this is particularly true of the *mulata*: "The *mulata* [of *negrista* poetry] may be *the* signifier of Cuba's [also Puerto Rico's and the Caribbean's] unity-in-racial-diversity, but she has no part in [it]. For the mestizo nation is a male homosocial construct premised precisely upon the disappearance of the feminine" (165). On the other hand, in an account of the traditional exclusion of female voices from nationalist literature, Silvio Torres-Saillant (70) writes that "in organizing a discourse of Antillean liberation and cultural emancipation around Caliban's self-assertiveness, Caribbean thinkers have often preserved one tradition of oppression, that which excludes women from the realm of constructive action." Torres-Saillant includes discussion of Fanon's vehement rejection of literature written by

Caribbean women, and serves to illuminate Sánchez's parody of Palés. Torres-Saillant does so by referring to Joan Dayan's investigation of Haitian scholars' devaluation of the work of female writers as well as male Haitian writers' removal of women to a spirit-world, where (as in Palés's poetry) they serve as muses, or embodiments of nature and its forces (Torres-Saillant 71). In short, women have served as the inspiration for poetry, while their own poetic voices have been stifled. This is uncomfortably reflected by the narrative us of the third-person in this story, combined with the highly sexualized physical description of Caridad's dancing, reminiscent of the dancing *mulatas* in Palés' poetry, particularly in his *Tuntún de pasa y grifería* (1937), and the stifling of her voice by Carmelo. At the same time, the prominence of the grandmother and her voice contest the invisibility of women and the assertion of male lineage Kutzinski identifies in the project of *mestizaje*, exemplified for her (166-69) by Nicolás Guillén's poems "La canción del bongó" [Song of the Bongo Drum] (1931) and "Balada de los dos abuelos" [Ballad of the Grandfathers] (1934). In "Aleluya negra," the black grandmother well and truly comes out of the kitchen where she has been hidden and does so with an ironic vengeance.

At the very least, "Aleluya negra" problematically acknowledges the historical violation of Caribbean women's desire for personal, political, cultural, and racial representation, while registering their ever more daring resistance to their exclusion across the generations represented by Caridad and her grandmother, whose desires, resourcefulness and pleasures are bound to pain and prohibition.

2. "¡JUM!:" ONE OF US IS NOT ONE OF US

The background to "Aleluya negra" is socioeconomic; but social divisions and alliances, as well as political exclusion, take place on the stage of Caribbean ethnicity and culture, within a particular historical context. Similarly, in "¡Jum!," questions of race and sexuality are given an urgent topicality by allusion to a particular period of Puerto Rican history and economic development while telling the story of a homosexual who is persecuted to death by his rural community. Mob violence against a sexual minority doubles as a brutal re-enactment of the rifts and alliances produced by Puerto Rico's economic transformations during industrialization. If in

"Aleluya negra" censure is only apparent and enables a covert expression of self-assertion, in "¡Jum!," self-assertion takes a degraded form. Marginalized from the channels of meaningful political action, affiliation can only be achieved indirectly, through an act of desperate physical violence, represented by the sacrifice of a surrogate white.

The protagonist is reprimanded for the supposedly inappropriate ostentation of his Sunday best (55). His sporting of a waistcoat, whose ornamental clovers and lacey trimming (55) would anyway be considered suspect by a homophobe, takes place on workdays (55) and puts into question the cooperative work ethic that unites a rural community. Indeed, the punishment for his incomprehensible disloyalty is marked by his not being permitted a name (cf. Lugo-Ortiz 126). He is simply known as "el hijo de Trinidad" [Trinidad's son] (55). On the other hand, the characters named are predominantly working people or, in the case of one Eneas Cruz, active in ominous community enterprises, such as surrounding the protagonist's house with barbed wire (56). All these characters shun the anonymous protagonist. As in "Aleluya negra," the use of a diminutive "negrito" (58) perhaps sets the protagonist apart, as a mulatto, from the "negros" (57) of his community.

Any animosity felt by blacks towards mulattoes in Puerto Rico goes back to the greater freedom and higher status of mulattoes in the period of slavery on the island. Making full use of their distinct advantage over blacks, mulattoes have since then more fully integrated socially, commercially, and politically in *criollo* society. Of related interest is Guillermo A. Baralt's account of a documented case, perhaps representative, involving black resentment towards a mulatto slave overseer. Baralt reports (148-49) that the mere fact that he was a mulatto was enough so that the slaves and freedmen working under him should be disobedient. The hostility of the black slaves and workers towards Clotter, the overseer whom they considered a mulatto lackey, finally led them to murder him. This is one of two documented examples recorded by Baralt of slaves turning against mulatto overseers. A more recent example of the conflicting interests between black and mulatto Puerto Ricans is provided by the failure, in the 1930s, of the Nationalist Party, led by a mulatto, Pedro Albizu Campos. By appealing to a nostalgic Hispanism, whose benefits were traditionally more accessible to mulatto Puerto Ricans, he alienated blacks on the island, who associated a Hispanic past with the restrictions of slavery. As I will show in the next chapter, they assertively rejected Albizu's patrician nationalism by embracing an emergent working-class movement that represented them more forcefully than ever before.

The historical context I have just given is undoubtedly illuminating and has already drawn the attention of certain intellectuals.[12] But there is need for more rigorous research in the area of contemporary relations between and the respective status of black and mulatto Puerto Ricans. With such a lack of up to date sociological research literature might provide some useful illustrations of relations between these groups.

In 1958, a young Luis Rafael Sánchez performed as an actor in Francisco Arriví's *Vejigantes* [Carnival Demons], a play which is not only exceptional in its concern for black issues but which foreshadows Sánchez's own concern for these in his subsequent writing. The plot concerns a young Puerto Rican *mulata*'s passing for white at the instigation of her mother, in an attempt to catch a white American husband. The play indicates the advantage of being a pale-skinned mulatto for the large number of Puerto Ricans who have had to suffer racism while seeking their fortunes as *spiks* in white America. However, its portrayal of a darker-skinned grandmother's farcical concealment every time her granddaughter's suitor visits bears more relation to the melodramatic tradition represented by Douglas Sirk's *Imitation of Life* (1959) than to the racial realities of present-day Puerto Rico.

Outside the stories I look at in this chapter, Sánchez's own work underplays any differences between blacks and mulattoes. Meanwhile, the short stories here can be of little help. The absence in them of the modern technology and machinery so prominent in all contemporary Puerto Rican life suggests that they are set well before the time of their writing, when memories reaching back to the slave period would have been fresher. More recently, Kelvin A. Santiago-Valles ("Puerto Rico" 142) has observed that, with the expansion of a non-white middle class since the Second World War, tension has arisen between the light mulattoes in the middle classes

---

[12] On historical relations between blacks and mulattoes on the island, see J. L. González ("Literatura e identidad nacional" 46-47), Blanco (*El prejuicio racial* 123-26), and Díaz Quiñones ("Tomás Blanco" 65). On Albizu's alienation of black Puerto Ricans, see Scarano (692).

proper, dark mulattoes and blacks in the lower middle classes, and the growing, largely black, underclass of unemployed Puerto Rican men. [13] In my own limited experience as a visitor to the Island, I have found it very hard to detect or hear any complaint of prejudice between blacks and mulattoes, though the pragmatic advantage of lighter skin when seeking employment is a commonplace, and, as Arlene M. Dávila observes (*Sponsored* 83-85), purported claims of a "lack of prejudice" on the island have much to do with the denial of racial inequalities by the discourse of *mestizaje* promoted as part of the "cultural nationalism" of Puerto Rican politics and institutional culture (Dávila, *Sponsored* 69-73). [14] In any case, if not actually mulatto, Trinidad's son is tainted by his presumed association with the white world, reviled for being a "negrito presumío" (stuck-up *negrito*) (58). Homophobia and race resentment on the part of the protagonist's village reinforce each other in the mob's assertion at one point that "los negros son muy machos" (blacks are real men) (56). If blacks are real men, then, by contrast, effeminate homosexuality may be attributed to whites. [15] Therefore, the protagonist's branding as white equates with his branding as homosexual.

Recourse to sexual and gendered discrimination has been central to political struggle in twentieth-century Puerto Rico. It has been observed that colonial and class conflicts during the first decades of American colonialism were disputed by, among other means, a masculinization of one's own group at the cost of feminizing one's enemies. [16] I would suggest that, in "¡Jum!," the blackness of the protagonist's persecutors and their marginalization from a working-class identity assures that theirs is an impotent masculinity. I come to this conclusion by presuming that the story is set at an early stage of American colonization, suggested by the protagonist's use of an American perfume, "*Come to Me*" (58), and the techno-

---

[13] The situation of middle- and lower-class mulatto or black Puerto Rican women should be studied separately, since their employment and sociopolitical profile has generally increased as part of the changes brought about by an industrialization process that has favoured female laborers, and as a result of liberal reforms and a women's movement originating in the Sixties. See Ríos, Silvestrini, Santiago-Valles ("Puerto Rico" 143).

[14] A useful discussion to Puerto Rico's "shade discrimination" and helpful references to the few previous studies are provided in the introduction to Kinsbruner (1-18).

[15] A point already made by Vázquez (*Por la vereda* 126-27).

[16] Santiago-Valles (*"Subject People"* 63-67, 82-83, 95, 155).

logical invisibility already mentioned. Hence, it is significant that village life is portrayed at a time when a working-class identity and, along with it, black rights emerge (albeit unevenly) and become established in the factories, docks, and modernized sugar estates or refineries of rapidly expanding coastal municipalities.[17] At the rural margins of an incipiently capitalist Puerto Rico, the blacks of Sánchez's story are at the farthest remove from the resources underpinning both the paternalistic masculinism of *criollo* elites and a black working-class identity. Indeed, it is their detachment from these that allows me confidently to date the story. For, from the moment when the Federal Government assisted New Deal initiatives to be implemented on the island as compensation for the ravages of the Depression, increasingly populist local governments pursued a policy of land and labor reforms that increased the political importance of the rural sectors (Scarano 7-14, 676-83).

As Puerto Ricans distanced from both the unifying ideology of *criollo* paternalism or proletarian solidarity, the village rallies around a binding heterosexuality, summoned by means of the abjection of a token homosexual, a process examined in unprecedented depth by Agnes I. Lugo-Ortiz. Trinidad's son stands in, not for the parodically feminized other used in the political language of the labor disputes discussed by Santiago-Valles, but as testimony to his community's emasculating exclusion from participation in the urban struggles of the working class. The story illustrates one of the social transformations experienced by blacks as a result of the change of colonizer. Baralt has shown that, during the semi-feudal slavery of Spanish domination, it was rural blacks who were more prominently militant than the largely domestic black slaves of the towns. Conversely, the source of concerted unrest came to be resituated in a budding, urbanized, proletariat. The convergence of workers in municipalities constituted the first step of a process that culminated in the mass migration to the cities that resulted from Puerto Rico's radical transformation, initiated in the 1940s, from an agrarian to an industrial economy.

The physicality of direct masculine violence portrayed by Sánchez testifies to the village's barred access to a political language, whether it be the *criollo* elite's metaphorical expression of patriarchy or the working class's manipulation of the signs of gen-

---

[17] Santiago-Valles (*"Subject People"* 41, 105-09, 117-18, 139-42, 151, 203-07).

der and sexuality. A very early example of this manipulation is described by Santiago-Valles (*"Subject People"* 103-04), who gives an account of a demonstration, in 1901, by unemployed laborers. One of these was dressed as a transvestite version of a leading politician (Luis Muñoz Rivera), who, in his guise as a homosexual drag queen or "loca," was not only believed to represent an unmanly lack of *cojones*, making him an indecisive leader, but could also symbolically bear the brunt of the demonstrators' diatribes.

The protagonist's silence, as well as, one might add, his decision to leave (56), may be considered a defiant refusal to play his role in reinforcing the identity of the mob. Unlike the demonstrator in drag, he refuses to be one of the boys. In fact even if he chooses affiliation, there is no possibility of his survival. He cannot be involved in any playacting unless he leaves for the city, as he attempts to do. And even there, if Santiago Valles's account is anything to go by, it seems that his homosexuality can only be degradingly subsumed as, again, a negative reinforcement of new Puerto Rican identities made possible by class struggle. Even the liberating masquerade of a later work, such as *Quíntuples*, whose potential is implied by a character's travelling bag full of make-up and costumes (58), seems preempted by the pantomime of a demonstration such as that detailed by Santiago-Valles. However, whatever its initial intention, this urban visibility itself still provides the marginal figure with possibilities for the political diversion suggested by the later play. The protagonist of "¡Jum!" certainly wishes to join those in the city, in an economic version of Caridad's attempt to recuperate from her ethnic incompletion by allying herself with another group. More than this, his escape and fulfilment depend on an inversion of "Aleluya negra." This time, the protagonist really has to run away from the blacks of his pre-modern community instead of embracing their primality. On the other hand, the village's detachment from Puerto Rico's economic transformation, rather than evoking the strength of ancient traditions or the Arcadianism of rural self-sufficiency, this time implies regression. With no access to a meaningful civic language, the community reverts to an unqualified primitivism, more violently incoherent than the cultural assertion of Afro-Antillean traditions and language depicted in "Aleluya negra." Moreover, without representation, conflict cannot be mediated by the language of politics. Blood sacrifice substitutes the detached humor of drag politics.

Homophobia's grotesque predominance is marked by the insults that hound the protagonist and fill the text with an extreme hatred signaled by dehumanizing intention, repetition, and orgiastic verbal distortion (60):

> Llegó al río.
> –¡Mariquita!
> –¡Mariquita!
> –¡Mariquita!
> El agua era fría y la sangre era caliente.
> –¡Cochino!
> –¡Marrano!
> –¡Cochino!
> Los satos asquerosos se quedaron en la orilla. Las sombras también. Y las voces hirientes.
> –¡Mariquitafiesteramariquitafiesteramariquitafiestera!
>
> [He arrived at the river.
> "Little faggot!"
> "Little faggot!"
> "Little faggot!"
> The water was cold and his blood was hot.
> "Pig!"
> "Filthy swine!"
> "Pig!"
> The filthy mongrels stayed on the bank. The shadows too. Also the mutilating voices.
> "Missfaggotypartypansymissfaggotypartypansymissfaggotyparty-pansy!"]

The deformed language here signals how the traditional disadvantage of blacks under colonialism, to whose class-inflected languages of historiography, ethnography, law, commerce, journalism, and politics they have had limited or no access, is most acutely suffered by rural Puerto Rican blacks. [18]

Lugo-Ortiz (116-18) has associated the mob's defensive tribalism with Puerto Rican homophobia in the 1960s, which she lucidly identifies as a reaction to the sociopolitical instability and weaken-

---

[18] On blacks' continuing subjection to these languages, even after their emancipation from slavery, and on blackness as a loaded marker in early American colonial discourse, see Santiago-Valles (*"Subject People"* 44-46, 74, 87, 105, 122, 156).

ing of traditional models of authority in the areas of sexuality and gender. However, to understand the story's violence, I believe it is important to inform Lugo-Ortiz's reading with a historical appreciation of the villagers' relationship to the urbanized working classes and traditional mulatto privilege. Thus, Lugo-Ortiz's association (129) of the "verbal language" of the village with expressions of modern Puerto Rican nationality and identity is misleading, since she fails to discuss the representational advantage of incipiently urban blacks over rural blacks. Meanwhile, the community's persecution of a scapegoat on the basis of his association with leisured, hence privileged "blancos" ("¡Jum!" 57) highlights the resentment and political impotence of his persecutors, who are spurred on to assert themselves through homophobic sexual persecution. Barred from the symbolic world of politics, they retreat into a pre-symbolic world of ritual.

Lugo-Ortiz's definition (125) of this ritual as Dionysian is well argued, but her inference of a complementary Apollonian dimension is in my view doubtful. While it is true that the mob's "Dionysian hunt" (125) approximates, albeit as a travesty, the communality that is the foundation of the Apollonian spheres of culture and hence politics, the village's actions increasingly, as I will show, distance them from these.[19] I disagree with Lugo-Ortiz's (125) attribution of the following phrases to a "communal *verbum*" (125, my emphasis): "se vestían las lenguas con navajas" [tongues were dressed with blades] ("¡Jum!" 57); "una sombra le asestó la palabra" [a shadow stabbed the word at him] (58); "el murmureo era dardo y lanza" [the murmuring was a dart and spear] (58); "voces hirientes" [mutilating voices] (60). Instead, I interpret these phrases as examples of the mob's primitive and sacrificial tribalism and reject Lugo-Ortiz's identification (124) of a "word of the law, of the community as law." I believe that, for want of a better word, the mob's sub-verbalism precludes the "word of the law," whose unavailability eventually undermines cohesion. Furthermore, I shall challenge Lugo-Ortiz's identification of a "*verbal richness* through which the community [tentative at best] becomes one" (128, my emphasis, my aside).

---

[19] Incidentally, the distance here between Dionysian orgy and Apollonian civilization is a graphic illustration of the classic dichotomy of civilization and barbarism debated by Latin American intellectuals since the nineteenth century and discussed in my next chapter.

Ritual is highlighted by the repetitious chanting of the mob's insults, which constantly fail to develop reiterated single utterances into sentences but which, through incantation directed in unison to an outsider ("¡Mariquita! ¡Mariquita! ¡Mariquita!"), constantly reassert the boundaries of its would-be community. Several times, the virtually static enunciation of a string of synonymous variations replace the semantic development of meaningful communication. For example:

> –¡Patito!
> –¡Pateto!
> –¡Patuleco!
> –¡Loca!
> –¡Loqueta!
> –¡Maricastro!
> –¡Mariquita!
> [...]
> –¡Madamo!
> –¡Mujercita!

> ["Patsy!"
> "Nancy!"
> "Fancy-boy!"
> "Queen!"
> "Queeny!"
> "Faggotballs!"
> "Miss Faggot!"
> [...]
> "Madame!"
> "Little woman!"
> (55-56)

> –¡Remilgado!
> –¡Blandengue!
> –¡Melindroso!
> –¡Añoñao!
> ["Prim Jim!"
> "Softie!"
> "Prissy Missy!"
> "Sissy!"]
> (58)

The villagers' most complex utterances, as in the opening paragraph, are reported second-hand (55):

El murmureo verdereaba por los galillos. Que el hijo de Trinidad
se prensaba los fondillos hasta asfixiar el nalgatorio. Que era ave
rarísima asentando vacación en mar y tierra. Que el dominguero
se lo ponía aunque fuera lunes y martes. Y que el chaleco lo lucía
de tréboles con vivo de encajillo. ·

[The murmuring was gurgling out from the back of their throats.
That Trinidad's son tightened his buttocks to the point of suffo-
cating his fanny. That he was a queer bird, swooping from holiday to holiday on earth and sea. That he wore his Sunday best
even on Mondays and Tuesdays. That he sported a vest with ornamental clovers and lacy trimming.]

As the only proof of the villagers' linguistic proficiency is their static, largely one-word utterances, it is hardly possible to attribute the
relatively more sophisticated reported speech to anyone but the
omniscient narrator. Even if this mediation is dismissed, then such
articulations can, at best, only take the tentative forms of the villagers' "murmureo" [murmuring] or their faltering condemnation:
"en altibajos" [humming and hawing] (55). Meanwhile, the over-
flowing passion of the primitive, unarticulated sub-language with
which Trinidad's son is insulted ("¡Mariquitafiesteramariquitafi-
esteramariquitafiestera!"), as well as the mob's increased anger
when their victim attempts to leave confirm a paradoxical desire for
the outsider.

If it is against a necessary threat that the villagers hope to build
their sense of community, then the victim's silence is provocative
because, by refusing to reply, he mutely echoes the absence of political dialogue that excludes his persecutors. The mob's reiterated
variations on a single meaning rebound as disruptive echoes, with
the assailants' verbal assault boomeranging on itself. And all this is
made possible by the silence of Trinidad's son, who surrenders
none of himself to the would-be community that attacks him but,
like an amplifying sounding board, merely deafens them with the
aggressively hollow sound of their own brutality. As violent as it becomes, their increasingly frustrated ranting finds no response. Any
hope of dialogue drowns with the protagonist at the end of the story, and the unity of the mob disintegrates into childish gibberish as
the only binding pretext for community dies:

El agua era tibia, más tibia, más tibia. Las voces débiles, más débiles, más débiles. El agua hizo glu. Entonces, que no vuel-va,
que no vuel-va, que no vuel-va, el Hijo de Trinidad
glu . . .
que
glu . . .
no
glu . . .
vuelva
glu . . .
se
glu . . .
hundió.

[The water was warm, warmer, warmer. The voices weak, weaker, weaker. The water went glug. Don't let the him come back,
don't let Trinidad's son come back, come back, come back.
glug . . .
don't
glug . . .
come
glug . . .
back
glug . . .
he
glug . . .
drowned.]
(60)

3. "Los negros pararon el caballo:" Islands Apart in the Stream of History

The divisions traced in the stories I have looked at so far reap-
pear only to be defused by stealth in "Los negros pararon el caballo." The blackness described here does not take the form of a self-
amputating pretext to vent the desperation of colonial impotence,
as in "¡Jum!," but instead is the site of violent betrayal by a cruel
dictatorship.

The story takes place on a fictitious island subject to the tyrannical rule of a father and son, referred to as Bebé, and their private
militia. Within the Haitian setting implied, the story concentrates

on the forced enlistment of villagers, who are transported to the capital to celebrate Bebé's birthday and to pledge their allegiance at gunpoint. Fiction reenacts the well-documented transportation of peasants to Port-au-Prince as part of stage-managed displays of loyalty to Papa Doc Duvalier. [20]

In terms of Sánchez's development as a writer, "Los negros" stages a tentative early demonstration of irony as part of a political strategy to develop historically informed but unpredictable identities. Such irony is employed by the characters of recent works like *Quíntuples* and, as I will demonstrate in the next chapter, *La importancia de llamarse Daniel Santos*. The necessary historical knowledge that informs any possible struggle for change is cogently portrayed by Sánchez. Gathered together in the main square of the story's island capital, and under the watchful eye of Bebe's militiamen, one of the villagers remembers long years of tyranny: "la cosecha de años duros, quince son los años duros, catorce de vivas al Padre y uno de vivas al Hijo" [the harvest of harsh years, fifteen in all, fourteen years of *vivas* to the Father and one of *vivas* to the Son] (94). Under such oppressive conditions, the narrator admits that opposition must be cautious if it is not to succumb to superior force (94). His avowed surreptitiousness demonstrates an experienced knowledge of the limits of public discourse as, when cheering the dictator, the narrator admits that "una onza de letra más y se ganaba el castigo" [just one breath more than required and you earned punishment] (94). The wry humour of these disclosures emerges from the ironically confidential tone of a narrator who addresses the reader directly in the formal *Usted* form, thus conspiratorially undermining the terms of his ostensible public display of loyalty. In deadpan fashion and with dramatic irony, the narrator describes Bebé's acclamation by his subjects as "la felicitación merecida" [the well-deserved congratulation] (94) on "la fecha memorable de su cumpleaños" [the memorable date of his birthday] (94). The culmination of this loaded ovation is an absurd birthday cheer: "Feliz cumpleaños, Presidente Bebé" [Happy birthday, President Bebé] (95). Irony underlines the dissimulation under whose guise political struggle is able to take place and the climax of the story is reached when, disguised by enthusiastic cries of support, there is an assassination attempt against Bebé. Though this

---

[20] Diederich & Burt (169-70, 187, 213, 233, 305).

fails, it is set up to provide the story with a hopeful ending based on the wry unity of Bebé's subjects, whose outward passivity conceals unified political resolve.

The colonially fractured blackness of "Aleluya negra" and "¡Jum!" reappears in "Los negros," initially in the form of a figurative language that traces the violent disarticulation of black communities in the Caribbean. Bebé's betrayal of his people is written in the color of his skin. Realizing that an attempt has been made on his life, his fear makes the color drain from his face, so that "por una vez dejó de ser negro" [for once he stopped being black] (95). In a sense, his physical symptom shows his separation from the ethical responsibilities that result from a blackness that refers beyond mere skin pigmentation to particular historical relations. Blackness is a political signifier rather than an essence. Historically, black ethnic identities and cultures have survived by resisting oppression. Therefore, Bebé can be said to cease to be black by having become an oppressor himself. And, if by blanching he does not become white, perhaps he momentarily becomes pale enough to be taken for a mulatto, so that Bebé's association with being mulatto revives historical Haitian conflicts. If pride in being Haitian is founded on the distinction of being the world's only nation to have been founded by slaves, then Haitian mulattoes cannot fully share in that pride. Though many fought on the side of the slaves during the slave revolution of 1791-1804, the mulattoes were mostly the offspring of white slave owners and black slaves, often educated in France and, right up to the outbreak of revolution, competed with white creoles as great landowners and exploiters of slaves (Mintz 76-77). C.L.R. James has recorded not only the periods of real cooperation but also the complex frictions and internal conflicts between mulattoes and blacks during the revolutionary period itself. [21] Significantly, it was mulatto collaboration with white counter-revolutionaries and mulatto vacillation in the form of a reactionary adherence to long-established privilege based on slavery that dealt an emerging Haiti's abolitionist revolution some of its major setbacks. [22] Furthermore, James has observed that "the advantages of being white were so obvious that race prejudice against the negroes permeated the minds

---

[21] James (96-100, 115-17, 122-29, 135, 149, 161-73, 207, 219-35, 270, 295-97, 306).

[22] James (96-100, 115-17, 122-23, 164-66, 270, 295-97, 306).

of the mulattoes who so bitterly resented the same thing from the whites" (42-43). Qualifying this statement, Sidney W. Mintz has warned that racial discrimination in Haitian society is far from clear-cut and, in elite circles has traditionally been superseded by, among other things, European criteria of education, language, religion, economics (82). These criteria largely determined the emergence of a post-revolutionary ruling elite. The upbringing of many mulattoes ideally prepared them for entry into this emergent elite, whose authoritarianism and exploitation has been continued to modern times in Haiti (Diederich & Burt 26-27, 35, 58-59). In a discussion of the contemporary distribution of power in Haitian society, James Ridgeway writes (27):

> Ensconced at the top of Haitian society is a mostly mulatto oligarchy, composed of a few thousand families who continue to embrace a sort of feudal life that it is hard to believe exists at the end of the twentieth century. The less than one percent of the population represented by these "ruling families" controls over 44 percent of the wealth in Haiti. . . . These families have used the army, the Tonton Macoute, and the overall power of the state to maintain themselves in a sort of decadent splendor, and have long been a reactionary force in Haitian politics, often aligned with the Duvalierists.

Rumor also has it that in 1991 it was pressure from the rich mulatto class that incited the military coup against the elected president, Jean Bertrand Aristide.

Yet again, the infra-racial division between Caribbean blacks and mulattoes, explored in the previous stories I have discussed, hampers the possibility of a unified Caribbean identity asserting itself at the local level. Instead, I will show how Sánchez displaces that hope to the imagined space of regionality. Moreover, if Sánchez traces the fissures of a violent history, he does so in search of an all-empowering Caribbean identity, whose fragments are startlingly reconciled by Sánchez at the end of the story, through the ingenious use of a multiple narrative point of view.

Two interchangeable narrative perspectives are employed by Sánchez: the first-person singular and first-person plural. Their interchangeability obviously enough implicates the individual narrator in the community for which he speaks. It is even possible to go further and include the narrator as one of those killed when, after the assassination attempt, the militiamen fire on and kill many of the crowd.²³ The use of the first-person plural in the following sentence certainly makes the life or death of the narrator ambiguous: "Arrastrados como a perros, así así nos sacaron a los que habíamos muerto" [dragged away like dogs, just like that they removed those of us who had died] (96). However one reads the outcome of the massacre, the eventual return transportation of the villagers, dead or alive, at the very least blurs the boundaries between life and death, animate and inanimate. The survivors are loaded onto trucks, which haul them away, "como a fruta amontonada, como a piedra de cantera, como a mierda al basurero" [like piles of fruit, like quarry stones, like shit to the rubbish dump] (96). The living of present action are united with the dead by a shared history.

Throughout the narration, communal experience prepares the ground for the implication of Puerto Rican readers in the concerted action anticipated by the story's ending. Describing the events of the story, three times the narrator affirms the truth of his account by startlingly addressing the reader in the second-person singular, with the informal plea "créame" [believe me] (94, 95). Published in Puerto Rico, the story is thus made by Sánchez to follow in the footsteps of fervent Caribbeanists such as the Cuban José Martí or his Puerto Rican counterparts, Eugenio María de Hostos, Emeterio Betances, and Luis Palés Matos. In emulation of them, he has his narrator directly address Puerto Rican readers' potential sense of a pan-Caribbean identity and history of Independence struggles and revolution. But like his role models, he perhaps overestimates this potential, since Puerto Rico, unlike Cuba for instance, has never had its own experience of a concerted Independence struggle nor of revolution, fought for by all classes and racial groups.

The writer manipulates an anticipated sense of identity in the vain attempt to cut across the class barriers separating the peasant narrative voice and the educated reader. The story ends on a hopeful note, with a statement of faith in the eventual overthrow of both dictator and divisive oppression: "Volvimos a Nombre de Dios a esperar. La próxima vez lo enterramos" [we returned to Nombre de Dios to wait. We will bury him the next time] (96).

"Los negros pararon el caballo" presents hope, in the form of common aspirations forged out of a common history, as the positive

---

²³ Carmen Vázquez Arce (*Por la vereda* 174-75) supports this view.

counterpart of the unconfessable allegiance or exclusion portrayed in "Aleluya negra" and "¡Jum!" Still, even the unity to which Sánchez finally appeals is only made possible as the result of a mass killing. In the Caribbean, optimism can only ever be founded on the perpetual mutilations of its history. In a further turn of the screw, even the vibrancy, the sunny Caribbean temper favored by classic Hollywood and travel brochures, appears a violent overcompensation for the hungry loss at its center.

4. CONCLUSION

Violence sets the scene of all three stories. A possible rape is followed by a lynching, while the ferocity of both is capped by a mass execution. Any conception of Caribbean blacks as a homogeneous group uniformly oppressed under colonialism and united by popular culture disappears. Instead, a network of discursive relations is traced, implicating inter- and infra-racial power relationships as well as shifting loyalties, and duplicitous survival, a process identifiable throughout Sánchez's work.

However, the redemption of an ambiguous Caribbean identity is attempted by means of the integrating optimism of "Los negros pararon el caballo." Sánchez seems to imply that mutual recognition of the bitter lessons of a common Caribbean history of subjection–from Haiti's cruel dictatorships to Puerto Rico's paternalistic colonialism–unites all Caribbean people, regardless of their differences. Thus, the writer again brings Palés Matos to earth by contextualizing the poet's celebration of a common Caribbean culture, founded by him somewhat vaguely in a mystical Afro-centric "tipo espiritual homogéneo" (Palés Matos, *Poesía completa* 219). But, what of working-class Puerto Ricans, blacks, women, and the newly educated professionals and entrepreneurs that emerged as a result of the opportunities offered by modernization? I will further demonstrate in the next chapter how they actually found hope in the prospect of American colonization. And, to what extent is the experience of a common history of domination shared, if at all? How so, when domination has been so different and historically heterogeneous for the various strata of Puerto Rican society, the rural mob of "¡Jum!" and the burgeoning proletariat described by Santiago-Valles? When, under American colonization, however uneven, the gains experienced by the groups just mentioned have traditionally pitted them against the Hispanist discourses of formerly landed classes now dispossessed? These are questions that repeatedly pose themselves throughout this book; questions whose complexities I shall further trace in the following chapters.

"Los negros pararon el caballo" is an early work that tentatively points forward to Sánchez's subsequent development as a writer. The pan-Caribbeanism of "Los negros" seems to foreshadow the optimistic internationalism I shall examine in Sánchez's 1988 novel, *La importancia de llamarse Daniel Santos*. Though "Los negros" was first published in 1972 in the San Juan journal *Sin Nombre* [Without Name] (11.4: 77-78), it first appeared in the fourth edition, in 1984, of Sánchez's short story collection. The fact that the writer decided to include the story in the collection at this time, only four years before the publication of his second novel-length text, is evidence of his growing pan-Caribbean and pan-American optimism from this period of his career onwards. However, unlike "Los negros," I shall now go on to demonstrate how the novel never attempts synthetically to unify Caribbean identity but situates its internationalism precisely in the heterogeneous space of Hispanic Caribbean culture.[24]

---

[24] In terms of "¡Jum!" and Sánchez's work in general, I fully agree with Lugo-Ortiz's statement that "'el pueblo' [the people], a pivotal concept in nineteenth-century bourgeois theories of the nation-state, which has been reappropriated by left- and right-wing populist rhetorics alike in Latin America, is inscribed [by Sánchez] as a problematic–not heroic–agent" (130). However, I would claim that, in "Los negros," Sánchez projects a regionalism that indeed exploits the populism to which Lugo-Ortiz refers.

CHAPTER 4

FROM *LA GUARACHA DEL MACHO CAMACHO* (1976) TO *LA IMPORTANCIA DE LLAMARSE DANIEL SANTOS* (1988): MODERNITY, POPULAR CULTURE, AND THE POPULAR HERO

> There can be little doubt that nationalism as a founding ideology is a characteristic peculiar to marginal and dependent societies.
>
> (González Echevarría, 'The Case' 11)

> Uno se pregunta si la cultura popular ha ocupado y por lo tanto humanizado el espacio urbano, o si el espacio urbano ha constreñido y quizás impuesto a la cultura popular una deshumanización.
>
> [One wonders if popular culture has taken over and thus humanized urban space, or if urban space has constrained and perhaps forced the dehumanization of popular culture.]
>
> (Ortega, in Rodríguez Juliá, Interview 142)

L UIS Rafael Sánchez has disclaimed any relationship between his 1976 novel, *La guaracha del Macho Camacho* [Macho Camacho's Beat], and his other novel-length narrative text, *La importancia de llamarse Daniel Santos* [The Importance of Being Daniel Santos] (1988) ("Los motivos del lobo" 103). I shall argue that *La importancia de llamarse Daniel Santos* develops a view of a unifying and assertive popular culture that intensifies his earlier depiction, in *La guaracha del Macho Camacho*, of a popular culture which defies exclusive models of Puerto Rican identity promoted by bourgeois authoritarianism. Moreover, Sánchez goes a long way toward reconciling the class conflicts presented in *La guaracha*.[1]

---

[1] All translations into English of *La guaracha* are taken from Gregory Rabassa's 1981 translation of the novel.

Sánchez's novelistic debut presents the interrelated lives of a corrupt Puerto Rican senator, Vicente Reinosa, his repressed upper-class wife, Graciela Alcántara, his working-class mulatto mistress, La China Hereje, and his wastrel son, Benny. Narrative progression is minimal since the action is centered around a massive San Juan traffic jam, from which the narration constantly digresses by means of flashbacks, fantasy, daydreams, as well as cross-cutting between episodes and characters. On the other hand, *La importancia* is a generically hybrid text, what the narrator terms a "fabulación" [fabulation] (5), or what one reviewer has defined as the fusion of a journalistic chronicle, novel, essay, dramatic dialogue, testimony, and travel journal (Colón Zayas 515). In several Latin American towns and cities, the narrator carries out research and interviews fans of the bolero singer Daniel Santos, as part of an investigation into the legend surrounding the historical Puerto Rican artist. In the second book, even the semblance of narrative development is absent. Instead, the text is largely constituted by fans' fictional reminiscences concerning the significance to them of the singer, as well as the narrator's own admiring reflections. Hence, *La importancia* is ostensibly a compiled homage to Daniel.

Though humor and a playful use of enjoyably rhythmic vernaculars are common to both books, the sly optimism of the second text contrasts with the bitter-sweet wit of the first. It seems that this difference of perspective involves an evolution from Sánchez's depiction of a combative popular culture in the first novel. There, Puerto Rican popular culture, lived out in the commonplace settings of daily life, defends a vernacular communality against a threateningly impersonal modernity represented by the city. In contrast, through the second text's depiction of Latin Americans' personal identification with the figure of a popular hero, Sánchez confidently recognizes the traditional geopolitical subordination of all Latin American classes. Indeed, he portrays the creative transformation of such subordination into a forceful assertion, only incipient in the first novel, of a multiple but unified Latin American communality made possible through the complex sharing of a common cultural space. In the process of such a portrayal, the narrative perspective seems to embrace the politically incorrect or even taboo aspects of popular culture with even greater relish than in the first novel, with the result that *La importancia* was met by a less enthusiastic, even hostile, critical response than *La guaracha*.

1. CITY SPACE/BODY SPACE

If the growth of Puerto Rican cities marks the shift from an agrarian to an industrial economy, then the urban traffic jam that constitutes the central motif of *La guaracha* is perhaps a metaphor for Puerto Rico's stagnation under American capitalism.[2] In this situation, the incapacity of official politics to conceive a postcolonial project that might fulfil national aspirations is countered by a type of Bakhtinian carnivalization, or "permanente fiesteo" [movable fiesta] (*La guaracha* 23), of modern capitalism and its commodities.[3] Carnivalization takes place according to the physical terms of the human body as the center of popular communal life and is best exemplified by the *guaracha* of the title.[4] The song, "La vida es una cosa fenomenal" [Life is a Phenomenal Thing], not only provides the mass media with a vehicle capable of taking the country by storm but also provides its listeners with what is described as a "dogma nacional de salvación" [national dogma of salvation] (31).

Commodification does not limit itself to the promotion and broadcasting of hit songs but pervades all levels of Puerto Rican life, stimulates a consumerist attitude to the world, and propels personal relationships. At one point, the sexual act takes place as a sequence from a pornographic film (140-42). Also, La China Hereje first meets Vicente in a supermarket (203-06) and later fulfils his sexual fantasies in the hope that he pay for her home decoration

---

[2] See Díaz Quiñones ("Los años" 119-34), García, Ortega ("Teoría" 16), Paravisini (22), Rodríguez Juliá (*Puertorriqueños* 146-47), Scarano (749-72, 806-25, 854), Vázquez Arce ("Salsa" 31-34). Of particular interest is Chadwick's discussion (63-67). According to him, Sánchez's association of the hit *guaracha* of the novel's title with the traffic jam relates to Marxian commodity fetishism and Walter Benjamin's "homogeneous, empty time" of (capitalist) history, where the illusion of desirable novelty serves to constantly reinstate capitalism (Chadwick 64).

[3] See Bakhtin (*Rabelais* 5-15, 24, 28-30, 71-75, 82, 88-89) for popular culture's parallel relationship to the official culture of social, religious, artistic institutions, as well as political and economic constitutions. In this context, I believe carnivalization involves a dependent, delimited (*Rabelais* 94-95) and ostentatiously excessive remoulding of official culture that "denies, but . . . revives and renews at the same time" (11). Consequently, my use of the term suggests a constant negotiation with rather than a "temporary liberation from the prevailing truth and from the established order" (10) or the "suspension of all hierarchical rank, privileges, norms, and prohibitions" (10). Such constant negotiation suggests the daily life of the marketplace (4, 15-17, 153-54) rather than the occasional liberties of feast days (90, 96).

[4] See Bakhtin (*Rabelais* 18-22, 48). The *guaracha* is a popular form of Caribbean music.

(83, 139, 201). Again, Benny's professed admiration of his father is based on cupboard love (74), while Vicente substitutes the difficult responsibilities of fatherhood with extravagant gifts to his spoilt son (ibid.). Identity itself is modelled according to the consumption of images of media and show business stars. At the same time as Graciela takes Jacqueline Onassis and Elizabeth Taylor as her role models (165), La China Hereje models herself on the Puerto Rican cabaret queen, Iris Chacón (56). Thus, Graciela's middlebrow tastes situate her as middle-class, while La China's distinctly lowbrow role model identifies her unmistakeably as lower-class. Graciela's and La China Hereje's respective class statuses are further distinguished by their media consumption. Graciela mostly follows her role models' careers through the society pages of international magazines, such as *Time* (161-63), while La China Hereje idolizes the images of Iris Chacón circulated by popular Spanish-language leisure and show business magazines, as well as televised variety shows (17-19). Further irony is added to these examples of class through consumption by the fact that Graciela is portrayed as the epitome of upper-class Puerto Rican society. The downturn in the fortunes of her class is represented both by her family's need to associate their interests through marriage with those (as I shall speculate) of the socially inferior Vicente, and the dumbing down of the high cultural tastes expected of Graciela's social origins, through her consumption of the Americanized media products of what might be construed by the Hispanic ideologues I shall go on to discuss as a commercialized, imported, inauthentic, technocratic age (Dávila, *Sponsored* 74-79, 89, 124-25, 192-93, 196-99, 201 217-20, 259-60).

Even religion is commodified in Benny's prayers to his Ferrari (132, 185-86), and politics are reduced to catch phrases, such as "Vicente es decente y su honor iridiscente" [Vince is a prince and with honor ever since] (218), which are produced for the consumption of potential voters. Certainly, if human and social relationships are commodified under capitalism then the latter's process of modernization transforms the natural environment into an urban dystopia, the "desamparada isla de cemento nombrada Puerto Rico" [this unprotected concrete island named Puerto Rico] (34-35). However, the transformations undergone by modern Puerto Rico are never definitive.

It is true that the song "La vida es una cosa fenomenal" disguises the less than ideal conditions of everyday life in the Puerto Rican colony through the escapism of its infantile lyrics (256). But, as far as the music that carries these lyrics is concerned, "las trompetas hablan de cálidos encuentros de una piel con la otra, las trompetas hablan de ondulaciones lentas y espasmódicas" [the trumpets speak of the hot encounter of one skin with another, the trumpets speak of low, spasmodic undulations] (20-21). Despite its packaging and apparent message, popular music clears a space for the inscription of the body, pleasure, and personal relationships in the capitalist mass media whose success, it is true, may on the other hand be founded on allowing space for such inscription. This is the very point Joseph Chadwick makes in his Marxist reading of the novel (esp. 67-73, 79). For him, identification forms part of the illusion of and necessary investment in commodity fetishism, where social relations are eclipsed by the seemingly self-sufficient false consciousness resulting from capitalist modes of production. Nevertheless, within the tentative space cleared by music, the undulating slowness of the rhythm suggests the implied dancer's control as a subject rather than passive consumer. The spasmodic nature of the suggested and suggestive dance points to the dancer's potential for spontaneous violence motivated by the daily physical discomfort of dependency on an imported economic and political system whose First World aspirations Puerto Ricans cannot or never should fulfil.

Though the trumpets of the *guaracha* have a political sound, the vehicle of politics throughout is the pleasurable fellowship reclaimed in everyday life. The immediate outlet of a bus passenger's despair, arising from the disparity between the dream of capitalist progress and the feeling that "el país no funciona" [the country doesn't work] (21), is not provided by established political processes, discredited by being represented by Vicente and other sleazy political figures satirized in the book. Instead, alienation from official channels of action leads the other travelers on the bus, those who do not form part of the more privileged class of car owners, to occupy their own space in a spontaneous outbreak of dancing and singing to the piped-in *guaracha* that transforms despair into popular culture's movable feast (21-22). A feast that allows a wilfully unproductive respite from the constraints of labor through a knowing consumption of mass culture that divertingly represents the popular interests indicated in the novel.

The communality of the bus scene may be contrasted to La China Hereje's seclusion in the flat where she acts as Vicente's sexual servant, a juxtaposition highlighting the island's uneven development as well as the incomplete alienation of daily life. On the one hand, pockets of communality stage resistance to the commerce of individuals as consumers or commodities and, on the other, La China individually seeks self-fulfilment through identifying with the fetishized images of Iris Chacón she consumes. These are beamed across the nation and invested with humor by the text (18):

> Me han comentado que a Iris Chacón le pusieron la cámara en la barriga y esa mujer parece que se iba a romper de tanto que se meneaba, como si fuera una batidora eléctrica con un ataque de nervios.

> [They told me that they'd put the camera on Iris Chacón's belly and the woman looked like she was falling apart from so much wiggling, like she was an electric mixer, like she was an electric mixer with an attack of nerves.]

La China herself occupies several spaces, each of which testifies to the uneven capitalism of the island. The opening passage of the main text of the novel is a troubling illustration of living under capital in a colonial capital (13):

> La verán esperar sentada en un sofá: los brazos abiertos, pulseras en los brazos, relojito en un brazo, sortijas en los dedos, en el tobillo izquierdo un valentino con dije, en cada pie un zapatón singular. Cuerpo de desconcierto tiene, . . . cuerpo que ella sienta, tienda y amontona en un sofá tapizado con paño de lana, útil para la superación de los fríos polares pero de uso irrealísimo en estos trópicos tristes: el sol cumple aquí una vendetta impía, mancha el pellejo, emputece la sangre, borrasca el sentido: aquí en Puerto Rico, colonia sucesiva de dos imperios e isla del Archipiélago de las Antillas. También sudada, la verán esperar sudada, sudada y apelotonada en un sofá sudado y apelotonado.

> [You'll see her sitting and waiting on a sofa: her arms open, bracelets on her arms, a small watch on one wrist, rings on her fingers, over her left heel an anklet with a trinket on it, on each leg a knee, on each foot a striking big shoe. A restless body, . . . a body that she sits down, lays out, and plops onto a sofa upholstered with a woolen material that's useful for overcoming polar chills but most unreal for any use in these tristes tropiques: the sun carries out an ungodly vendetta here, it stains the skin, prostitutes the blood, roils the senses: here is Puerto Rico, the succes-

sive colony of two empires and an island in the Archipelago of the Antilles. Sweaty too, you'll see her waiting sweaty, sweaty and plopped onto a sweaty and ploppy sofa.]

As Vicente's sexual slave, her physical seclusion in the flat he keeps for their assignations fetishizes her as just another investment, another commodity in the marketplace. Accordingly, her body parts are juxtaposed indiscriminately with jewels and shoes, while the boundaries between her body and the sofa are fluidly merged by sweat. Her restlessness, the discomfort of waiting for Vicente on a sofa unsuited to the tropics testifies to the violent adjustments required by capitalist colonialism. But, the dismemberment illustrated by the passage is refuted by her inclusion, as a dancing passenger, in the fellowship of the communal body celebrated on board the traffic-jammed bus. This pleasurable sense of community translates into a political solidarity, again located in the unofficial space of the neighbourhood scenes where La China and her neighbour, Doña Chon, relish gossiping and cooking traditional Puerto Rican delicacies to be savoured by a group of local strikers whom the women feed.

The portrayal of popular culture in *La guaracha* might lead one to consider that Puerto Rican popular culture denotes processes taking place outside and in opposition to an elitist high culture. However, the portrayal, in *La importancia*, of mass culture, its varied reception, certain values, such as machismo, shared across class boundaries, and the appropriation of high cultural discourse by non-elite Puerto Ricans, such as Daniel Santos, demonstrate the invalidity of reductive binary oppositions between popular and elite Puerto Rican culture.[5]

2. The Hero of a Thousand Barrios

In *La importancia de llamarse Daniel Santos*, the socially disempowered, "público populachero" [common populace] (64) enjoy sharing a popular Latin American culture where the communal is

---

[5] *La guaracha* has received more critical attention than any other work by Sánchez. From the many studies available, I recommend Alonso, Aparicio ("Entre"), Barradas (*Para leer* 65-151), Ben-Ur, Chadwick, Cruz-Malavé ("Repetition"), Gelpí (*Literatura* 17-45), González Echevarría ("La vida"), Ortega ("Teoría"), Paravisini, Parkinson Zamora, Ramos.

always individualized and which validates their aspirations alongside those more privileged than they; allowing representation but
also contestation of social differerence between Puerto Ricans.
Meanwhile, the multiple aspirations of Latin American communities avoid dispersion by being reconciled in a legendary hero, a
"leyenda continental" [continental legend] (68) invested with hope
and collective strength. A focus is identified where "las miradas
convergen en la imagen destinataria de los sueños públicos" [looks
converge on the central image of public dreams] (68) and which is
never reductive of "las muchas voces que apadrinaba su voz" [the
many voices engendered by his (Daniel's) voice] (68). The particular-
ization of the fabled singer is parallelled by the reclamation of distinct Latin American cities not only as human spaces but human
spaces with their own histories and hence names. One of Daniel's
Nicaraguan admirers writes to the narrator from "las arterias de pul-
so escaso que hacen el cuerpo de Managua" [the fluttering arteries
that feed the body of Managua] (67). In the same way the geogra-
phies of distinct Latin American cities are configured by their inhabitants' pride in belonging to and sharing particular neighborhoods
and streets (64), the dispersed communities formed by these inhabitants are united by the differentiated but collective memory (75) that
belongs to the survivors of the violence and deprivation suffered by
the majority of Latin Americans (3), who forge their dreams and desires on the common stage of their communal aspirations (74).

If myth, as the narrator asserts, is where the *pueblo* dreams (74),
then popular culture, in its capacity as a Freudian dream (74), is
perhaps the stage where the conventionally prohibited is enacted.
Consequently, as a popular symbol, Daniel's career gives rise to a
black legend of drink, drugs, women, and prison. When the narrator recognizes that dreams drift free from inhibitions (74), he acknowledges that popular culture flouts the rules of politeness, de-
cency, and good taste adhered to by the easy morality of the ruling
classes satirized in *La guaracha* by the portrayal of the affected Graciela Alcántara and hypocritical Vicente Reinosa.

By using a series of popular vernaculars in his chronicle of first-
hand reports, the narrator gives free rein to a barrage of enjoyably
coarse language, sexual imagery, and an admiring portrayal of
Daniel's monumental machismo (e.g. 124-29, 134-35), all of which
have angered some critics (e.g. Alvarado, López, and Ramos). However, I believe that, in fact, the narrator is expressing his sympathies

with what, through a lowlife brazenness (135), opposes oppressive social inequality and the entrenched official culture that upholds it (82-83, 109-10).

As a popular hero, Daniel, "el Bohemio . . . , el Jodedor . . . , el Desobediente" [the Bohemian . . . , the Cocksman . . . , the Disobedient] (110), offends by not lending himself to assimilation into the easy categories of conventional virtue misrepresented by corrupt politicians and, as a mulatto "mito cimarrón" [outlaw legend] (134), he offends the bourgeois myth of *criollo* virtues traditionally promoted by the upper-class powers in Puerto Rico (González, "El país" 26-29, 35-39; 1989c: 63-64, 73-76). If popular culture is the place where the disavowals of a bourgeois morality are defied then the masculine adultery encouraged by the machismo of Daniel's songs (84-85, 124-29) is only "insolente" [insolent] (129) when it flaunts itself as an ostentatiously defiant lower-class way of life (129). For the powerful "mandamás" [grandee] (129) such adultery is undertaken surreptitiously, with the discretion of a Vicente Reinosa, a hypocritical paragon of Catholic virtue (*La guaracha* 31). Popular culture is not an exclusively oppositional space since the preoccupations of social strata normally segregated find common ground (*La importancia* 87-88). On one level, the success of Daniel's songs depends on the appeal of their machismo to heterosexual Latin American men of all classes who, through these songs, seek to recognize ideal selves to which they aspire either defiantly or guardedly.

Armando Figueroa (198) disapprovingly notes that Sánchez represents Daniel Santos with distorted masculine and Caribbean stereotypes. But may not Sánchez's recourse to stereotypes with powerful resonances in Puerto Rican culture constitute a strategically offensive position from which to attack the conventional messianism of Puerto Rican paternalism (Gelpí, *Literatura* 20-25) and the supposedly virtuous machismo traditionally promoted by revered writers such as René Marqués?

In his 1960 essay, "El puertorriqueño dócil" [The Docile Puerto Rican], Marqués argued that Puerto Ricans' supposed feminine docility, largely attributed by him to the Anglo-Saxon importation of a supposedly matriarchal social model (175), should be countered by a patriotic return to the masculine values rooted in a Hispanic tradition. That Marqués should condemn modern Puerto Ricans' rejection of tradition has as much to do with certain class affiliations as with a supposed anti-colonialism. Following the defeat of the Spanish in 1898, US colonialism seemed to provide a relatively more liberal framework in comparison with conditions under Spanish rule.[6] Greater rights, accompanied by growing social mobility for Puerto Rican women and recently emancipated blacks, as well as the consolidation of emerging working and non-landowning professional, merchant, and artisan classes, promised a modernizing transformation of social hierarchies (Carrión, "The Petty Bourgeoisie"). However, these advances seem to be scathingly identified by Marqués as elements of a supposedly destructive "democracia" [democracy] (156-57). In reaction to the burgeoning freedoms of the groups above, Marqués dismisses their understandable pro-Americanism by attributing it to a reaction to the traditional authoritarianism of Spanish rule (166 n27). This justified reaction has, according to Marqués, led these groups to be blinded to the injustices of American society (166-67). As Díaz Quiñones has observed ("Tomás" 40-44), the unfavorable portrayal of conditions in America, as compared to those on the island, was a commonplace of *hacendado* discourse which attempted to refute the popular classes' antithetically favorable predisposition to the tenets of American egalitarianism.[7]

Sánchez's Daniel constitutes a humorous vulgarization of the supposedly noble virility–rooted in a Golden Age or Classical Arcadia–Marqués believed was necessary in the emasculating context of

---

[6] On this point see Carrión ("The National Question" 69-71), J. L González ("El país" 27-28, 32-36), Grosfoguel (6-7), Mattos Cintrón (201-03), and Scarano (612-14, 636-42, 649-54). More recently, the work of Kelvin A. Santiago-Valles (49-62, 204-06) qualifies this view. He suggests that, though by associating themselves with reformist American movements the groups I have mentioned could claim rights they had never had before, living conditions for most Puerto Ricans during the first decades of American colonialism were the same, only marginally better, or even worse than before. New rights of expression (Santiago-Valles 112-15, 119), including eventually the vote for women (Scarano 654), took place within the context of what Santiago-Valles calls the "dispossession" of Puerto Ricans in relation to "inordinately brutal and excruciating" (51) socioeconomic changes (53-54). Through the establishment of a capitalist system, these substantially deprived Puerto Ricans of the mutual support structures (31, 39) and intimate trade relations of rural precapitalism (Scarano 612).

[7] On the other hand, there might be some truth in Eduardo Seda Bonilla's assertion, cited by Zenón Cruz (1: 126), that blacks' unprecedented political representation was only made possible by the ironically egalitarian American assumption that all Puerto Ricans were racially inferior. As I will further demonstrate in the next chapter, the predominance of the degraded *criollo* classes was no longer clearcut, since in American eyes they were merely more fully reformed versions of the potentially reformable inferiors in their charge.

modernizing US colonialism ("El puertorriqueño" 175). For instance, Marqués writes of the "último baluarte cultural desde donde podía aún combatirse, en parte, la docilidad colectiva: el *machismo*, versión criolla de la fusión y adaptación de dos conceptos seculares, la *honra* española y el *pater familiae* [sic] romano" [the last cultural bastion from which collective docility can still, if only partly, be combated: machismo, the *criollo* version of the fusion and adaptation of two secular concepts, Spanish honour and the Roman paterfamilias] (175). Sánchez ironically confirms Marqués' assertion that only in their literature have Puerto Ricans shown the requisite masculine "agresión" [aggression] in defence of traditional machismo against the threat of matriarchy in Puerto Rico ("El puertorriqueño" 175; see also 194).

Sánchez's concern with bad language, gross sexuality, and machismo is far from gratuitous. Instead, in ironic dialogue with Marqués, it portrays a form of popular self-assertion taking the form of "el machismo a todo tren" [breakneck machismo] (*La importancia* 123): histrionic sexual aggression that attempts to compensate for the degrading status of Latin American men who, as Third-World, colonized, or tentatively democratized subjects of, in all cases, economically dependent nations, are incapable of measuring up to Marqués' nostalgic and imperially masculine ideal.[8] Traditionally subjected to rather than agents of dictatorial masculine dominance (*La importancia* 109), Latin American men are "los hijos, los nietos, los bisnietos de los fusilados y los desaparecidos; los hijos, los nietos, los bisnietos de las dictaduras que reducen a puré cremoso los cojones de la disidencia" [the sons, the grandsons, the great grandsons of the executed and disappeared; the sons, the grandsons, the great grandsons of the dictatorships that crush the balls of dissidence into creamy purée] (110). Traditionally marginalized in the public sphere of History, Latin American men transpose the domination they suffer there into their domination of personal relationships through an "afecto opresivo" [overbearing ardour] (125) rooted in the triumphalist male physicality that finds its high priest in Daniel. The resultant masculinity resides in the display of a combination of virility and aggression against submissive women (124-26). The socio-political frustrations that lead to

---

[8] Marqués' nostalgic machismo is discussed by Barradas ("El machismo"). Gelpí ("La cuentística") examines Sánchez's confrontation with Marqués' work.

such grotesque masculinity are evidenced by the authoritarian language that underscores their aspirations. They appear as "machos creyentes en el machismo dogmático, infalible, papal entonces" [macho believers in dogmatic, infallible, and, therefore, papal machismo] (125).

Sánchez focuses extensively on the obvious physical marker of threatening macho virility. But though the narrator may gloat, comic deflation or, if one prefers, detumescence is achieved through an exhaustive visibility (126):

> Parecer varón es lisonjearse, belicosamente, el güevo con los nombres variados de instrumentos contusos–la daga, la lezna, el espadín, el sable, el tolete, el jierro, la vara, la tranca, la porra, el cipote, la fisga, el marrón, la macana, la bayoneta, el bate, la estaca, la maceta, el macetón, el *destroyer*.

> [To look a man is militantly to fondle one's dick with the various names of offensive instruments–machete, awl, sword of honour, sabre, bludgeon, rod, bar, cudgel, truncheon, prick, harpoon, black beauty, club, bayonet, bat, stake, mallet, sledgehammer, destroyer.]

I would suggest that the repeatedly attempted representation of the penis betrays a desire "militantly" ("belicosamente") to assert command over a constantly embattled Latin American phallocentrism associated with the unofficial authority of machismo. The reiterated naming of the penis may indeed be related to Freudian negation or *Verneinung*.

In a discussion of Freud's 1925 paper, "Negation," Martin Thom considers that negation involves "the truth of the subject's desire and the knowledge he or she has of that desire" (166). Accordingly, desire, contained by knowledge of it, may be voiced in a language that names desire before disowning it.[9] Conversely, for Sánchez, Latin American men's aspiration to authority constantly surfaces as just that, mere aspiration. Largely unfulfilled in history, except in the narcissistic dictatorships of grotesquely flamboyant strongmen such as Batista, Trujillo, Somoza or Pinochet (110), this aspiration irrationally reinstates itself against a knowledge of histor-

---

[9] Freud ("Negation" 235) gives an example, observed during analysis. A patient may negate a desire for his mother in the following manner: "You ask who this person in the dream can be. It's *not* my mother."

ical underprivilege. Hence, in *La importancia*, there seems to be a reversal of Freudian terms. For Sánchez, it is emasculating historical knowledge that is perhaps warded off through an excess of desire spilling into a history that will not yield to the fantasy of self-sufficient integrity. Instead, history returns as an unbearable, castrating knowledge that shadows fantasy and limits the latter's purchase on history to ephemeral reenactments of violent, totalitarian domination. These take the form of either the phallic frenzy of machismo or the insecurely reiterated assertion of distorted brute force on the part of the dictators just named, who were, as backward Backyard cousins, sustained unreliably by foreign interests. The animality of these dictators suggests both the brutality of machismo and the degradation from which such brutality arises, in reaction. They are: "El gorilón de turno . . . El gorilón canallón que succiona las vidas. El gorilón militarón de la cuenta bancaria en suizo ascenso. El gorilón santurrón que se apodera del reino de este mundo" [The savage ape of the moment . . . The ruthlessly savage ape who greedily devours lives. The jack-booted gorilla with the bank account in Swiss ascent. The sanctimoniously savage ape who lords it over the kingdom of this world] (*La importancia* 109). I also detect an underlying image in these lines of the Third-World circus animal's dependence on the commands of an unseen First-World circus master. The extended naming of the penis and the reiterated animalization of unnamed dictators fall short of historical glory under the weight of historical dispossession and result in repeated, bitterly bathetic deflation which must constantly be warded off.

It would be right to argue that patriarchy, even in its extreme form of violence against women, is present also in the masculine behavior of the developed world of the formerly or currently colonial powers. For example, such masculinity may be modelled on the arrogant First World muscle-flexing of a right-wing US patriarchy whose scale makes Marqués' "machismo versión criolla" look limp by comparison. The metropolitan counterpart is founded on real power with international reverberations going back to an assertion abroad of a Manifest Destiny and its accompanying paternalistic rhetoric (Santiago-Valles 63-67). Modern manifestations of such supremacism are the fundamentalist rhetoric of extremist Republicanism, its crusading anti-feminist, anti-abortion *Moral Majority* and, most relevantly, the continuing paternalism of United States foreign policy in the Caribbean and Latin America. Obversely, though appealing to a universal patriarchy that transcends geopolitics, Puerto Rican machismo is, I have argued, a theatrical compensation for the degraded representation of Puerto Rican and Latin American men in the political sphere, a reflex to unconsciously perceived dispossession of supposedly inherent masculine authority. Unlike men, women perhaps do not labor, or more importantly are not allowed to labor, under the illusion of their supposedly innate supremacy. For them, compensation for underprivilege is only allowed to take the form, in *Quíntuples*, of Dafne Morrison's subterfuge, her sister Bianca's hysterical struggle for masculinity, or Carlota Morrison's threatening matriarchy.

The singer's *machista* prowess is commemorated by the narrator as a series of tales recounted to him in accompaniment to Daniel's songs (*La importancia* 123), which are heard in countless Latin American bars and billiard halls (122-23, 124-26). The stage thus set, Sánchez goes on to examine the portrayal of penises in literature and film, from Herodotus (127) to *Empire of the Senses* (128). What takes the place of inaccessible First World or bourgeois authority is "un texto dictador y absolutista [que] totalizan el güevo y los textículos" [a dictatorial, absolutist text totalized by the dick and texticles] (128). By highlighting machismo as but one, mostly oral, version of a series of cultural texts, histrionic *machista* arrogance is deflated by a pun that underscores machismo as a text of economic and political impotence rather than an unconquerable essence.

In any case, it is clear that an exclusively heterosexual reading is untenable, when the exhaustive assertion of male physicality may also be read as a homoerotic discourse, where masculinity is staged as a baroque display of machismo taking place and imitated in all-male environments (125-26), and whose seductively coded exhibitionism between men is at the very least sexually ambiguous.[10] If, as the narrator informs us, male friendships are defined by a terse restraint from affection (125), "parecer varón instruye un histrionismo rudimental" [to look a man demands a rudimentary form of performance] (125-26). Therefore (126):

---

[10] Such ambiguity is already present in *La guaracha*, as has been pointed out by Efraín Barradas (*Para leer* 141-42 n8). On the other hand, the homoerotic display of *La importancia* reconciles machismo with homosexuality in a way that circumvents Barradas's discussion of machismo's exclusion of homosexuality ("El machismo" 75): "El homosexual, más que la hembra, es el anti-macho esencial. El macho se manifiesta plenamente cuando subyuga y fecunda a la hembra" [The homosexual, more than the female, is the essential anti-macho. The macho fully reveals himself when he subdues and impregnates the female].

si el voladizo de las tetillas configura los triunfos atléticos de los pectorales la camisa se entreabre en los pezones. Si una rampante vellosidad ocupa el pecho la camisa se desabotona hasta el ombligo. Si el tendido de venas entre las muñecas y los codos revela que se está dando duro a las pesas la camisa se arremanga. Si la justedad del calzón perfila el tamaño responsable del güevo la camisa se anuda en la cintura.

[if the curve to the nipples shows off the athletic triumphs of the pectorals the shirt is half opened down to the chest. If a rampant hairiness covers the chest, the shirt is unbuttoned down to the navel. If the track of veins between the wrist and elbow show that one is pumping a lot of iron the sleeves are rolled up. If the tightness of one's underpants outlines a worthy size of dick the shirt is tied up in a knot around the waist.]

The bisexual appeal of Daniel's machismo is underscored by the interview with three homosexual drag queens (21-25). One of the "locas" unconvincingly assures the narrator that Daniel was never a practicing homosexual: "él nunca estuvo al alcance del pecado nefando" [he never came close to committing the unspeakable sin] (24). The use of the term, "el pecado nefando" by an unashamed homosexual turns homophobic moralizing inside out. Inversely, and in the same way Catholic morality may institutionally contain (for example, in confession) forbidden pleasures, one of the queens is described as "Madre Superior de los Polvos Desperdiciados" [Mother Superior of the Wasted Fucks] (21-22), so that a sense of sinfulness provides the humorous context for friskily titillating tittle-tattle. Within the campness of this scene, reminiscences of a licentiously decadent Havana, and the enjoyably coarse flirtatiousness of the interviewees, the categorical assertion of Daniel's macho restraint playfully throws doubt on Daniel's heterosexuality, at best implying closet homosexuality.

Though Daniel was apparently untainted by *the* unspeakable sin, his arrival in Havana was preceded by the fame of unspecified but terrible sins, sins that he shared with the "hermana" [sister] of one of the "locas" (23). Just as Daniel's sins are obscure, so the sex of the "hermana" is ambiguous, since the "locas" use the feminine gender to address each other, and since the name of the "hermana," "La Reina de Belleza" or "The Beauty Queen," could refer to a man or a woman in the context of the scene's transvestism. Indeed, the interviewees are dubiously described as a flighty damsel with a masculine gendered name, "Cisne Negro," "Blanche DuBois," and the plushly named Velia Gina Raquel. Furthermore, though La Reina was the lover of a rampant lesbian ("tortillón siniestro") (24) when Daniel met her, the gender and possible sexual bending of the scene does not exclude a sexual liaison between a male transvestite and a butch lesbian. Finally, does not the description of La Reina's lustrous blonde mane spilling down her shoulders like a glass of champagne (23) conjure up the caricaturesque masquerade of movie femininity, à la Veronica Lake or Marilyn Monroe, so beloved of male transvestites in wigs and falsies?

Exclusive heterosexuality is ultimately highlighted unfavorably against the highest achievements of Western civilization. If homosexuality is a sin, it is associated with the greatness of Leonardo Da Vinci, Michelangelo, and Socrates (24). In view of Daniel's status as a hero, his greatness grants him a place alongside the great men above and his sexuality is by implication juxtaposed, even identified, with theirs. With great irony, therefore, Sánchez replies to Marqués's rallying cry for Puerto Rican men to reaffirm their universal greatness as heirs to a Roman tradition of machismo. If Sánchez acknowledges a masculine legacy of European civilization it is to the homoerotic sensibility of Michaelangelo's sculpture he looks, as in *The Dying Slave* or even his *David*, rather than to the system of patriarchy underpinning Greek and Roman dynasticism.

If machismo slips from heterosexuality to homosexuality, essentialist masculinity to masculine and feminine masquerade, what of women in relation to a machismo whose violence would initially seem to exclude them from popular culture or admits them at the price of their submission to misogyny? Ana D. Alvarado, María Milagros López, and Wanda E. Ramos perhaps rightly mourn the book's "foreclusion" [sic] (2) of a "polysemous femininity" (6), sung by the celebrated performers La Lupe and Nydia Caro, as well as "the women's boleros sung in kitchen coffee shops . . . or beauty parlors" (6).[11] And, what of the boleros that substitute "the masculine *o* of the masculine- penned bolero and replac[e] it with the

---

[11] Alvarado, López, and Ramos (2) translate and cite the following quotation from J. D. Nasio's "La foreclusión y el nombre del padre" to describe "foreclusion:" "The foreclusion is not an exclusion but the nonarrival of something asked for, the noninscription of where that something should have been."

feminine *a'* (6)? Yet, "foreclusion [sic] is not . . . exclusion" (J. D. Nasio, cited in Alvarado, López, and Ramos, 2), so that I shall argue that the dynamic participation of women in Latin American culture is indicated, albeit latently, by Sánchez's text and by the term "foreclusion," what I take to be an incorrect rendering of the French word "forclusion," translated into English as "foreclosure" (Laplanche and Pontalis 166).

By conceding Martin Thom's assertion that foreclosure is "linked to the signifier that it does not affirm" (168), one is allowed to entertain the possibility that, because of such a "link," foreclosure on the part of machismo is defenceless against other "unsymbolized" (171) voices for which it cannot be held responsible and by which it is perhaps uncontrollably stalked. Uncontrollably so since, in foreclosure, intolerable perceptions are not subject to repression. Thus, refused admission to the unconscious, there is, in Laplanche's and Pontalis' words, a "decathexis of what is perceived" and "a withdrawal of significance—a refusal to lend meaning to what is perceived" (168). For Freud, "it was the same as if it [the latter] did not exist" (qtd. in Laplanche and Pontalis 168). Thus, foreclosure is more vulnerable, or open, than Freudian negation, since the former is weak where the latter is strong, inasmuch as foreclosure, unlike negation, cannot repudiate that of which it has no stated knowledge.

At this point, I conclude that, opposed to masculine-gendered self-control the bolero's emotional exorbitance perhaps allows possibilities for women and homosexuals to recognize themselves in a space that ostensibly excludes their interests. Possessed by their pleasure in the music and singing, any listener may possess the bolero, so that each member of the audience, male or female, heterosexual or homosexual, rich or poor becomes their own authority in the realm of the senses (*La importancia* 87-88). [12] There, individual suffering and longing not only find their cultural catharsis in the bolero but also a site whose resident passion may be diverted to un-

---

[12] Since writing this chapter it has been brought to my attention that my observations concerning the permeable hybridity of the bolero coincide with those of Frances R. Aparicio in part 3, largely on the bolero, and part 4, on the reception of Latin American music of her *Listening to Salsa: Gender, Latin Popular Music and Puerto Rican Culture* (1997). I was unaware of her work at the time of writing but believe that the fact that, working independently, we both took similar views perhaps strengthens my arguments.

precedented ends. Thus, the fragmentary, non-totalizing form of *La importancia* perhaps underlines the appeal to individuals of the bolero (Rowe and Schelling 111, 219). If so, the emotional investment made by Daniel in singing may provide each of his listeners with the vehicle to supersede the repugnant, albeit ambiguous, social codes of many boleros' lyrics. His songs present permeable sites where emotion, by means of its openness to being mediated according to each interlocutor's needs, may be rechannelled into anti-authoritarian ends.[13] In this sense, Sánchez presents the bolero as, in Doris Sommer's terminology, a "foundational" text that, through "erotic passion . . . bind[s] together heterodox constituencies" in a kaleidoscopic communality that foresees a prospective national or regional identity I shall go on to discuss (Sommer 14).

3. THE FRESH COUNTRY AIR OF BIG CITY BARS, BARRIOS, AND CINEMAS

In *La importancia de llamarse Daniel Santos*, modernity is mediated by the entertainment palaces of Latin American cities whose modernity is centered in the body and its pleasures, "los cabarets y las salas de fiesta que suman la geografía cambiante de la nocturnidad tienen la ciudad capital en su garganta [la de Daniel]" [the cabarets and dance halls that comprise the shifting geography of the nocturnal landscape have their capital city in his (Daniel's) throat] (38). The constitution of a capital city of pan-American popular culture (39) is founded in Daniel's performance and translates the mass culture and fetishes of the US metropolis or grander neighbours, like Mexico, into its own terms. Clark Gable, Porfirio Rubirosa (a renowned Mexican playboy), and Robert Redford are associated with Daniel and localized in "todo hombre que fue el Clark Gable o el Porfirio Rubirosa o el Robert Redford de su esquina o su balcón" [every man who was the Clark Gable or Porfirio Rubirosa or Robert Redford of his street corner or balcony'] (38). Modernity is further incorporated by Daniel's performance, "en primera persona singular" [in the first person singular] (40), of a *guaracha* entitled "La televisión pronto llegará" [Television Will

---

[13] Iris M. Zavala's *El bolero: historia de un amor* is essential reading for anyone interested in the bolero.

Soon Be Here] (41). By being transformed into an "estilo personal e intransferible como el sudor" [a style as personal and untransferable as sweat] (41), the modern world can be assimilated by a premodern communality founded on direct human relations and surviving in Latin American cities, which have undergone rapid and hence incomplete modernization (cf. Santiago Valles, *"Subject People"* 31, 38-39, 42-43). Consequently, we read that Venezuelans, Cubans, and Puerto Ricans are people who enjoy themselves collectively (*La importancia* 41), and note the village air of the big city (28).

Daniel himself is a symbol of the liminal spaces of partially industrialized Latin American urbanism. His origins lie in the shanty town of Tras Talleres, on the outskirts of San Juan, "barriada periférica de un país periférico" [a peripheral neighbourhood of a peripheral country] (84). The *barriada*'s liminality is underlined by its strictest definition as part of a city or village with its own name but which does not constitute an officially recognized administrative sector (Moliner 352). Such a definition is reinforced by the *barriadas'* contextualization in Puerto Rican history as working-class neighbourhoods that illegally occupy public land. The *barriadas* have traditionally straddled an illegitimate, transitional space necessitated by the incomplete migration to the city which results from a level of industrialization only partially able to accommodate the Puerto Rican work force and fulfil its expectations. The survival of intimate rural relations and solidarity in an urban setting are made possible by the interstitial status of the *barriadas*, where the extended family dwelling serves as a halfway house and refuge for country cousins who arrive looking for work in the city (82).[14]

Nevertheless, if Daniel's live performance perfectly exemplifies the popular assimilation of modernity, then do the relationships of an industrialized world disrupt popular culture's defence of communality? In a bar in Lima (30-33), Daniel rejects the amorous advances of a good-time girl who requests that he sing for her. He does so by citing a clause in his contract with a radio station forbidding impromptu performances. Yet, when she tries a different tack

---

[14] On the *barriadas* as transitional spaces related to the failures of industrialization, see Scarano (600, 614, 616, 639, 670-71, 674-75, 709, 747, 750-51, 772, 794, 804-09, 814-18, 830-32, 838-39). On the communality of the *barriada*, see Santiago-Valles ("Puerto Rico" 146-47). For a discussion of shanty towns within the broader Latin American context, see Rowe and Schelling (102-03).

from the fan worship of a recently established Latin American music industry and challenges him to an old-fashioned drinking competition, Daniel readily complies (31). [15] Thus, communal relationships, typified by a very Caribbean invitation to participate in a spontaneous, non-professional musical performance, ultimately evade the legally binding commercial obligations of the modern world. For these are deployed by Daniel in a tantalizingly subtle game of hard-to-get which culminates in another form of popular performance, the barroom drinking contest (32-33). I would suggest that the rules of modern capitalism are thus assimilated through an apparent adherence to their impositions which only enhances what one of the narrator's interlocutors identifies as the Caribbean's persistently defiant "estilos de subdesarrollo" [styles of underdevelopment] (37).

Daniel's knowing underdevelopment relates to the cultural debates the Cuban critic and poet Roberto Fernández Retamar discusses in his 1971 essay, "Caliban: apuntes sobre la cultura de Nuestra América" [Caliban: Notes Toward a Discussion of Culture in Our America]. As part of his argument, he turns his attention (46-55) to Domingo Sarmiento and notes that in his 1845 book, *Facundo,* and more overtly in his *Conflicto y armonía de las razas en América* [Conflict and Harmony of the Races in Latin America] (1883), Sarmiento proposes that Latin Americans should abandon their inherent barbarism and embrace the progressive modernity of Europe and North America. [16] For Fernández Retamar, Sarmiento's position aligns him with the traditional subservience of the colonized intellectual, identified by the Cuban with the Shakespearian Prospero's servant, Ariel (23-27). On the other hand, Daniel's example suggests that "underdeveloped" communal relationships may

---

[15] On the Latin American music industry as part of a process of modernization, see Flores ("'Bumbún'" 85, 90) and Rowe and Schelling (98-99, 134-35, 215, 233).

[16] Edwin Williamson considers such a view 'crude and tendentious' (290). He believes that Sarmiento was not referring to an innate barbarism but rather to the particular post-independence violence of Latin America's populist dictatorships. Though Williamson's argument merits more attention, Fernández Retamar's more extensive exposition, backed up by evidence from Sarmiento's text and the heated debate between Sarmiento and José Martí, makes his argument more convincing. Certainly, Fernández Retamar's position is, I would suggest, supported from the outset of *Facundo,* where Argentinians' supposedly indifferent recourse to violence is attributed to the geographical accident of birth in a vast land of barbarous frontiers, climatically conditioned differences of character, and racial degeneration.

be upheld by colonized Puerto Ricans and Third-World Latin Americans in a subtle defence of identity. This invests Sarmiento's civilization/barbarism dichotomy with emancipatory possibilities for the popular subject, identified by Fernández Retamar (30, 34) with the Shakespearian figure of Caliban.[17] Moreover, while in the previous chapter I suggested that "¡Jum!" points to the inevitable location of meaningful popular identities in an urban environment whose modernity is contrasted against a primitive rurality, Daniel further complicates matters by his simultaneous urbanism and underdevelopment. He ironically manipulates and advantageously blurs Sarmiento's terms, so that clearly delineated binary oppositions are no longer possible as a result of Daniel's manipulation and rejection of the exclusions central to all versions of Sarmiento's discussion.

Fernández Retamar's mounts his attack against the colonization of Caribbean intellectuality by means of a radical appropriation of terms first used in José Enrique Rodó's seminal essay, *Ariel*, which was fittingly published in 1900, and since then has occupied a central place in all discussions of Latin American modernity. The essay takes the form of an address by a venerable teacher to his students on their responsibilities as future leaders of their nation. Juan Flores ("The Insular Vision") has convincingly argued that this classic served as a blueprint for Antonio S. Pedreira's *Insularismo* which, like Rodó's work, is dedicated to the youth of his country. Their cultured idealism was to embody the elevated spirit of Ariel. Both writers strive to instil an evangelizing patriotism with the hope of

---

[17] Any discussion of a Latin American or Caribbean Caliban must address Juan Duchesne Winter's criticism of Fernández Retamar's enlistment of the above figure. Duchesne Winter (73) considers this enlistment an attempt to justify Castroist authoritarianism, which is exercised in the name of the people it claims to represent: "Hablo por Calibán en Calibán, lo que me autoriza en tanto Calibán que soy al hablar" [I speak for Caliban in the name of Caliban, which gives me the authority of the Caliban I become as I speak]. Duchesne Winter asserts that Latin American identification with Caliban arises out of the desire for authority of bourgeois intellectual elites, which legitimize their entitlement by a recourse to Shakespeare as well as Marx. Thus, these elites may hold the intellectual high ground of high culture "al servicio de las clases explotadas" [in the service of the exploited classes] (Fernández Retamar 40). Meanwhile, according to Duchesne Winter's view, the latter's voices are subsumed by the authority of those responsible for "la extensión de la educación a todo el pueblo, su asentamiento sobre bases revolucionarias" [the administration of education to all the people, and its foundation on revolutionary principles] (Fernández Retamar 92).

saving what they perceived was the ailing spirituality of European culture against the supposed barbarism threatened by the brute technological utilitarianism being advanced by a Calibanesque North America.

To locate the authority of Fernández Retamar's voice, one inevitably turns to Roberto González Echevarría's disassembly ("The Case") of the magisterial character of *Ariel*'s narrative voice. González Echevarría identifies this as the defensive complaint of a tentatively hegemonic bourgeoisie against an unsettling and foreign modernity. The Cuban-American scholar probes the violent defensiveness of this voice (echoed so faithfully and just as desperately by Pedreira) with the intention of bringing out the ideological vulnerability of its unsustainable authoritarianism. In this sense González Echevarría's critical deconstruction parallels authoritarianism's dispersal into the many voices of *La importancia*, ranging from a highbrow narrator-cum-author prone to learned literary humour, as in the very title of the work, and the popular voices of his interviewees. The confusion between narrator and author is intentional. The projection into the text of the typically patrician perspective of the Puerto Rican writer who is faithful to the hispanism of Latin American literary tradition allows a detached displacement of that rhetorical position, so that this becomes one more voice situated against so many other voices which could have been silenced or interpreted by the author, in the same way populist Puerto Rican politicians and nationalist intellectuals have assumed the position of spokesmen for their people.

In a Puerto Rican context, Sánchez's contending network of voices resound in the debate concerning civilization and barbarism, which involves complex considerations of class, sexuality, gender, and race. Although, for blacks, women, workers, and the new professional and merchant classes, association with the United States offered the possibility of a way forward along the road to civilization and away from the colonial barbarism of the past, for an influential proportion of the established bourgeoisie such association implied a profound threat. Disaffection steadily took root in the former coffee and, to a relatively lesser extent, sugar plantation-owning families, who, already in decline in the latter stages of Spanish rule, could not compete with the exclusive establishment and domination of large-scale US sugar production as part of a capitalist monopoly. Eventually, the descendants of the *hacendados* became a predominantly administrative, business, and professional class with sharply reduced political power.[18] It was with such a reduced, class-specific position of dependence that influential figures such as the radical Nationalist Party leader Pedro Albizu Campos, the self-styled spokesman for independence José de Diego, the writer René Marqués, and the visionary intellectual Antonio S. Pedreira aligned themselves. Though of varying political complexions and social backgrounds, all the above figures converged in their use of a rhetoric of civilization and barbarism that betrays a nostalgia for the power the *hacendado* class wielded in the feudal or slave plantation days of Spanish colonialism, represented in *La guaracha* by the parodically *castiza* [true-blue] Graciela.[19] Such nostalgia informs the bitterness of the *hacendado* class towards what they perceived as US barbarism in relation to their interested portrayal of the cultural and spiritual superiority of a Spanish civilization to which their own nationalism would prove a worthy, even if sovereign, successor.[20] It is partly such an elitist class perspective that definitively cost Albizu's Nationalist Party the support of the militant new Puerto Rican working class in the 1930s.[21] Albizu's stance is in this respect surprising, since it was the US authorities on the island who supported non-white candidates for important political posts against racist *hacendado* opposition, from the ravages of which Albizu's own career in the nationalist movement had gravely suffered (Zenón Cruz 1: 117-19). Of course, one should not discard the view held by independentists, including perhaps Albizu, that what might appear a demonstration of a US sense of social justice was merely a cynical strategy of divide and rule, which operated by exploiting racial tensions (Zenón Cruz 1: 119-20).

---

[18] On the decline of the *hacendados* as a result of the US transformation of the Puerto Rican economy, see J. L. González ("El país" 27), Grosfoguel ("Puerto Rico" 5-6), Quintero Rivera (*Conflictos* 18-19; *Plebeyos*), and Scarano (582-90, 592-93, 632-33).

[19] See J. L. González ("El país" 14, 17-18, 25-33). As an example of the complexities of colonialism, it is interesting to note that Graciela models herself on the media icons projected by a US press.

[20] See Flores ("The Insular" 20-24, 33-34, 39-40, 46) and J. L. González ("El país" 17-18, 30-31).

[21] See Scarano (692); García (4-6); Mattos Cintrón (203-04).

The dependence of the *hacendado* class under US colonialism is best represented by José de Diego's ambivalent position as a colonial intermediary. In his lifetime (1867-1918), José de Diego was both one of the principal voices of Puerto Rican independence as well as a lawyer who prospered fighting against workers' rights in the service of the largest US sugar refinery in the Puerto Rico of his time. José de Diego's evolving interests and dependence, representative of his class, informed the radically conflicting phases in his rhetoric, which shifted from repugnance to glorification of the United States. [22]

The nationalistic hesitation just described finds a fictional voice in Vicente Reinosa's rhetoric. This veers between two poles. Firstly, he flaunts a flowery Castilian, whose degraded cultural status is underlined by Vicente's clandestine recourse to it in the private moments of his sordid affair with La China Hereje, above whose working classness he thus attempts to place himself (*La guaracha* 82, 85, 86). But, secondly, knowing which side his bread is buttered on, he is prodigious in his use of the marketing slogans, so typical of American advertising and political campaigns. [23] By means of these, he promotes himself politically as a faithful servant of American business and political interests and supporter of the war in Vietnam (29). Ultimately, however, nostalgic nationalism collapses under the strain of its attempted reconciliation with a new colonial situation and, with it, Vicente's efforts to sustain his overripe verbosity. The bathetic result of attempting to adhere to nostalgically grandiose ways in the cramped (84) American-style "furnished studio" (86), his and La China Hereje's love nest, is the foundering of the values communicated by the language to which Vicente clings as if to a leaking life raft. After a lengthy passage of Ciceronian oratory (85), of which La China Hereje "no entendió ni papa" [didn't understant squat] (85) and for which José de Diego was mocked by one of Puerto Rico's leading satirists of his day (Flores and Campos 115), Vicente stutters to a halt. In expounding the importance of his furnished studio (85-86), he explains that his is:

---

[22] See J. L. González ("El país" 30-31), Flores and Campos (111-23).

[23] Roberto González Echevarría ("La vida" 94) has observed how, with a duplicity similar to that of de Diego, the slogans describing Vicente Reinosa are corruptions of the epic epithets used to exalt the Spanish hero of the *Poema de Mío Cid*.

> Un furnished studio que utilizo . . . para urgir, clamar, para reclamar el socorro generoso de las musas y pergeñar las cuartillas lumbradas de amor patrio que leo en el podio senatorial . . . . Furnished studio en la mejor tradición de la humildad que utilizo, que utilizo, que utili, que utili, que uti, que uti, que u, que u.

> [A furnished studio that I utilize . . . to urge, to claim, to reclaim the generous aid of the muses and draft the fiery pages of patriotic love that I read on the senatorial podium . . . . Furnished studio in the best tradition of humility that I utilize, utilize, utili, utili, uti, uti, u, u.]

Though Vicente's rhetoric aspires to that of the *hacendado* class, the passage might also indicate that, like Pedreira (a salaried university professor), he is not of that class, an impression created by, in contrast with his wife, a lack of references to any aristocratic Spanish pedigree. But, while Pedreira was of the traditional petit bourgeoisie discussed by Dávila (*Sponsored* 109), Pantojas-García, and Carrión ("The Petty Bourgeoisie"), Vicente might be a self-made representative of what the same authors describe as the new petit bourgeoisie that emerged in the 1950s and became "associated with civil administration, the service sector, and nonproductive forms of labor" (Dávila, *Sponsored* 109). As a social climber, Vicente seeks the cultural prestige of *hacendado* cultural values while, as a cunning political manipulator, he makes the effort to employ Hispanophile rhetoric, whose terms still form the cultural capital of political discourse on the island (Dávila, *Sponsored* 24-94). Perhaps analogous to the satire in Sánchez's essays of middle class presumption, discussed in my next chapter, Vicente's pretensions prove greater than his capabilities (indicated by his stuttering) and are illustrative of the inferior education of the "new" petit bourgeoisie compared to its "traditional" counterpart, represented by a master of language such as Pedreira (Dávila, *Sponsored* 109).

By contrast, like the figure of the colonized Caliban, at the centre of Fernández Retamar's discussion (26-36), Daniel's fluency in the language of colonialism, Prospero's language, allows him to redefine that language to his own measure and pleasure. But, while Fernández Retamar's Caliban uses the language of the colonialist/Prospero to vehemently oppose him (11-12, 30-36), a playful Daniel shrewdly negotiates with colonialist terms. Indeed, it his lower-class, mulatto background that affords Daniel an ambiguous, disabused perspective in relation to terms of civilization and barbarism which are quite different to those of the *hacendado* class. Such a perspective allows him to engage positively with the terms of American capitalism. However, in spite of his ability to find pleasure in capitalist modernity, the collective ordeals of the working class, of blacks under American colonialism, then Free Associated Statehood, cannot be forgotten and inform Daniel's defiance, "la discrepancia de su modernidad" [the discrepancy of his modernity] (*La importancia* 53), whose "agresión" [aggression] (53) is tempered by wit. [24] Therefore, while the life of La China Hereje highlights capitalist colonialism's blind spots through the disparity between her aspirations to stardom and her daily life, Daniel, I would suggest, represents a knowing strategy of self-assertion whose wile and aggressive power is founded on the historical consciousness of his class and racial group.

4. CONCLUSION

In the intensification that takes place between the two books–from the depiction of a defensively opportunistic local popular culture to the portrayal of popular culture as a defiantly unifying Latin-Americanism–Sánchez avoids imposing brute dogmatism concerning complex issues of cultural hegemony. This he achieves in the later text by portraying a positive popular assertiveness that is ironically undercut, firstly by being identified as a histrionic reaction to the vagaries of oppressive Caribbean and Latin American history. Secondly, the gendered, sexualized nature of popular culture as a disputable space is underlined by the deflation of masculinist terms through possible homoerotic readings of Latin American machismo and emotional reinvestment in the bolero by female listeners.

La importancia portrays many-leveled dialogue in the form of daily microhistories enacted locally in multiple locations. In the introduction, the narrator describes the text we are about to read as nothing more than fabulation ("fabulación nada más") (5); a

---

[24] On the failures of modernization under US colonialism, see Flores ("Puerto Rican Literature" 146), Flores, Attinasi, and Pedro Pedraza Jr (168), Flores and Campos (131-37), Scarano (743-47, 768-75, 806-09, 817).

hybrid, *mestizo*, and frontier narration which ignores generic rules. Hybridity is achieved through the supposed transcription of the digressive voices of the narrator's interlocutors, within a dense, knowing text which, like *La guaracha*, is full of literary allusions. Similarly, the main part of *La importancia* culminates in the lyrics of a popular song, "Amor" [Love], which not only constitute marks of orality, lyrics to be performed by a singer, but also a tenuous script on which to freely improvise, like the established cultural conditions daily interrogated by popular culture. These lyrics are the textual constituent of both the legend of Daniel Santos and a literary work. The term "fabulación" itself indicates the literary through *fábula,* or plot, tale, fable; and popular oral discourse through *fabulación,* or conversation, with the two levels merging in conversation's translation into an archaic term *(fabulación),* whose only acceptable contemporary context is literature, and *fábula's* alternative meaning of "gossip." Armando Figueroa believes (199) that the hybridity of *La importancia* attenuates the desirable vernacular purity of the narrative voice in *La guaracha*. However, I would suggest that a process of hybridity is already initiated in the first novel, where popular voices are already combined with parodies of the literary masters. *La guaracha* constitutes the complex matrix from which the second book emerges. Furthermore, why does Figueroa's disapproval of *La importancia's* intertextual "guiño[s] intelectual[es]" [intellectual winking] (198) and "complicidad elitista" [elitist complicity] (199) not extend to *La guaracha?* Far from being a transparent populist celebration of "lo puertorriqueño para los puertorriqueños" [Puerto Ricanness for the Puerto Ricans] (199), *La guaracha* is often a difficult text appealing to educated readers.

In *La importancia*, "fabulación," as an ever-renewable and contingent "amorcito instantáneo" [instantaneous fling] (205), provides the means for modernity and pre-modernity, dominant and subaltern, textual and oral to converge–*enamorarse* [fall in love]–and be redeemed as hybrid popular spaces of, by turns, shared or contested pleasures that engage with as well as supersede social, sexual, and cultural restrictions. It is precisely the porousness of popular culture, with its openness to individual aspirations, that allows Daniel to rewrite the conception of the mythological strongman depicted by the novel of dictatorship (cf. Ortega *Teoría* 37-41). Such a porousness also makes his songs the democratic counterparts to the authoritarianism of institutionalized Puerto Rican culture (Cachán 182), represented by ideologues of national glory through strong masculine leadership, such as Antonio S. Pedreira and the paternalistic government of the legendary Luis Muñoz Marín. [25] Whereas authoritarianism ultimately only allows the allegiance or alienation of those excluded from authority, participation in popular culture permits the daily assertion of private or unrepresented group desires in a public space. Furthermore, institutionalized Puerto Rican culture has uncomfortably promoted the nostalgic ideals of an independent Hispanic utopia while at the same time, its representatives have enjoyed the middle-class benefits of Association with a supposedly barbaric capitalist superpower. Ultimately, the questionable nationalism of official culture is countered by the hybrid appeal of popular heroes and shared public symbols like Daniel Santos.

Broad-ranging and differentiated reclamation becomes the positive counterpart of the cultural/class segregation depicted in *La guaracha*, where, though materially advantaged, the class to which Vicente and his family belong is excluded from the "permanente fiesteo" [movable fiesta] of the lower classes. Vicente is plagued by the *guaracha* that has taken the country by storm and starts humming it contritely and without pleasure, isolated in his car (9, 98-99, 149). Meanwhile, Benny's fantasies concerning his Ferrari excite him to masturbation, described in its unattractive furtiveness (133) as a counterpart to the juxtaposed episode of La China Hereje's enjoyable childhood memory of her masturbation of three cousins (137-38). Moreover, Graciela's preoccupation with the lifestyles of the rich and famous only leads her to jealousy and an attack of hysteria (161-65), a counterpart to La China Hereje's ability to at least find pleasure in her identification with Iris Chacón (56). Significantly, the *guaracha's* accompaniment of Graciela's hysterical attack (163) contrasts with La China's previous enjoyment (eg. 14, 22) of the music Graciela considers too repulsively low-class (226).

Vicente's project for a pantheon dedicated to the founders of the Puerto Rican homeland (38)–to be represented by Washington, Lincoln, and Jefferson–, Graciela's worship of Hollywood stars,

---

[25] On the ideological investment of these two figures, see Gelpí (*Literatura* 9-12, 20-25) and Vázquez Arce ("Salsa y control" 18).

and Benny's fetishism towards his Ferrari are telling. All are examples of the bourgeoisie's replacement of the negotiated pleasures of popular culture with the uncritical aping of North American or European models of History or the high life, as part of what Frances R. Aparicio has described as "the efforts at racial and class discrimination that are still prevalent among a large part of the Latin American bourgeoisie" (*Listening* 204). The wholesale imitation of these models again sits uncomfortably with the *hacendado* nationalism to which I have referred. Yet, in spite of contradictions, the assumed elitism, or condescension, of official culture is the ideal towards which bourgeois culture, however banal, aspires. For instance, the prime arena for Graciela's social exhibitionism takes place in the context of the annual Pablo Casals classical music festival, even though the latter is heavily subsidized to keep ticket prices low, and held at the University of Puerto Rico, Río Piedras, an unpretentious and accessible cultural center. Such elitism precludes the inter-class participation of popular culture which constitutes the optimism of *La importancia*. Also, in a cruel parody of the folklorism promoted by the Institute of Puerto Rican Culture, participation is replaced by Graciela's condescending collection of Puerto Rican art, from her point of view charmingly quaint artifacts of supposed lower-class underdevelopment (223-24). However, on reflection, it becomes clear to her that she cannot include the work of Puerto Rican painters such as Myrna Báez, Antonio Martorell, and Lorenzo Homar. Their work cannot be tamed into inert objects of decoration but rather contests elitism's taxidermic appropriation of high culture, through dialogue with popular forms and localized exploration of international high art aesthetics. This scene and others in *La guaracha* contrast with the participatory hybridity of *La importancia*, a work that should be associated with the work of not only the above artists but–as José Luis González has suggested in relation to Sánchez's earlier work–with the "plebeyista" [plebeianist] work of the graphic artist, José Rosa ("Plebeyismo" 85-97). [26] But,

---

[26] José Luis González cogently distinguishes between the elitist populism of official Puerto Rican culture and the defiantly dialogic "plebeyismo" of Rosa and Sánchez: "Popularismo es selección desde arriba de formas de abajo que no aspiran a ser modelos. Plebeyismo es creación de modelos desde abajo y su imposición hacia arriba" [Popularism is selection from above of forms from below that do not aspire to become models. Plebeianism is the creation of models from below and their imposition on those above] ("Plebeyismo" 92).

Sánchez's more inclusive portrayal of Latin popular music in *La importancia* problematically coincides with, since the 1980s, the increasing patronage by the dominant social sectors, official institutions, and corporations, as well as patriots of all classes, of more romantic, less strident and politicized forms of salsa; previously considered a lower-class counter-cultural music and discriminated against by being associated with black Puerto Ricans and Nuyoricans, but now internationally celebrated. Partly in populist opposition to the penetration of American rock and pop, which are especially popular among young, white, middle-class Puerto Ricans and represent the island's incorporation into US media networks, and to Dominican *merengue*, which now occupies the devalued but highly popular space previously occupied by salsa, the latter has been officially validated as an authentic representation of Puerto Rican culture, culminating in the "Puerto Rico es salsa" concert, which took place at Expo 92 in Seville on the evening of the National Day of Puerto Rico, on 23 June (Aparicio, *Listening* 650-82; Dávila, *Sponsored* 194-95).

In conclusion, Sánchez's ironic dialogue with important Puerto Rican cultural debates lends Daniel's appropriations a historical gravity, which, by being centered in a compelling protagonist rather than a dispersed cast of characters, is all the more cogent in the second book. Paradoxically perhaps, Daniel's protagonism allows the representation of a Latin American identity for Puerto Ricans that takes them beyond the stifling dysfunctionality of the Puerto Rican family represented in *La guaracha*. The more unbounded affirmation of popular culture depicted in *La importancia*, published twelve years after *La guaracha*, should be contextualized in the generally greater optimism of subsequent works, such as *Quíntuples*. Sánchez's growing optimism should be considered part of a general shift in recent work by Latin American intellectuals, who perhaps have reacted against earlier pessimism concerning cultural imperialism (McAnany 6-8, 11). They now seem to increasingly view "cultura popular" (McAnany 8-14, 19 n27) as a dialectical subaltern process that has little to do with passive dependency and much to do with negotiation. Nowhere is the difference between the two books clearer than in their endings. *La guaracha* ends with the death of Nene under the wheels of Benny's Ferrari, a literally senseless act involving the two most verbally incoherent characters in the book (Cerna-Bazán 64). *La importancia* ends with a scene where, against the lush foliage of the former maroon territory of the Yunque National Park, and accompanied by an electronic version of Beethoven's Fifth and Daniel Santos' boleros played on a beat box, the lovemaking of a boy and girl literally consummates the liberating hybridity of "Amor."

CHAPTER 5

WRITING CLASS: THE ESSAYS

Sánchez's essays have, until recently, taken the form of occasional, journalistic pieces, and often concern literature, music, and cinema. In these, he often discusses artists and writers in relation to whom he has shaped his own work, from Fellini ("Cine de nuestro tiempo: *La Dolce Vita*") [Cinema of our Time: *La Dolce Vita*] (1961) to Luis Palés Matos ("Las señas del Caribe") [Marks of the Caribbean] (1993). As in the rest of his work, Sánchez's central concern has been to examine the questions that arise from Puerto Rico's colonial situation. Sánchez's priorities throughout his career are signaled by the fact that his most productive period as an essayist has been during the 1970s when he published his most vehemently anti-colonial articles in the socialist newspaper, *Claridad*, under the series title, "Escrito en puertorriqueño" [Written in Puerto Rican]. In "La generación o sea" [The You-Know Generation] (1972), he attacks what he considers the colonial undermining of language and institutions. In "La gente de color: cariños y prejuicios" [People of Color: Affections and Prejudices] (1972), he speaks up against racism. In "Literatura puertorriqueña y realidad colonial" [Puerto Rican Literature and Colonial Reality] (1974), he discusses Puerto Rico's colonial status and national identity. Meanwhile, in "El debut en Viena" [The Debut in Vienna] (1975), Sánchez considers the tawdry bourgeois values that accompany colonialism. More recently, in "La guagua aérea" [The Flying Bus] (1983, 1994), "Puertorriqueño he nacido" [Puerto Rican Born and Bred] (1991), and "El cuarteto nuevayorkés" [The New York Quartet] (1993) he writes about the international invisibility of Puerto Ricans, the prejudice faced by them in the US as well as the ties that bind them to the island. As I have already indicated, Sánchez's developing views in the essays cannot be isolated from their place of publication. Therefore, my discussion will pay attention to the essays' critical perspective in relation to the political slant of the organs in which they were published.

In 1994, Sánchez published *La guagua aérea*, a collection of his essays that arguably excludes his more openly polemical work, but that provides a broad sample of his various interests as an essayist. I shall not deal here with the title essay and its film version as I have discussed these extensively in a previous chapter. I shall concentrate instead on the other essays just mentioned, identifying the specific cultural debates with which Sánchez engages and their representation in his plays, short stories, and novels.

I shall suggest that the connecting thread between the related but broad-ranging matters discussed by Sánchez is a concern with the role of class in processes of national and cultural identity. As always and especially in Puerto Rico, class questions are complicated by the historical nodes of contention constituted by gender, race, and sexual issues on the colonized island. Furthermore, the professed class affiliations expressed by Sánchez in the essays prove to be a minefield, whose varyingly successful navigation by him I shall explore with the aim of examining the difficult location of the intellectual in Puerto Rican struggles for national identity. The increasing self-consciousness with which Sánchez writes about Puerto Ricans ("Las señas del Caribe") (1993) demonstrates his mature awareness of his difficult role as a writer. In short, Luis Rafael Sánchez not only foregrounds the cultural and political context for his other writing but also increasingly highlights his own difficult position as an observer of Puerto Rican life.[1]

For the purposes of this chapter, Sánchez's essays prove to be most illuminating when read in terms of the development, over a period of over thirty-five years, of his preoccupation with class and the growing problematization of his role as a social commentator. Therefore, I shall be dealing with the essays under separate thematic headings while, at the same time, following a broadly chronological order.

---

[1] Efraín Barradas (*Para leer* 82-101) has already studied the "auto-intertextualidad" [autointertextuality] between Sánchez's essays and *La guaracha*.

1. A YOUTHFUL COMMITMENT TO ART: "CINE DE NUESTRO TIEMPO:
LA DOLCE VITA" (1961)

This early essay is a raw example of the moral preoccupations
and ambiguous class affiliations I shall trace in Luis Rafael
Sánchez's essays. Certainly, a crude Marxism is at play here, which
will have a significant bearing on the writer's development as an intellectual. At this stage, the social significance he attaches to his
subject and his didactic tone may be associated with the Italian
Left's adoption of Fellini's film as a faithful mirroring of a deca-
dently bourgeois society, with Sánchez's essay occasionally reproducing the rhetoric probably favored by the Italian Communist
Party who, according to Richard Mayne's testimony, "ran debates
and lectures to explain the film's 'exposure of bourgeoise [sic]
decadence.'" More directly, Sánchez's deployment of pathological
figures of speech coincides with the famous description of the film
attributed to Fellini by several newspapers and magazines at the
time of the film's release: "*La Dolce Vita* puts a thermometer to a
sick world" (Rev. of *La Dolce Vita*). [2] At a local level, like many
Puerto Rican intellectuals before him, Sánchez even aggravates
symptoms of social malady to lend urgency and authority to his di-
agnosis. [3] He applauds what he considers the film's unflinching depiction of a society covered in festering wounds ("presentación de
una sociedad completamente vestida de sucio y llaga") and admires
Fellini's unmasking of middle-class escapism. However, there is little sign here of the great ironist Sánchez would become. The young
Sánchez is markedly more Catholic and less skeptical than the Italian master toward the dogmas that would remedy social ills. Furthermore, by making a conservative appeal for a return to basics,
Sánchez's high moral tone slips into a curious rhetoric amalgamat-

[2] For example, in his April 1961 review of the film for *Esquire* Dwight Mac-
Donald uses the same quotation. Meanwhile, Fred Majdalany in the London *Daily
Mail* of 7 Dec. 1960 wrote: "An earlier Roman satirist, Juvenal, considered his mission 'to excise the ulcers of a festering age.' Fellini is less surgical. He is content to
identify the ulcers with a bitter humour and hint at the sadness behind it" (N. pag.).
For a useful sample of reviews from the time of the film's release, see Fava and
Vigano (101-05). For further discussion of the frenzied Italian reception of Fellini's
film, also see Burke (85) and Leprohon (167-70).
[3] On diagnostic pathology as a traditional means of lending authority to intellectual discourse in Puerto Rico, see Gelpí (*Literatura* 9-12).

ing the fashionable existentialism of the Puerto Rican literature of the time, particularly evident in the work of René Marqués, and religious language.[4]

Paradoxically, religious language in its turn incorporates the essay's Marxist rhetoric, so that Sánchez provides an idiosyncratic reconciliation between the language of the Italian Left who championed the film and that of the Church's condemnation of the film's supposed immorality, condemnation which formed the basis of an attempt to have the film banned (Bondanella 132). This uneasy blend of discourses even reemerges later in Sánchez's 1968 play, *La pasión según Antígona Pérez*, which portrays the semi-religious martyrdom of a heroine whose persecution is representative of that of left-wing Latin American liberals and revolutionaries of the period. Meanwhile, an apparent appeal to universal sentiments is made in that play with the use of an epigraph attributed to Camus, which states that there is nothing for which it is worth giving up what one loves most: "Nada en el mundo merece que se aparte uno de lo que ama más."

Unlike Antígona, the protagonist's central problem is a loss of faith and meaning in his life. If Marcelo, played by the great Mastroianni, is infected by the incurable disease of *la dolce vita* ("la enfermedad de la dolce vita, ya incurable"), Sánchez interprets his malady as a spiritual one, a form of desperate limbo ("limbo desesperado"). His nihilism is described as a universal problem, a wound shared by all men and women condemned by modernity to live an existential Passion in this degenerate age.[5] Developing his argument, Sánchez states that it is the protagonist's ethical and sentimental corruption by his world that makes him deaf to the voice of salvation ("la voz de la salvación"). By amalgamating the rhetoric of the Left and Right, Sánchez parallels Luis Muñoz Marín's attempts to appeal to all Puerto Ricans through the populist Partido Popular Democrático, with whose views *El Mundo*, which published Sánchez's article, was closely associated.[6]

---

[4] Sánchez discusses the fashion for French existentialism in Latin America and Puerto Rico during the 1950s in his interview with Rabassa (188-89).

[5] Sánchez writes: "se abre la herida por donde sangrará esta sociedad enferma, que no es romana precisamente, sino humana" [the wound opens through which bleeds this sick society, which is more human than exactly Roman].

[6] From the establishment in 1952 of the Free Associated State, the PPD has attempted to coopt independentists, annexationists, progressive modernists and con-

The universal moral values to which Sánchez appeals ultimately sublimate difficult questions of class and politics, enabling the young Sánchez to state that it is immorality rather than sociopolitical problems that ail the society portrayed in Fellini's film: "En *La Dolce Vita* el grupo social no cuenta. No hay problema de sistema o partido . . . . Lo que sí hay es desmoronamiento de valores" [In *La Dolce Vita*, it is not the social group that matters. The problem is not one of systems or parties . . . . It is one of a collapse of values]. This is an unmistakable example of how, to be taken seriously, the intellectual has to assume the respectable voice of tradition. Sánchez, the struggling writer, feels obliged to inappropriately deny the troubling class transformations that have both threatened the patrician classes from which most Puerto Rican writers have been drawn, and allowed a figure like Sánchez himself to achieve prominence in modern Puerto Rican society. I hope to show that such blanket moralizing is interestingly still present in some of Sánchez's later essays, while increasingly absent from his most recent non-essay work. Furthermore, at this early stage in his career, Sánchez not only shares the fashionable existentialism of writers such as Marqués but also their accompanying pessimism, what Efraín Barradas has called "El derrotismo existencialista" [existentialist defeatism] ("El machismo" 73).

Consequently, with his reading of *La Dolce Vita*, Sánchez subscribes to the intellectual tradition I discussed in my chapter on another film, *La guagua aérea*, whose conservatism is founded on a nostalgia for the supposedly pure virtues believed to be lost to the alienation of a decadent age. Via his identification of Marcelo's alienation, Sánchez ultimately considers the core of Fellini's film to be the longing for purity as a way of human (rather than Puerto Rican) redemption in the world: "La comunicación no se logra. La vida dulce lo ha devorado [a Marcelo]. No hay escape . . . . He ahí lo significativo de este cine: tratar de llegar a algo *esencial* que re-

servative patriots, through a political rhetoric that combines the militancy of revolution, modernizing cosmopolitanism, and exaltation of supposedly eternal Puerto Rican and Hispanic cultural values (Scarano 712-29, 733, 794-97). However, by the 1960s such populism was beginning to crumble, with disenchanted groups forming unlikely alliances with radical groups. Consequently, Sánchez's use of hybrid rhetoric not only reflects the PPD's mainstream language of reconciliation but also the disenchantment of the Catholic Church, which briefly flirted with the Independence Party (PIP), a factional party composed of left-wing militants, and idealistically Hispanic critics of Puerto Rico's Americanization (Scarano 782-85).

sulte identificable con el hombre como habitante del mundo"
[Communication is not achieved. The sweet life has devoured him
(Marcelo). There is no escape . . . . Herein lies the key meaning of
this film: to try to arrive at something *essential* that might be identifiable with man as an inhabitant of his world'] (my emphasis). I
shall show how Sánchez's preoccupation with supposedly universal
man and his universal environment continues in certain later essays
with a defense of national identity as an essential birthright. On the
other hand, as I have already demonstrated in the previous chapters
of this book, in *Quíntuples* and *La importancia de llamarse Daniel
Santos* Sánchez portrays a more complex national identity which
emerges from multiple struggles taking place in different locations
within culture and society. Therefore, the essentialism that has led
many critics such as, for example, Eliseo Colón Zayas ("La problemática"), to discuss Sánchez's work in terms of a Puerto Rican
"nature" ("el ser puertorriqueño") has been superseded by
Sánchez's exploration of social survival and cultural improvisation.

The shift in Sánchez's work between *existential essentialism* to
postmodern situationism may be examined in his treatment of parallel scenes in Fellini's film and *Quíntuples*.[7] Impressed by *La Dolce
Vita*'s depiction of the falsification of a religious miracle, as the cen-
trepiece of a sensational televison spectacle, Sánchez much later, in
Quíntuples, reworks the idea of the religious event as mediafest. In
the play, Mandrake Morrison's reconstruction of the Biblical story
of the Flood is informed by direct reference to Fellini. However,
though in the play universal belief, in its capacity as a commodity,
presents the colonial subject under its authority with creative possibilities to renegotiate the terms of his national and personal history,
in this early essay Sánchez uses the media miracle to denounce the
modern world's loss of faith.

---

[7] By using a contradictory coinage such as *existential essentialism*, which uncomfortably combines a philosophy of self-invention through ethical action and an
unshakeable faith in eternal identities, I wish to convey the ersatz ideology upheld
by writers such as René Marqués. According to him, Puerto Ricans were to recover
their supposedly innate Hispanism through the ethical exercise of a traditional code
of *machista* honour.

2. The Non-Tenured Writer: "La generación o sea" (1972)

Sánchez increasingly lays bare his complex affiliations in relation to the class structure of Puerto Rican cultural hierarchies. But the growth of Sánchez's honest awareness of his role as a writer should be measured against his persistent recourse, some eleven years after the Fellini essay and beyond, to the ostensibly unimpeachable redoubt of his role as an apparently authoritative and objective observer of the Puerto Rican middle classes. Again, he makes clear his intention to dissociate himself from them in the essay, "La generación o sea." However, the anecdote with which he begins is gleaned from his unmistakably middle-class experience as a university professor. The anecdote concerns the verbal ineptitude of one of Sánchez's students, whose poverty of expression is sustained by the constant repetition of the corrective phrase, "o sea," roughly translatable as "I mean," "what I mean to say is . . . ," and which is equivalent to the verbal crutch, "you know," used by inept speakers of English. [8] Sánchez presents this as an example of the limited expressive ability of many of his countrymen, who are torn between the Old World cachet of a precious Hispanism and the promise of assimilation into an American way of life. [9]

Sánchez is clear as to whom he blames for Puerto Ricans' inability to use language not only as the most direct means of engagement with one's experience of life but also as an instrument of political power (53). He attacks the ambivalence of colonial education (53). Respectively at home and in school, language is distorted in the re-

---

[8] Sánchez refers to his student's "repetición, una, diez, cien veces de la frase *o sea*, utilizada como angustioso recurso de ciego de la lengua que adelanta ese torpe bastón inseguro y vacilante; o sea que reclama la palabra distante que ni llega ni alumbra" [repetition, once, ten, or a hundred times of the phrase *you know*, used as the anguished resource of a linguistic blind man who tentatively reaches out with that crude and hesitant walking-stick; I mean to say that he lays claim to an unreachable word that neither shows itself nor lights the way] (51). Benny's incoherence, in *La guaracha*, perfectly caricatures such verbal incompetence (e.g. *La guaracha* 74).

[9] Between "casticismo maltrecho, refulgente de mantones, castañuelas y zetas que quiebran oído" [shop-worn traditionalism, redolent of shawls, castanets, and deafening lisps] (52) and the "log cabin del buenazo Lincoln y árbol de *cherry* del perdonado por verdadero Jorge Washington, huevo de *Easter* y brujas de *Halloween*" [good old Lincoln's *log cabin* and the *cherry tree* of a Washington forgiven because of his honesty, *Easter* eggs and *Halloween* witches] (53).

lentless baby talk children soak up from those who raise them, or is neglected under the perhaps expedient bureaucratic lie concerning the bilingualism of a largely American educational system (52-53) (Scarano 606-09). [10] Childishness, marked in Puerto Rican Spanish by the indiscriminate use of the diminutive (53), and the backwardness of characters such as Benny and La China Hereje's retarded child, Nene, in *La guaracha*, or Baby Morrison, in *Quíntuples*, perhaps represent for Sánchez the difficulties of growing up as a Puerto Rican. If so, childishness stands in for the underdeveloped dependence of any colony while, simultaneously, his righteously critical point of view of an infantilized Puerto Rico merges with the paternalistic perspective of a Pedreira. [11] Certainly such a tradition of paternalism is strongly implied by Sánchez's gendering through synecdoche of the direct culprits responsible for Puerto Rico's immaturity. Not only does he point an accusatory finger at mothers, aunts, grandmothers, schoolmistresses, headmistresses, and priests but makes sure to identify them as a group by the skirts they are all supposed to wear ("faldas de la madre y la abuela y la tía y la maestra y la principal escolar, faldas del cura" [mother's and grandmother's skirts, the aunt's, teacher's, and headmistress's skirts, as well as the priest's skirt] (53). While the attribution of feminine responsibility for the island's stunted development harks back beyond Pedreira to discourses that precede him Sánchez's attack is immediately anteceded by René Marqués's criticism of what he identified as Anglo-Saxon colonialism's matriarchal social system, which I discussed in my chapter on the novels.

---

[10] (Scarano 606-09). On bilingualism as part of the question of the biculturalism of Puerto Rican education, compare Marqués ("El problema") and Sánchez ("El cuarteto" 29-31). In "La generación" Sánchez highlights Marqués's belief ("El problema;" also "El puertorriqueño 181-82) that institutionally sanctioned bilingualism favours English at the expense of Spanish. Consequently, Puerto Ricans are left stranded between both languages, with a firm grasp of neither, resulting from, on the one hand, a disinclination to live their everyday lives in a foreign language (Marqués, "El puertorriqueño" 183) and, on the other, inadequate teaching of their native tongue. In later essays, such as "El cuarteto nuevayorkés," or in the multi-registered ornateness of his literary language, Sánchez either rejects the dominance of English at the level of popular culture by branding it "El Difícil" ("El cuarteto" 29-31), incorporates it in vernacular registers as *Spanglish* ("La guagua"), or contrives to have it overshadowed in his literature by an ironically baroque style of learned Spanish (Barradas, *Para leer* 71-74, 76).

[11] Efraín Barradas ("Jangueando" 191) comments that Sánchez is virtually abandoned by his characteristic humor in this essay and adopts the tone of a sermon ("sermoneo").

Clearly, the reason for Sánchez's attention to be focused so fully on female figures of authority and the skirted, hence feminized, priest, is rooted in the past. Furthermore, by skewing the burden of lapsarian morality towards Eve's familiar role of responsibility, such a focus again obscures the question of class, the issue at the heart of the mainstream Marxist agenda once more implied, albeit ambiguously, by Sánchez's language and vehement condemnation of bourgeois decadence. That women should figure so centrally is hardly surprising since Sánchez's social criticism relates to long-standing debate about the role of women in Puerto Rican nationality and is an extension of nineteenth-century liberal ideas circulating throughout Latin America concerning social justice for the subjects of the newly established republics (Rojas Osorio 138; Williamson 203, 235, 238-39). Most relevant to my discussion is a consideration of the social role projected for women in the thinking of the renowned liberal thinker and independence activist, Eugenio María de Hostos. [12]

In his 1873 essay, "La educación científica de la mujer" [The Scientific Education of Women], Hostos's considers the potential of women as nurturers of national identity. According to him women essentially are motivated by their emotions and, if trained, may instil a fiery appetite for the political values enlightened, rationally nationalist leaders will subsequently require of their emancipated but obedient subjects. Hence, for Hostos, the education of women is a vital first step in the creation of patriotic (masculine) citizens. Meanwhile, feminine emotion is considered an ephemeral catalyst for the education of rational future citizens of an independent postcolonial world, won through their patriotic love of Independence. Women's instrumentality in building the nation subordinates them

---

[12] Eugenio María de Hostos (1839-1903). A pro-independence patriot and campaigner for the abolition of slavery, as well as a sociologist, novelist, essayist, historian, critic, and journalist, he collaborated with the Cuban revolutionaries of his day and lived most of his life in exile from Puerto Rico. After disillusioned attempts to reform the conditions of Puerto Rico's colonial status, he eventually advocated the founding of an independent confederation of Caribbean islands. His political work was complemented by his theoretical and practical work as an educational reformer, largely in Chile and the Dominican Republic. There, he held important posts as, among other things, an educational administrator and professor of constitutional law. Hostos is one of the major figures of Puerto Rican intellectual, political, and pedagogical history. The most important recent discussion of his thoughts concerning the role of Puerto Rican women in the island's independence is that of Rivera Nieves (El tema).

by drawing attention away from their own needs to the supposedly manly needs of the nation envisaged by Hostos, in which theirs is merely a foundational role. Yet if, as instruments, they are to be trained by enlightened fathers of the nation-to-be, such as Hostos, their success or failure reflects on the power of the masculine authority that guides them. In view of this, perhaps Sánchez should have redirected blame away from the "skirts" he mentions in this essay and failed mothers, like La China Hereje and Graciela Alcántara, in *La guaracha*.[13] If one agrees with another descendant of Hostos, Mandrake Morrison, that it is the writer not the work that counts, then the "authors" of these women should be called to task: the husband who abandons La China Hereje, and Vicente, who uses her and is unfaithful to his wife, Graciela.[14]

Throughout his life Hostos was concerned with promoting reason as the ultimate civilizing force. He also gave up a promising career as a novelist in favor of writing related to ostensibly utilitarian political aims. According to Hostos' rationalism, although women lit the emotional fire that fueled reason, theirs was an inferior, ever-dangerous domain that could undermine reason if feminine emotions were not "scientifically" harnessed. Similarly, the nurturing, maternal emotions of the "skirts" Sánchez admonishes threaten to smother what he considers the emancipatory possibilities of the language he seeks to promote ("libertad social de la palabra") [social liberty of the word] (54), by means of the implied reformation of the essential but sorely wanting role of women as teachers and mothers. However, if Sánchez aims here to affirm Puerto Rican nationality, later, in *Quíntuples*, he not only questions the very terms of such a nationality but also highlights the inappropriateness of Hostos's scientifically (res)trained and socially responsible woman. In contrast to the earlier essay his characterization of Carlota Morrison highlights the crisis and reworking of established representations of women as good wives, mothers, and teachers, rather than subjects of their own.

---

[13] La China Hereje neglects her handicapped son, who, unprotected, is abused and finally killed, while Graciela not only spoils the wastrel Benny, for which Vicente is equally responsible, but also addresses him in the baby talk Sánchez disparages in this essay.

[14] When I mention Mandrake Morrison, I am thinking precisely of his statement, "la obra no es la obra; la obra es quien la obra" [the work is not the work itself; the work is knowing how to work it out] (*Quíntuples* 50, 53).

To conclude, in this essay Sánchez identifies a use of language which is the negative counterpart of the popular language celebrated in "La guagua aérea" or "El cuarteto nuevayorkés." In a previous chapter on "La guagua" I have shown how Sánchez revels in a vast, rough-and-ready language ("idioma vasto y basto") ("La guagua," 1994, 15) that affirms an oral working-class communality. Meanwhile, in "El cuarteto" Sánchez is elated by the market of 14th Street in Manhattan, where not only Puerto Ricans but Spanish Americans of all nationalities meet in the sort of cosmopolitan capital city only dreamt of by Bolívar; where Americans are united in and by their Spanish language: "Los espacios venturosos del idioma español" [the fortuitous spaces of the Spanish language] ("El cuarteto," 27).

In "La generación o sea" Sánchez suggests (54) that the ravages of colonialism most gravely affect the middle classes who, as the speech of the cited student demonstrates, become incoherent caricatures, torn between an unfulfilled Puerto Ricanness and a half-digested American culture. It is they who assiduously attend university, meetings and parades of civil organizations, like the Future Housewives of America; all shrines to their vacuousness. For Sánchez, it is in these organizations that "la tontería se eleva a categoría, la frivolidad también" [foolishness is promoted to prestige, along with frivolity] ("La generación" 54). And, returning to the island's colonial subjection, it is an American educational system that Sánchez believes hobbles Puerto Ricans' progress towards fulfilling a national project whose traditionally gendered parameters hark back to Eugenio María de Hostos. Furthermore, Hostos's authoritative tone of leadership, based on the ostensibly correct appreciation of objective truths by a rational positivist, is not only echoed by orthodox Marxist criticism (Williams and Chrisman 8). At this stage in his career, and seemingly uncompromised by any class affiliations, Sánchez too would be seen to stand apart from the main object of his condemnation: the colonized middle classes.

3. BACKGROUND AND TRADITION: "LA GENTE DE COLOR: CARIÑOS Y PREJUICIOS" (1972)

The objectivity to which Sánchez aspires in "La generación o sea" clearly collapses in "La gente de color: cariños y prejuicios." Here, Sánchez oscillates between racial and class concerns emerging, respectively, from his humble origins and his present position as a dissident, middle-class intellectual who (distinctly from the dedicated artifice of his major work) may be associated in his essays with the tradition of critical bourgeois realism (cf. Hutcheon 180). In this essay, middle-class Puerto Ricans again are taken to task; this time for their racist self-promotion by dint of euphemistic but degrading discrimination. The essay begins with a discussion of the controversy surrounding the 1972 Miss Puerto Rico Competition, when its director allowed the participation of black contestants. Sánchez writes that this development was opposed by "las clases que tienen la frivolidad por dogma" [the classes which adopt frivolity for their dogma] (20), presumably the middle classes.

The resulting controversy is identified by Sánchez as a display of his society's disguised racism. In Puerto Rican society not only is race a taboo subject but racism is concealed by empty legislation, denial, and condescending rather than openly aggressive forms of address for blacks: *"quemadita, bien quemadita, trigueño, trigueño oscuro, trigueño quemado, trigueño pasado, trigueñote, trigueñota, indio, aindiado, caoba, azabache, sepia, morena, morena oscura, morenota"* (22).[15] These terms seemingly express the non-discriminatory *mulatez* of the island, as opposed to the racist, incorporative *mestizaje*, proposed by Pedreira and discussed in my third chapter. But, in fact, by way of a colonial mimicry which I shall go on to describe, the pluralism described in this essay sets color apart against a zero degree of whiteness which the upper middle classes spuriously profess in opposition to the blackness of those who are Puerto Rican but "not quite like *us.*" In Sánchez's words (27), "la gente de color se define cuando se la opone a la gente sin color, o la gente de piel blanca" [people of color are defined in opposition to people of no color, or white-skinned people]. This, in my outsider's experience of Puerto Rican life, does not stop *blanquitos* (white, upper-middle class Puerto Ricans) from rhetorically slumming it in a reinforcement of *mulatez,* by addressing each other as *negra* or *negro.*[16]

---

[15] English, which tends to polarize race according to the absolute terms "black" and "white," cannot match Caribbean Spanish's subtle range of racial distinctions. Faced with Sánchez's virtually untranslatable passage, I have settled for the following rendition: "burnished, toasted, tawny, swarthy, sable, ebony, smoky, dusky, Indian, pale-Indian, mahogany, jet-black, sepia, brunette, dark brunette, raven."

[16] In a different context, William Rowe and Vivian Schelling state (18): "The difficulty with the idea of *mestizaje* is that, without an analysis of power structures, it becomes an ideology of racial harmony which obscures the actual holding of

Sánchez affirms that though the multiform blackness of Puerto Rico confirms the latter as a basically *mestizo* country (22), the use of this fact by *blanquitos* might only serve to foreclose racial conflict by, again, incorporatively denying black identities. Richard L. Jackson (18-21) has called such incorporative denial "the prejudice of having no prejudice." Consequently, according to Sánchez, Puerto Rican racism takes the form of conspicuous absences ("ausencias conspicuas") (22) that exclude blacks from the higher echelons of the island's administration as well as from the top jobs in the private sector while, until recently, race has been conspicuously undervalued in the thematic agenda of literature and scholarship.

But, considering Sánchez's background, how does one explain his subsequent alignment with a bourgeois *hacendado* discourse, referred to elsewhere in this study, if not by his divided location as a writer inserted into a literary mainstream founded on *hacendado* values? For, Sánchez contrasts the traditionally violent racism of the United States with the non-confrontational form he recognizes on the post-abolition island: "naturalmente, aquí no se linchan negros" [naturally, blacks are not lynched here] (22). He concludes that it is perhaps blacks' inexperience of physical racial violence on the island that misguidedly has allowed many of them to entertain annexationist sentiments. These sentiments he describes as nightmarish ("pesadillas") (22) and anti-historical ("antihistóricos") (22). How can Sánchez himself be so "anti-historical"? Only by aligning himself with the literary tradition embodied by a René Marqués. For Sánchez, like Marqués, ignores the historical attractions for blacks of annexation to the United States, discussed in my chapter on Sánchez's novels, and curiously repeats Marqués's misguided admonition of Puerto Rican blacks' pro-Americanism as an ill-considered overreaction to long years of Spanish authoritarianism ("El puertorriqueño" 166 n27).

Only Sánchez's split situation as an intellectual can explain his affiliation to Marqués's arguments. But, in the light of his latest

---

power by a particular group." And later (42), in a discussion of Brazilian *mestizaje,* they cite the black Brazilian playwright Abdias do Nascimento, who asserts that "the underlying objective of this ideology has been to deny blacks the possibility of self-definition by depriving them of the means of racial identification." Richard L. Jackson (2) has used the terms "racial amalgamation," "racial bleaching," or "ethnic lynching" to emphasize the underlying appropriation and violence of such supposedly egalitarian integration. One of the most detailed recent discussions of *mestizaje* and its myth of egalitarianism is provided by Kutzinski.

work which so subtly explores the colonial subject's adaptation of what oppresses her, his subsequent statements concerning black Puerto Ricans' attempts at passing for white still seem ingenuous. He condemns their use of wigs, hair straighteners, curling irons, creams, headdresses made of nylon stocking and other whitening devices ("La gente" 23). Sánchez concludes that the racial ideal on his island is classical Greek rather than Caribbean (23). Furthermore, the adoption of this racial touchstone–molded from the whitest of Mediterranean marble–testifies to the upper middle classes' desperate need for self-validation. The inspiration for the latter is perhaps made possible by an exclusive package tour, which allows a stop off in Greece as an extra cultural treat on the eve or morning after the night before the events described in Sánchez's essay "El debut en Viena," which deals with upper middle-class Puerto Ricans' obsession with celebrating debutantes' balls in Old Europe. To compensate for colonial dispossession, waltzing as Old Europeans is perhaps not enough, Hapsburg grandeur or not. At worst such grandeur perhaps attests to the antiquated obsolescence of a bygone age rather than the accruing value of antiquity. The wishful consumption of the universal and enduring classicism of Eternal Beauty privileges longevity and is endorsed by the Venuses de Milo standing by marbled San Juan swimming pools in the showy hotel lobbies of Condado and Isla Verde. More importantly, such consumption aims to cover over the all too historically contingent ravages to which the rise and fall of Austro-Hungarian Empires and, closer to home, the middle classes bear witness.

Perhaps the power of a zero degree is its invisibility. Zero visibility operates undercover, as an assumption never openly admitted. However, by being invisible against an all too visible blackness, it may be eclipsed by being brought out into the open in performance, against which the zero degree is defenseless. For to resort to violence or to condemn is to define one's position against that which is interdicted, and hence to become denaturalized by showing one's interests. Where Sánchez sees servile integration on the part of blacks, who should supposedly strive for self-sufficient integrity, maybe there is a coloring of terms whose status can only be guaranteed by a truth that goes without saying. Reluctant to give themselves away in defense, these terms are deauthorized by being displaced. Consequently, whiteness is, in fact, given away piecemeal in its negative repetition as a series of accessories, implying imitable artifice rather than natural virtues (wigs, curling irons, etc.), or a beauty openly contested in a pageant that, through re-presentation, alienates whiteness from any assumed essence.

Sánchez goes on to discuss (23) an all-time legend of Latin American music, Rafael Hernández. The latter, a pale mulatto like Sánchez himself rather than a "negro" as Sánchez refers to him (23), is criticized by the writer for not explicitly referring in his lyrics to the Afro-Antillean character of Puerto Rican culture: "No refiere líricamente la aportación negra a [la] preciosidad [de la cultura puertorriqueña], sea rasgos de carácter, sea el temple, sea el sentido profundo del ritmo, sea una sensualidad que no se agota en la salvajina y el sexo, sea en la belleza rotunda, la inteligencia, la sensibilidad" [He does not register in his lyrics the black contribution to [the] richness [of Puerto Rican culture], whether it be the features of its character or temper, or a profound sense of rhythm; whether it be a sensuality that cannot be exhausted in wild excess or sex; whether it be its resounding beauty, intelligence, sensibility] (23). However, if there is truth in Borges's gloss of Gibbons' observation that the one thing Mohammed does not have to mention in the Koran is a camel, it being so much part of daily Arab reality that it is taken for granted, then the extra-verbal features listed above by Sánchez are especially forceful. They are so imposing in the performances I have heard, by say Daniel Santos, of Hernández's most famous composition, "Lamento borincano," and confirm a local musical tradition so closely tied to Afro-Caribbean culture that it is unnecessary for Hernández to affirm that tradition in the lyrics of his songs. Therefore, Rafael Hernández is not, I would argue, as Sánchez suggests, a "víctima agradecida" [willing victim] (23) of white values with which he sought integration. I would rather have him be an artist so confident in his black cultural heritage that, as a mulatto, he is able to sing about the cross-fertilizations that produced him, by undercutting what Sánchez identifies (23) as ostensibly Hispanist lyrics with the Africanness of rhythms that remain unnamed.

With Rafael Hernández in mind I would suggest that, based on the fetishism of a classical ideal, the white bias of the Miss Puerto Rico contest does not mean that black Puerto Ricans' participation expresses their eagerness for integration at all costs. Instead, confident in their blackness, their wearing of white accessories or posing at passing provokes a reaction that shows up whiteness to be a mask of interests rather than the physical manifestation of eternal virtue. Unmasked as an arbitrary mark of discrimination by being worn over black skin, the race of those dispossessed of their whiteness is finally forced out into the open as condemnation and this time ironically marked against a blackness that does not have to be asserted, indeed is not at issue. Strange reversal when whiteness is the loaded term!

Finally, Sánchez concludes that the presumably white(ish) judges of the contest felt so threatened that they make sure to elect a whiter than white Miss Puerto Rico (23). What Sánchez omits to say is that, with her validity discredited at home, her exportation effectively results from her displacement as a Puerto Rican ideal which is suddenly contested and no longer taken for granted. Moreover, as an exile, this blonde Miss Puerto Rico would also be unable to find a cultural home in Greece since the very Puerto Rican desires she represents would be foreign there. However, by being located in the traditional role of the middle-class intellectual, the insider posing as dissident outsider, Sánchez is unable to acknowledge, as he does in his most mature work, the ironic potential of the stereotypes that bind all Puerto Ricans, whether they are beauty queens or writers, whatever their cultural location. For to have done so, he would have had to reflect on the paradox of his writing from a traditionally patrician critical perspective in this essay published by the Marxist, pro-independence Puerto Rican newspaper, *Claridad.*

4. THEORY AND THE NONCOMMITTAL WRITER: "EL DEBUT EN VIENA" (1975)

It is from the same critical stance I have just described that Sánchez launches his attack against the middle class in this fierce broadside against bourgeois pretension, which was also published in *Claridad.* Again, Sánchez's presumed outsider status leads here to a highly contradictory critical perspective.

He takes as his subject the trend amongst the upper middle classes of celebrating Puerto Rican debutantes' balls in Vienna, as part of what the writer presents as a misguided attempt to emulate the imagined lifestyle of an Old World aristocracy.[17] What at first appears a spectacular display of vanity is, for him (10), a clear expression of class desperation and a brazen example of the wish to belong. He reflects (11) that such aspirational longing materializes in a present without historical purpose, or even the mistaken pride in an independent creole identity enjoyed by the middle classes of other Latin American societies. The Latin American pride to which Sánchez probably refers was rooted in the eventual decline of the Spanish metropolis in relation to the increasing wealth, power, and aspirations of creole elites. Such aspirations found their voice in the promotion of Enlightenment values, with creole self-assertion culminating in the national consciousness that emerged through Latin America's Independence and, more recently, revolutionary struggles.[18] These struggles were never adopted with sufficient intensity by the less potent creole elites of Puerto Rico, though this did not halt the expression of a half-baked pride in an ostensibly independent though fiercely Hispanic creolism, promoted by Antonio Pedreira and other canonical Puerto Rican intellectuals, whose *criollismo* I have discussed in previous chapters.[19] The middle classes Sánchez discusses in this essay are not capable even of mimicking the gestures of an affirmative historical destiny.

Though Sánchez does not do so himself, I would parallel his discussion of historical dispossession with Jean Baudrillard's view of the postmodern age as a time when the historical dice have been cast and meaningful political action becomes impossible. This is so

---

[17] A parallel may be drawn here between such behaviour and, in *La guaracha del Macho Camacho*, Graciela Alcántara's upbringing as an imitation "Infanta de las Españas" (46), presented in society amongst a "cotillón de debutantes en la Casa de España [de San Juan]: ghetto de amenidades peninsulares y admiraciones criollas" [cotillon of debutantes in the Casa de España: a ghetto of peninsular amenities and creole wonders] (43).

[18] Williamson (116, 154-55, 163-165, 199-203, 204-05, 233-36. 437, 439, 452-53, 457).

[19] However, to avoid distorting omissions, one should not dismiss an influential liberal strand of the Puerto Rican creole elites, which since at least the nineteenth century was well in tune with the Independence struggles of the Spanish Caribbean (Scarano 425, 431-43, 530-32). Such identification was reinforced, for instance, by direct Puerto Rican participation in the Cuban struggles for independence (Scarano 529, 531-32). Furthermore, in the eyes of Puerto Rico's greatest spokesmen for independence, figures such as Hostos and Emeterio Betances, the desire and subsequent struggle for independence were the vital first steps toward the forging of a national identity, *not* the wishful expression of an already established nationality (J. L. González, "El país" 15-17; "Literatura" 72; "Bernardo" 113).

because social action takes place as the constant reaffirmation of the flexible, all-incorporating parameters of contemporary capitalist society (Baudrillard, *The Transparency* 3-13, 89-99). [20] In Puerto Rico's case questions of national identity reaffirm the island's dependence on the authority of colonialism. Official politics take place within a constitution that leaves the final word with an overseeing US Congress that must approve major political decisions taken in Puerto Rico–including the independence option–and whose membership excludes voting representatives from the island. [21] Thus, the heated referenda on Status that periodically take place are reproductions of the terms of a political process that takes place, or has already taken place, elsewhere. Perhaps for all Puerto Ricans history is virtually empty simulation without purpose or meaningful consequence. More specifically, earlier in this study I have shown how the middle classes of *hacendado* descent, whose former standing now takes the debased form of wealth enough to

---

[20] (Baudrillard, *The Transparency* 3-13, 89-99). On the preemptive nature of Capital's regulation of all possible responses within integrated "systems" that institutionalize a broad range of choices, see Baudrillard (*Symbolic* 10-20, 23-24, 31-32, 36, 56-60, 67-68). According to Baudrillard, the incorporation of dialectical structures by post-modern Capitalism anticipates and neutralizes the possibility of outside challenges to its hegemony. Consequently, in a "tactical division of the monopoly" (68), "power is only absolute if it is able to diffract into various equivalents, if it knows how to divide in order to become stronger" (69). Baudrillard's statements are supported by the survival of a modern system of inclusive democracy, whose representative system is anticipated by Benjamin's comments (234) on European Fascism:

> Fascism attempts to organize the newly created proletarian masses without affecting the property structure which the masses strive to eliminate. Fascism sees its salvation in giving these masses not their right, but instead a chance to express themselves. The masses have a right to change property relations; Fascism seeks to give them an expression while preserving property.

[21] On Puerto Rico's constitutional dependence, Cabán, Carrión, Fernández (*The Disenchanted* 72-73, 180-81; 1994: 280-82), McNamee Alemañy (208), Meléndez, Meléndez Dávila (213-14), Morales Carrión (148-49, 200, 302). The foreclosure of Puerto Rican political identity is highlighted by the actions of attorney Juan Mari Bras, a prominent independence leader. By renouncing his US citizenship in 1995, Mari Bras has forcefully highlighted the constitutional inadmissibility of Puerto Rican nationality by virtually becoming a stateless person in his own country. Certainly the dice are loaded when, though the 1917 Jones Act allowed Puerto Ricans to opt for Puerto Rican over US citizenship, the latter choice denied one basic civil rights and privileges. Meanwhile, the Immigration and Naturalization Service had to decide whether Mari Bras would have to apply for a visa to stay in his own country.

afford Viennese debutantes' balls, are doubly unentitled. Hence, by means of the debuts in Vienna, the upper middle classes desperately attempt to relive the privileges of an earlier imperial age in a further incorporation by simulation that appeals to class aspirations through capitalist fetishism.[22]

The historical dislocation of a displaced bourgeoisie is represented by their choice of Vienna rather than a Spanish city with presumably greater cultural affinities with Puerto Rico. But what is at play is not a celebration of cultural traditions with real historical and geographical coordinates. Instead, the kitsch ritualization of a prestigious, pre-digested European culture fuels their transcontinental social climbing. Sánchez pointedly dissociates himself from such "banalidad" [banality] (10) by peppering his attack with references to representatives of highbrow literature and cinema (Buñuel, Flaubert, Balzac, Böll); references whose erudite cosmopolitanism is perhaps intended as the positive counterpart of dislocated and indiscriminate bourgeois consumption. Sánchez's cosmopolitanism is backed up by an unfavorable comparison between the sobriety of true aristocracy and the vulgarity of Puerto Rico's middle class (10), to lend him an authoritative patrician advantage over the middle-brow tastes of the would-be jet-setters he vehemently condemns. These tastes are underlined when he recounts how, by renouncing its own history (11), the bourgeoisie attempts to compensate for its degraded status through conspicuous spending on the purchase of cultural fetishes from Old Europe: *The Blue Danube*, Mozart, Strauss waltzes (10). The ironically affected language he uses to describe how these Puerto Ricans perceive their Grand Tour conveys his contempt: "un próximo debut en la Viena venteada por la flauta mágica de Mozart y los valses de Strauss al azul del Danubio" [a forthcoming debut in the Vienna buffeted by Mozart's magic flute and Strauss waltzes to the blueness of the Danube] (10).

Sánchez's assault changes tack in a final paragraph where he conclusively routs those he ridicules by a complementary manoeu-

---

[22] According to Baudrillard (*Symbolic* 3-4, 10, 13-14, 19-20, 23-38), class structures merely allow capitalism to appeal to various interests. The aspiration of these to improved conditions won in competition with other classes merely become incorporated in an overriding process of negotiation that remains untouched by inevitably internal struggles for the most advantageous positions in society. For Baudrillard, such struggles take place according to pre-determined but flexible structures which always allow negotiation for improved contracts.

ver in counterpoint to his onslaught from a hitherto highbrow cultural position. He achieves this vertical pincer movement by aligning himself with the lower classes ("el pueblo puertorriqueño que padece la calle durísima" [the Puerto Ricans who suffer on the mean streets] (11). For Sánchez, the *pueblo*'s aggressively clear-sighted affirmation that "este país está del culo" [this country is up shit creek without a paddle] (11) constitutes a sort of "credo moral" (11), whose unrecognized militancy harbors political awareness, as well as constituting a social manifesto based on an understanding of history.

By delivering a coup de grâce on escapist middle-class aspirations so sharply caricatured in *La guaracha*, the vulgar cadences of a popular Puerto Rican expression, echoing the bus passenger's recognition that the country doesn't work, in *La guaracha*, should carry all the offensive force and historical resonance of the popular culture represented by Daniel Santos. But Sánchez initially seems to occupy a no-man's land of critical objectivity, before affirming his popular sympathies, and leaves himself open to the criticism of being a slumming cultural aristocrat. He thus runs the risk of eliding the difficult, specifically located mediations and negotiations between high and popular culture which he demonstrates in the two novel-length texts to which I have just referred. Such elision is suggested by his unproblematized representation of popular culture as instantly accessible to the learned bourgeois writer. A further difficulty is that the essay both implies a postmodern dependence of identity on images while sparing the ostensibly clear-sighted critic of dependence from such blinded consumption. Hence, postmodernism merges problematically here with, again, a privileged Marxist or dissident exteriority to the object of criticism.[23] In the conclusion of this chapter, I shall further discuss this incongruous coincidence of divergent theoretical frameworks in Sánchez's essays.

---

[23] Julio Ortega (*Teoría* 33) has referred to this presumption on the part of Puerto Rican literature as "una 'buena conciencia' humanista y didáctica" [a humanist, didactic, "good conscience"] and "didactismo crítico y político de los años sesenta" [critical and political didacticism of the 1960s].

5. The Writer of his People: "Literatura puertorriqueña y
realidad colonial" (1974), "Puertorriqueño he nacido"
(1991), "Nuevas canciones festivas para ser lloradas"
(1994), "Las señas del Caribe" (1993)

By following the trajectory of these four essays, the frequently
backsliding overall development of Sánchez's essay writing may be
highlighted definitively. "Literatura puertorriqueña y realidad colonial" is one of Sánchez's most overt expositions of the detached
critical stance I have identified earlier. This presumes that the writer may have unmediated access to the truth of his society through a
detached appreciation of society's most authentic elements. The
"truth" thus gleaned gives him the leverage to attack those set up as
that society's most "inauthentic" groups. "Puertorriqueño he nacido" goes on to dehistoricize this truth with the aim of counteracting
the destabilization of national identity under colonial dispossession.
Finally, with "Nuevas canciones festivas para ser lloradas" [Festive
New Songs Full of Tears], Sánchez's essay writing coincides with
his most recent non-essay work by presenting national identity in
the context not of eternal truths but of opportunistic survival tactics under dependency.

Just as popular culture has the final word in "El debut en
Viena" truth as it is spoken on the street also informs "Literatura
puertorriqueña y realidad colonial." There, the writer's duty under
colonialism is illustrated by one of the most notorious social events
of the 1950s. Like the scene in *La guaracha* where La China sweats
uncomfortably on a sofa made for a colder climate, the incident exemplifies the unbridgeable disparity between metropolis and
colony, and actually occurred on 6 January 1952, during the Christmas season, when an airplane was chartered to carry snow to San
Juan. The snow was finally dumped in a sports stadium, an enor-
mous snowman was built, and hundreds of hitherto snowless Puerto Rican children were bussed in by the hundreds to enjoy a white
Christmas. Sadly, due to the inevitable tropical heat the snow and
snowman soon melted inspiring one child to exclaim that the snowman was turning to shit. [24]

---

[24] "El muñeco se está volviendo mierda" ("El debut," 1997: 178). According to

I presume that for the hesitantly Yankified middle classes (not overtly addressed in this essay) these San Juan Christmas celebrations would have served to foreclose the violent dependency of Puerto Rico's relations with the United States through the sublimation into myth of a colonial inferiority complex ("inferioridad impuesta" [imposed inferiority] (14). This "mito idílico" [idyllic myth] (14) becomes a displaced colonial pride, whose pro-Americanism, like Vicente Reinosa's, alternates ambiguously with the nostalgic *criollismo* of Pedreira. Again, as in "El debut," false pride in an "idyllic myth" compensates for the middle classes' devalued status, this time not through consumption of Old World kitsch but instead through the consumption of New World kitsch. Consumption turns the violent impositions of colonialism into participatory delights. These assuage the degrading subjection of the entire Puerto Rican nation through its seasonally benevolent framing within the magnanimous paternalism of a United States dressed up as Santa Claus, whose generous gift to the underprivileged may be applauded by the Puerto Rican middle classes. Their travels to Vienna perhaps have made them blasé to the charms of snow. They have the satisfaction of not being the direct recipients of gifts representing an imposed dependence: for a white Christmas snow from the North is essential, but who needs snow in the tropics? They stand apart not only by being adults, unlike the children who were to enjoy snow in San Juan, but also by sharing the middle-class pleasure of giving to the poor.

Once again, middle-class Puerto Ricans may have deluded themselves of their dissociation from a painful dependency, but it is just such self-delusion that Sánchez and, according to him, writers must attack with mordant force (14). But, in attempting to do so here, Sánchez also purports to stand outside the situations he describes with eyes supposedly open to guide the blind for whom he writes: "el ojo negado al sosiego" [an eye denied to complacency] (14). For him, the young bystander's irreverent exclamation as he watched snow turning to shit sets the tone for all responsible Puerto Rican intellectuals by exposing the absurd denial of their situa-

---

Efraín Barradas's account of the incident, the child was immediately joined by a chorus of children who chanted, "mierda, mierda, mierda" (Barradas, "Puerto Rico" 45). Concerning the first arrival of ice in nineteenth-century San Juan, the first ice cream parlors, and the incident of the snowman referred to here by Sánchez, see José Luis Vega.

tion in the form of the middle classes' attempts to pass as sophisticated First Worlders. Taking their cue from the innocent forthrightness of the child above, writers and artists must seek truth with the corrosive integrity and incisive wit (15) associated with the popular irreverence of Caribbean street humor, "relajo y guachafita" (15), represented in all Sánchez's work, but most forcefully in *La importancia de llamarse Daniel Santos.*[25]

In Sánchez's view, the writer must join "street-level" Puerto Ricans, of whatever age, one of whom is *La guaracha*'s discontented bus passenger, whose assertion that the country doesn't work politely repeats that of "este país está del culo." He or she must demolish the mitigating lies concerning Puerto Rico as the best of all possible worlds: "Socavar la broma oficial de nuestra libertad oficial" [Undermine the official joke about our official liberty] (15). For Sánchez, these lies are promoted by the dispossessed middle classes and bourgeois national leaders like those represented by Vicente Reinosa, who proclaim the official liberty sanctioned by the very designation of Puerto Rico as an Estado Libre Asociado. The defiant humor prescribed in this essay finds its most forceful counterpart in Sánchez's second novel-length text. But there is an important difference in the way such humor operates there. In the essay, it is clear that the transparency of the child's observation is potentially that of Puerto Rican writers, as pristine champions of an objective truth that shatters injustice. In contrast *La importancia* follows both *relajo*'s and *guachafita*'s more surreptitious turning to advantage of colonialism's historical impositions, as well Sánchez's subversion of intellectual traditions in which he is inescapably implicated.

The search for clear-cut oppositional positions continues in "Puertorriqueño he nacido" (1991). Here, Sánchez cursorily underlines historically determined aspects of the Puerto Rican identity, such as its African elements, Spanish language, and relationship to the United States. Nevertheless, he ultimately detaches the above elements from the historical process out which they have arisen to conclude his essay with an expressed desire for self-sufficient Puer-

---

[25] *Relajo* and *guachafita* are untranslatable. They refer to the bitter-sweet, playfully deflating humour–most often related to violent or tragic events–so characteristic of all the Caribbean. A helpful discussion of these terms is provided by López-Baralt ("La prosa").

to Ricanness, asserting his identity as "Puertorriqueño sin más. Puertorriqueño, y punto" [Puerto Rican, no more no less. Puerto Rican, period]. Defiantly he testifies to his commitment to a free-standing national identity which may be invulnerable to the inevitably unequal struggles of history. Through such bold self-affirmation based on a definitive break from historical Puerto Ricanness he perhaps hopes to counter what he identifies in this essay as the international non-recognition of Puerto Rico as separate from the United States.

The contradictory historical disengagement attempted in "Puertorriqueño he nacido" is countered by "Nuevas canciones festivas para ser lloradas," an essay which incorporates, in broader discussion of recent Puerto Rican politics and literature, a slightly but significantly altered version of the entire text of the 1991 essay. The apparent rehistoricization of Puerto Ricanness undertaken in "Nuevas canciones" aligns it far more closely with the latest of Sánchez's non-essay work though, surprisingly, the 1994 collection of essays, *La guagua aérea*, informs the reader that "Nuevas canciones" was first published in 1984, before "Puertorriqueño" (*La guagua* 191). Therefore, in terms of the overall development of Sánchez's essays, "Puertorriqueño" is an example of backsliding.

Firstly, "Nuevas canciones" is far less defensive than "Puertorriqueño" by being more open to the mixed evolution of Puerto Rico's cultural heritage. Sánchez embraces this evolution more fully and contextualizes it not only in the island's African heritage and Spanish language but also in Puerto Ricans' love of a Yankee tradition of economic and political liberalism. No more telling contrast could be found with the essentialist blackness Sánchez attempts to impose over Rafael Hernández's very historical *mulatez* in "La gente de color." Secondly, the struggle for decolonization suggested by "Nuevas canciones" is more persistently presented as a constant dialogue, in fact polylogue, between the many elements of Puerto Rico's sociopolitical and cultural history.

Here, there is no recourse to birthright, decolonization promises no final prize, since there is no conclusive Puerto Rican identity, as in "Puertorriqueño he nacido." The decolonized national identity presented in "Nuevas canciones" places greater stress on the subtle transformations and contacts made possible by the island's continuing history. It is the catalyst rather than product of history, and provides the pretext rather than conclusion of the essay. Unlike

"Puertorriqueño he nacido," "Nuevas canciones" does not defend the ultimate inviolability of Puerto Rican Spanish. Sánchez's defensiveness is tellingly revealed in "Puertorriqueño" when he steps into Marqués' boots to defend the "idioma español que [al puertorriqueño] lo ha puesto a vivir en guardia" [Spanish language in whose defence (the Puerto Rican) has been obliged to live]. Instead, "Nuevas canciones" celebrates the mutual enrichment of Spanish and English in the Caribbean. The 1991 essay's discussion of the violent linguistic distortions made inevitable by Puerto Ricans' enlistment of one colonial language, Spanish, in their struggle for survival under another gives way, in its twin essay to a reflection on the subversive adaptation that is possible in such a situation. In "Puertorriqueño" he refers to the "idioma español que el puertorriqueño *estruja, sacude, violenta*" [Spanish language which the Puerto Rican *wrings, shakes, violates*] (my emphasis). Alternatively, in "Nuevas canciones" Sánchez refers to the "idioma español que él *subvierte* con giros originales" [Spanish language that he *subverts* with original new twists] (177, my emphasis).

The toning down of confrontational imagery links "Nuevas canciones" with the more surreptitious cultural processes the writer depicts in his most mature work and is further marked by the fact that this and many of Sánchez's most recent essays were first published not, like his most vehement essays (e.g. "El debut en Viena" and "La generación o sea") in the polemically socialist and pro-independence newspaper, *Claridad*, but in the more conservative *El Nuevo Día*. This hardly means that Sánchez's development signals the abandonment of his hopes for a decolonized future and an alignment with *El Nuevo Día*'s overall support of the statehood option. Rather, I take this change of publishing outlet to indicate Sánchez's rejection of *Claridad*'s often stridently dogmatic critical perspective, which owes more than a little to the spurious objectivity of Marxist authoritarianism. Consequently, Sánchez plays a more tactical game of give and take so that, by initially toning down his language, he is able to deliver more profound criticism of Puerto Rican culture and society.

While it is true that there is a modification of Sánchez's approach between "Puertorriqueño he nacido" and "Nuevas canciones festivas para ser lloradas," in the second essay he still hopes that the future of his island will be of such self-sufficiency so as to be, in his words, "ni mimética ni epigonal" [neither mimetic nor derivative] (178). In the context of Sanchez's recent non-essay work, it is clear, however, that such integrity is extremely complicated, and that mimicry can have both negative and positive connotations, contested (among other terrains) according to race as well as class.

To broach the subject of mimicry, I return to "Literatura puertorriqueña y realidad colonial." If fanciful antics at Christmas, the most fanciful time of the year, seem trivial, Sánchez juxtaposes these, in the same paragraph (15), with the notorious endorsement by a Puerto Rican Legislative Assembly of America's presence in Vietnam which should be set against the deaths of 1,300 Puerto Rican soldiers in Vietnam and the registered mental disorders of 56% of Puerto Rican veterans of that war (Rodríguez Beruff 154). The patriotic fervor of the Puerto Rican Legislative Assembly outdid even that of State Legislative Assemblies in the United States, none of which approved US intervention in Vietnam. Reference to this example of Puerto Rican efforts to be more American than the Americans themselves is made in *La guaracha*, where we read that Senator Vicente Reinosa is a fervent supporter of the war (29).

I have already described a process of middle-class dissociation from lower-class or immature Puerto Ricans. [26] Another aspect of such dissociation is a bourgeois willingness to be accepted as a responsible partner in the colonial project, a partner who *chooses* to share the latter's ostensibly benevolent or civilizing enterprises rather than admit any (economic) coercion in following the master's lead. [27] The mimicry I describe culminates in the founding of the Estado Libre Asociado (1952), by means of which, under the tutelage

---

[26] Interestingly, recent research has demonstrated that the lower classes have been subjected to the greatest degree of infantilization, as well as feminization, in the colonial discourse of law and sociology (Santiago-Valles 52, 64-67, 95-97, 105, 155-56, 180-81, 249 n22). According to the above colonial terms, the upper strata of colonized Puerto Ricans have occupied an intermediate position between the paternal authority of the colonizer and the infantilized majority (155, 241).

[27] The interplay of class and colonialism has been studied by Kelvin A. Santiago-Valles within the context of the island's self-policing during the first four decades of American colonialism. He writes (157) of American commentators' and legislators' increasing acknowledgement of:

> the growing proficiency of the Creole propertied and educated classes in defining and regulating the backwardness of "their own" people, as exemplified among other things by the capacity of "native" intellectuals to carry out social diagnoses among the impoverished majorities of the island.

of the supposedly civilized metropolis, there could be a reinforcement of the colonial order by incorporation and regulated participation of creole elites in its enterprises. The permission to participate in its own capitalist colonialism–through an Americanized system of government whose decisions must be approved by an older and ostensibly wiser US Congress–could be seen by the colonizer as evidence of the reform of primitive foreigners, resulting from the success of colonialism. [28] On the other hand, the continuing dependence of the island, under Free Associated Statehood, serves to reconfirm the legitimacy of colonialism's mission to oversee the continuing "civilization" of its wards. Accordingly, the colonizer can never allow the colonized to be fully reformed, equal to and indistinguishable from himself, since colonialism's interests are always hierarchical. [29] Therefore, by aligning himself with a popular voice, representing the social strata who are to be lead out of their backwardness by the supposedly more enlightened elite, Sánchez disowns a certain bourgeois strand of Puerto Rican mimicry.

Alternatively, in his other work, for example *Quíntuples*, he shows how mimicry may be deployed disruptively by the colonial subject to remodel the oppressive stereotypes by which he or she is identified. [30] Meanwhile, in his mature non-essay work and essays such as "Las señas del Caribe" Sánchez consciously represents popular identities through an often learned literary language belonging to a bourgeois intellectual tradition. Thus, Sánchez highlights the impossibility of his speaking directly for the *pueblo* from his advantaged situation. In this, there is a marked difference from the work of a writer such as René Marqués, particularly in the use of Spanish. Whereas, for example, in his dramatic masterpiece, *La carreta*

---

[28] Cabán (21-23), Scarano (732-35). The early American administration's policy of supposedly enlightened reform of "natives" emerges from the nineteenth-century view of racial and cultural evolution, discussed brilliantly by Robert J. C. Young (32-35, 40-41, 47-50). According to this view, different human societies represented asynchronic stages of a single evolutionary process of civilization (the Great Chain of Being), culminating in a continually perfectible process of European and Anglo-Saxon Enlightenment.

[29] Homi K. Bhabha ("Of Mimicry" 86) refers to the colonialist's "desire for a reformed [yet] recognizable Other, as a subject of a difference that is almost the same, but not quite."

[30] As Bhabha observes ("Of Mimicry" 86), "mimicry is also [covertly] the sign of the inappropriate . . . , a difference or recalcitrance . . . .[,] at once resemblance and menace," or for Lacan (cited by Bhabha 85), "camouflage" for "warfare," by means of which the disadvantaged gains subjectivity within colonial power systems.

(1953), Marqués skillfully attempts to provide a direct phonetic transcription of rural Spanish, Sánchez rarely attempts the same, even in his most vehement advocacy of the Puerto Rican popular classes. Instead, he consistently renders their voice in a highly stylized literary elaboration of popular Puerto Rican Spanish. Therefore, while Marqués would claim all registers of his island's Spanish as part of his own authoritative repertoire of linguistic expertise, Sánchez increasingly accentuates the difficulty, contrivance, and his discreet distance from the *pueblo* he represents.

An increasing awareness of cultural mediation and his own position as a writer inform Sánchez's love of Afro-Caribbean culture and music. If his background allows him to rejoice in the common African heritage that unites the Caribbean and which he shares, it is from the vantage point of a cultural high ground that in "Las señas del Caribe," as in *La importancia de llamarse Daniel Santos*, he appraises it. In short, Sánchez's celebration disowns any claim to transparency. Indeed, the essay begins with a quotation, from Alejo Carpentier, rather than a direct representation of the topic in question: "El Caribe suena, suena escribe el cubano Alejo Carpentier" [The Caribbean sounds out, sounds out, writes the Cuban Alejo Carpentier] (41). In this way, Sánchez underlines the fact that he is presenting "signs" of the Caribbean and that Carpentier's work is a privileged re-presentation of Caribbean culture, an artifice mounted on what, at a popular level of expression, is already constructed. For Sánchez describes the subject matter of Carpentier's work as a cloth of interwoven cultural threads: "tejido cultural" [cultural cloth] (41). And through such a description, Sánchez avoids the representation of popular culture as an Arcadian origin to which he can nostalgically address, as if to a birthright, his own privileged appeal to a Caribbean identity.

Distanced from both his background and any bourgeois claims of transparency, Sánchez continues his essay by admiring the artificiality of the Puerto Rican poet Luis Palés Matos's *negrista* poetry. He does so by drawing the reader's attention to Palés Matos's consummate literary transformation of the physical manifestations in daily performance, specifically dance, of Afro-Antillean culture: "Admira cómo el bardo puertorriqueño *transforma, en cuidadosa reflexión*, la plural vivencia negra. Admira cómo enmarca la plural vivencia negra con la *onomatopeya rítmica*, el soneo de las maracas y las sabrosas percusiones de cueros" [admire how the Puerto Rican bard *transforms, into a careful reflection*, the plural black way of life. Admire how he frames the plural black way of life with his *rhythmic onomatopeya*, the beat of the maracas and the delicious percussion of hides] (43, my emphasis). [31] Sánchez then goes on to discuss the poetry of Pedro Mir, from the Dominican Republic, and refers to Mir's search for a "*signo* comunal de la antillanía" [common *sign* of Caribbeanness] (43, my emphasis), as well as the calculated crafts-manship of Mir's sparse rhetoric (44). In addition to Carpentier's and Palés Matos's exploration of Afro-Caribbean culture and its ex-pression in music, Sánchez recognizes Mir's identification of exile and migration as conditions experienced by all the inhabitants of the Caribbean. Yet again, however, Mir's contribution joins that of Carpentier and Palés Matos, as another example of representation, "retrato con palabras" [a portrait in words] (44). From his own self-aware position, Sánchez indicates that the writers named re-fract Caribbean cultural reality, which is presented by them from specific social locations in that culture, as mediated representations. Indeed, a key achievement of Sánchez's mature work is his success at tracing the myriad ways cultural reality is always refracted ac-cording to the multiple social situations of its participants.

Through his discussion of a Cuban writer, a Puerto Rican writ-er, and a writer from the Dominican Republic, Sánchez contextual-izes his own work within a regional literary tradition that recognizes itself as but one manifestation of a Caribbean culture whose space for multiple agents, socially privileged or not, is acknowledged by Sánchez's signaling of his own position *in relation to* other inter-locutors within a porous Caribbean culture marked by class and other divisions but not exclusive. One outcome of this is that the complementary cultural exchanges between learned and popular culture are highlighted in this later essay, as in the rest of Sánchez's mature work. Following on from a homage to some great popular singers, such as Lucecita Benítez, Juan Luis Guerra, Celia Cruz, Danny Rivera and Lucy Fabery, Sánchez discusses the incorpora-tion of literary culture by the selfsame oral popular culture that serves Caribbean literature as raw material, by mentioning the recital of Palés's poetry by popular orators (42-43). [32]

---

[31] I have already discussed Sánchez's parody of Palés Matos's writing in the third chapter of this book.

[32] Perhaps the most famous declaimer of Palés's poetry was Juan Boria, a black

Sánchez's awareness that, inevitably, Puerto Ricans are all variously compromised by the mediations to which culture subjects
them, as well as his sensitive deconstruction of his own situation as
a writer, makes "Las señas del Caribe" a far cry from the would-be
transparency of many of his earlier essays. While those appeal, in
meaning if not in form, to a naked truth told plainly, "Las señas"
shows that truth is always woven from the cloth that is available.
But then, more importantly, that the sensibility and invention of
Carpentier, Palés, Mir, Sánchez, and the Caribbean cultures they
represent, enable them to cut old cloth into new garments.

6. CONCLUSION

In this chapter, I have traced how Luis Rafael Sánchez's essays
have moved away from crude Marxism towards more subtly postmodern positions, hectoring moral imperatives to situationism, essentialism to mediation, and detached authority to compromised
implication. By doing so, Sánchez has had to navigate, often in contradictory ways, among several Puerto Rican intellectual traditions:
Hostos, 19th Century liberalism, *hacendado* discourse, the so-called
Generation of 1940 and their existentialism, as well as "native"
bourgeois mimicry.
    By choosing class as a defining interest in Sánchez's essays, my
allusions to Marxism and postmodernism must be qualified, since
these theoretical frameworks seem to have widely different attitudes
to the concept of class. Class is at the center of global Marxist concerns whereas, in the work of several, if not all, postmodernist theo-
rists class dovetails into and is often superseded by questions of
race, gender, and sexuality. In this way class becomes only one
amongst several elements that fluidly define the specifically located
individual or social group. [33] In Sánchez's case, the essays express

school teacher whose recitals of Palés' and Fortunato Vizcarrondo's poetry gained
great popularity from the 1950s to the 1980s. I have already referred to the reworking of canonical poetry by the composers and performers of danzas, boleros, and
tangos, in an earlier chapter on *Quíntuples*, where I discuss the character of Papá
Morisson.
    [33] See Hutcheon (12, 59, 61-69, 85-86, 134-35, 165-67, 172-77, 195-96, 198-200,
214, 216-17). On the different perspectives of Marxist and postmodern or postcolonial criticism, see Bhabha ("How"). On the hostility felt in black quarters, especially

the largely Marxist concerns of Sánchez's generation, who reached intellectual maturity in the 1960s, in the aftermath of the Cuban Revolution. But these concerns coincide in the essays with traditional Puerto Rican debates about, for example, gender, and Sánchez's own experience as a working-class mulatto who has come up in the world. [34] Since the traditional local debates I have mentioned and Sánchez's racially inflected class background relate closely, and often incongruously to postmodern concerns, it becomes clear that Sánchez's essay writing takes place within an incongruous appeal to disparate theoretical traditions. It is this incongruity that leads, for instance in "El debut en Viena," to a discussion where a postmodern reading suggests itself but where the postmodern implication of the observer in the cultural situations he observes is excluded by the privileged exteriority of Marxist criticism. [35] In a further twist, the Marxist perspective of "El debut" and "La gente de color" merges with a posture of dissident bourgeois realism.

The real development between Sánchez's early and more recent essays demonstrates that he has undoubtedly traveled a long way; but the route he has followed has been a tortuous one. His necessary recourse to multiple traditions is due to the fact that none can represent him completely, so that his trajectory parallels that of his characters' constant wandering to and fro between the different elements that make up their Caribbean identity. The dynamic process of having to span incongruous traditions and identities as a way of compensating for the incompletion of any one of them I call hy-

---

by women, towards postmodernism as the movement of a white, male, intellectual elite, see the sceptical essay by bell hooks. See also Waugh, for feminism as a qualified postmodern practice, which attempts to undermine the legitimation of patriarchy and its adherence to supposedly universal truths, while at the same time seeking legitimation itself by appealing to freedom, justice, and progress.

[34] On this aspect of Sánchez's life, see Vázquez Arce (*Por la vereda* 221-22). On Sánchez's affiliation to the political and intellectual upheavals of the 1960s, see Vázquez Arce (*Por la vereda* 16).

[35] On postmodernism's refusal of not only Marxism's but also bourgeois positivism's exteriority to a supposedly objective historical, ideological, or class referent, see Hutcheon (46, 50, 55, 74-77, 84-86, 92-97, 99, 105-06, 109, 117-19, 141-65, 172-79, 184-86, 208, 210-15, 222-24, 230). In its turn, any oppositional position, based on a criticism of class plays straight into the hands of the deconstruction undertaken by a cultural theorist such as Jean Baudrillard. For the latter, the exteriority of such an oppositional position is untenable, since simulation largely functions by encouraging critical oppositions. These merely reinforce ideology, however conflictively, by reproducing it as a disputable contract open to self-perpetuating dialectics. Hence, criticism gives body to the ideology it criticizes by operating with it in the form of chiaroscuro. See Baudrillard (*Symbolic* 3-4, 10, 24, 31-38, 46-47).

bridity. However, the hybrid basis of his critical perspective may allow him to have his cake and eat it. It may also explain the occasional backsliding into essentialism of a recent essay such as "Puertorriqueño he nacido" and, in "La gente de color: cariños y prejuicios," his assumption of bourgeois attitudes relating to an *hacendado* discourse. The latter elides the historically generated, black working-class consciousness Sánchez expresses so powerfully in *La importancia de llamarse Daniel Santos*. The fact that such discontinuity occurs in his essays but not in the development of his other work may be a result of writing in a genre that traditionally would attempt to speak transparently in the writer's voice on issues he would address directly.[36] Therefore, essay writing may reveal more of the writer's uncertainties and divided loyalties. In this sense, and within the context of Sánchez's overall development as a writer, the lag between his essays and other work, as well as the regressions I have examined in this chapter, would seem to mark the unresolved nature of his divided background. Indeed, it is only the more openly mediated genres of fiction and drama that paradoxically permit Sánchez sufficient dissociation to be able to put these divisions into ironical play in his more dispassionate non-essay work.

7. POSTSCRIPT

Since writing this chapter, revised versions of three of the essays I have discussed appeared in a 1997 collection of essays by Sánchez, entitled *No llores por nosotros, Puerto Rico* [Don't Cry for Us, Puerto Rico]. One question guided my reading of this book: does the foregrounding of cultural and ideological mediation I had traced in my chapter continue to intensify in the collection or does the latter still have recourse to the same appeals to transparency I have discussed earlier? A first reading leads me to believe that the collection is still an ambivalent mixture of both processes, though further study of the new book will need to be undertaken.

For example, while the new version of "El debut en Viena," which heads the collection, is substantially revised, Sánchez main-

---

[36] The foregrounding of the writer's supposedly authentic voice is frequently signaled by the editorial decision on the part of the newspapers and magazines that have published many of Sánchez's essays also to publish accompanying photographs or sketches of the writer. On this point, also see González Echevarría ("The Case" 16).

tains the same posture of critical exteriority to the class he criticizes and the same alignment with the lower classes. If anything, the vertical pincer movement I have already described is reinforced. So that, first he maintains the references to an increased number of highbrow artists, such as Buñuel, and simultaneously proves himself worthy of joining their ranks through a more detailed, extended, and subtle criticism of their work. He proves his *plebeyista* credentials by favorably asserting, with intensified condemnation, that those artists' satire is emaciated stuff compared to the boisterously clear-sighted criticisms voiced by the "pueblo puertorriqueño" on the mean streets of his island. Also, he concludes the new version of the essay by following his discussion of the "este país está del culo" commentary of his compatriots by enjoining his fellow writers to prove their patriotism by advocating a similar "denuncia pública" [public denunciation] (17) in their work.

Though more polished than its earlier version the same tone and stance is maintained, even intensified, in "Gente de color," along with lofty appeals to realist objectivity. Railing at one point against the concealed racism of his island, Sánchez exclaims (21): "¡De los derroches de la imaginación me cuide Dios que de los derroches de la realidad me cuido yo!" [God save me from extravagant imagination for extravagant reality is my thing!].

The claim to represent objective reality, apparent in its very title, is as fervent as before in the new version of "Literatura puertorriqueña y realidad colonial." The exhortation to artists to be "el ojo negado al sosiego" is even intensified in the new version by becoming the title of a section of the essay. There is still the call to create an "arte corrosivo para demoler las mentiras." Indeed, in the new section there is a paragraph including the following lines on the supposed transparency of Puerto Rican reality (172):

> Quiero detenerme en la palabra colonia. Por llevada y por traída, la palabra colonia parece un elemento retórico, un comodín demagógico que manejan los inconformes con la estructura puertorriqueña de gobierno, para ofenderla o desautorizarla. No lo es. La palabra colonia nomina, capazmente, la realidad política de Puerto Rico.

> [I wish to dwell on the word colony. By being used hither and thither, the word colony seems a rhetorical device, a piece of catch-all demagoguery bandied about by those malcontented with the Puerto Rican system of government, with the purpose

of insulting or devaluing it. It is not. The word colony more than adequately designates political reality in Puerto Rico.]

But, Sánchez's problematic complexity is leavened in the new version by his own reflection on the virtually irreconcilable tension between what he holds to be the nationalist imperative toward objectivity and literary realism and the inevitable mediations of ideology and literary form.

In a new section, entitled "Se ruega no vedar la novedad" [Kindly Do Not Prevent Originality] (173-74), he claims that two Puerto Rican novelists he admires, Enrique Laguerre and Emilio Díaz Valcárcel, represent two poles of modern Puerto Rican literature. In the former's case, a detailed naturalism, and, in the latter's, a more openly mediated, elliptical, and cinematic form. However, Sánchez asserts that cultural tradition, in the form of nineteenth-century realism, colors both writers' view of national reality. What is more, this section is followed by another, revised, section, entitled "De parte de las princesas muertas" [On Behalf of the Dead Princesses] (175-76), where a reference to the committed writer *par excellence*, Jean Paul Sartre, prefaces discussion of the epitome of contrived literary artificiality, Rubén Darío, whose poetry, according to Sánchez, constituted an act of political defiance with regard to bourgeois convention. Similarly, in a key section (33-35) of his revised essay, on anti-Puerto Rican jokes in the United States, "Abrazos, prejuicios y fronteras" [Embraces, Prejudices and Frontiers], Sánchez subtly examines the reductively mythical connotations of his assertion that "una nación es una narración" [a nation is at the same time a narration] (33), from his customary position of defensive nationalism in the name of "truth" and "authenticity."

In this new book, Sánchez still navigates the difficult route between the disparate locations he occupies. But the ever finer contrivance of the language he employs complements the greater autobiographical content and the consequent self-reflection he undertakes in essays such as "Fortunas y adversidades del escritor hispanoamericano" [Fortunes and Adversities of the Latin America Writer] and "Strip-Tease at East Lansing." Through such an uncomfortable engagement, he courageously foregrounds his loyalties and limitations by complicating the appeal to transparency of much of his essay work.

BEYOND PUERTO RICO: THEORIES OF SURVIVAL INTO A POSTCOLONIAL FUTURE

> Names are symbols of convenience and not paradigms of substance.
>
> (Lincoln 210)
>
> Not to write as parrots talk, but to speak as eagles silence.
>
> (Rubén Darío, cited and translated by Zavala, *Culture* 39)

T HOUGH Luis Rafael Sánchez is well aware of being a writer working in a colonial situation and though he presents different means of opposition, none provides a clear road to a postcolonial future. Thus the question of the possible inescapability of Puerto Rico's colonial status is raised and the passive reaction of audiences to the conservative film version of Sánchez's work I discuss in my third chapter suggests that improvisation or opposition are only two among many choices open to Puerto Ricans.

Within the local parameters defined by Kevin A. Santiago-Valles's reading of Homi Bhabha, my research has shown how the mimicry played out in Sánchez's work can have positive as well as negative connotations. In terms of Puerto Rico's history of capitalist colonialism, mimicry has both represented the assimilationist attempts by the middle classes to be more American than the Americans as well as popular cultures' diversionary hijacking of the only available locations of subjectivity. Meanwhile, improvisation, a strategy frequently portrayed in the writer's work, is itself a problematic process which, like individualization, may merely constitute alternative forms of investment in capitalist colonialism, an internalization of its terms.

Does improvisation reinforce the established by identifying restrictions that are not absolute but incorporate their own destabilization? Such a possibility is put forward by Jean Baudrillard, who, in his *Symbolic Exchange and Death* (6-49), suggests that the consumption that reinforces a capitalist system is constantly renewed by being adapted by consumers to their different needs. Meanwhile, in *The Transparency of Evil* (124-38), he suggests that such differentiation is related to the incorporation of Third World cultures through a device of cultural "difference." In this scenario, difference becomes a mere variation of a universal standard that "feeds on the differentness of other people" (132). In short, Baudrillard identifies the imposition of difference as a surreptitious way of reproducing dominant systems through diverting variation.[1]

At this point an objection may be raised to the relevance in the Caribbean of processes Baudrillard attributes to First World capitalism. However, the tolerant pluralism enshrined in the oxymoronic designation of Puerto Rico as a Free Associated State was established with the accompanying deployment of the full apparatus of American colonialism. At the beginning of the Cold War period, the United States committed itself to investing the extensive resources of its military and industrial might in setting up the island as a tropical showcase for capitalism, where Puerto Rico's success might be used as a symbolic weapon against the supposed fate of regressive underdevelopment promised to countries in the communist sphere of influence. Ramón Grosfoguel has demonstrated that during the establishment of the Free Associated State, the island enjoyed preferential treatment, in terms of federal assistance, over several American states.[2] Colonialism in Puerto Rico has gone hand

---

[1] At another level, it is desirable to uphold a universal standard of humanistic cohesion between diverse cultures. As Robert J. C. Young argues, "today's politics of cultural difference *must* also presuppose sameness and equality" (50, my emphasis). If not, one may play into the hands of a racism that claims to defend the human species against the supposed subhumanity of an irreconcilable alienness (124-25). Moreover, a humanistic standard not only prevents racism but also may disqualify excuses for non-intervention in atrocities perpetrated outside "our" cultural or ethnic grouping.

Referring to recent Puerto Rican cultural history, José Luis González ("Sobre la literatura" 146-47) discusses Governor Luis Muñoz Marín's political deployment of "cultural pluralism." By providing support for the foundation of progressive institutions, such as the Instituto de Cultura Puertorriqueña, radical cultural ideas were coopted into a pre-existing socio-political framework.

[2] Grosfoguel, Negrón-Muntaner, and Georas (4-7) contrast this phase in the island's capitalist development with the subsequent deterioration of the Puerto Rican economy in the light of its declining importance for US capital investment and as a cheap labour market, as well as the significant cuts in federal transfers as a result of the "fiscal crisis" in the metropolitan state. For further background information, see Carr (391-400).

in hand with the island's affiliation to a system of First World capitalism, even if it becomes clear in Sánchez's work that there is a time lag between such an affiliation and what is at best its incomplete institutionalization of a capitalist ethos. It is just such a time lag that allows Daniel Santos his ironic engagement with "civilized" modernity.[3]

On another level, and analogous to the colonial's poachings of First World structures demonstrated in my chapter on the novels, I have shown how improvisation often forms part of the opportunist reinforcement of colonial identities by means of segregation within colonial groups themselves. This is illustrated in the third chapter, dealing with three short stories where, as part of a complex of variously situated poachings, and in the historical context within which I place the short story "¡Jum!," the liberating masquerade portrayed in *Quíntuples* becomes a degrading pantomime of abject sexual deviance. Nevertheless, the ambiguities of Sánchez's texts are such that, even though the pantomime mentioned reinforced the political identity of black working-class Puerto Ricans at the cost of a persecuted minority, the pantomime's unavoidable visibility is the very basis for the subversive performances in *Quíntuples*.

Homi K. Bhabha has traced how the colonial becomes a subject not by resisting established representations of her but by opportunistically adopting them, a strategy demonstrated by the Morrison Family in *Quíntuples*. In this way, the incipient subject operates through "the uncanny fluency of another's language" (Bhabha, "Dissemination" 139). For Bhabha, therefore, hybridity emerges from a process of "splitting," where authoritarian representations are constantly displaced by "the repetitious, recursive strategy of the performative" (145). This process is not only illustrated by the vacillation between representation and dissipation enacted by the Morrisons, but is perhaps also the hope that motivates the tragically curtailed flight to the city of the protagonist of "¡Jum!" Beckoning him, it is the performative nature of modern urbanity that tentatively promises to return him his voice.

Bearing in mind my brief discussion of Bhabha's mimicry, how are his readers supposed to take what appears to be an inconsisten-

---

[3] On Puerto Rico's development as a capitalist showcase, see Ríos (100), Grosfoguel (9-10). For the Latin American context of the island's incomplete capitalization, see Franco ("Beyond Ethnocentrism" 361-62).

cy in the introduction to these ideas in his *The Location of Culture* (1994)? Seemingly against the grain of his work to set colonial hybridity in the context of discursive power relations and from his privileged position as a successful First-World intellectual, Bhabha is at one point in his work able optimistically to imagine "a [postcolonial] cultural hybridity that entertains difference without an assumed or imposed hierarchy" ("Locations of Culture" 4). For Bhabha, the transposition of dominant cultures undertaken by colonial groups constitutes hybrid border crossings that imply "going beyond" established power relations (4) to, in Trinh T. Minh-ha's words, "elsewhere-within-here" (330). Bhabha's optimism is understandable from the hindsight of a perspective that takes in the "going beyond" of a politically postcolonial India. On the other hand, a celebration of "going beyond" appears premature from the weaker positions offered by a Caribbean political situation that takes in totalitarian dictatorship, authoritarian tyranny, neo-colonial dependence or, in the case of Puerto Rico, a continuing colonialism.

From the perspective of Caribbean politics and history, George Lamming would question Bhabha's faith in hybridity: "Provided there is no extraordinary departure which explodes all of Prospero's premises, then Caliban and his future now belong to Prospero." [4] Such a statement underlines a Caribbean intellectual's painful awareness that the mere fact of hybridity is not enough to go beyond the powerful terms of colonial subjectivity. In my third chapter, it becomes clear that hybridity emerges as a highly problematic concept when related to Puerto Rico's colonial history of constitutionally incorporated resistance. Furthermore, as I show in my chapter on the essays, Sánchez's heterogeneous location as an intellectual is also often ideologically compromised by incorporation. That this is so is due to a particular critical stance with regard to traditional discourses of nationality, towards which Sánchez occasionally gravitates; a stance implicated in a dynamic structure of supposedly detached critical opposition already foreseen by the bourgeois realist tradition that underpins those very discourses of nationality. However, while colonial resistance at all levels runs the constant danger of incorporation, I still maintain that such resistance in its turn poses a profound threat to any incorporative system.

---

[4] Cited in Fernández Retamar ("Caliban: Notes" 12-13).

In my introduction, I affirmed that one of the purposes of this book was the contextualization of the theoretical questions it raises in the "contested history of the island." Sánchez at his peak is always sensitive to the shifting ideological network of interests and power relationships that have defined the limits of Puerto Rican struggles for nationality throughout the island's history. But, at the level of the cultural processes investigated in this study, the contestable terms of such a history open up the question of the role of history as a conceptual matrix, so subtly deconstructed by Homi Bhabha.

Bhabha has traced the surreptitious intervention of subordinate identities in colonial discourses that constantly seek legitimation by appealing to the supposed continuity of Tradition, National Identity, Civilization, Race, and Masculinity. In this respect, Bhabha confirms Frantz Fanon's assertion (88) that: "All forms of exploitation resemble each other. They all seek the source of their necessity in some edict of a Biblical nature." Inversely, the supposedly pristine authority of these institutions can only be confirmed by the exercise of a discourse that aims to establish the colonizer's representative identity at the cost of representing an inferior other, who serves as a distinguishing colonized object to a colonizing subject. The accumulation through time of these confirming acts of colonial assertion aims to become History. However, it is this very discursiveness which allows representation for both the colonizer and the colonized, who, by functioning as a differentiating sign of colonial discourse, comes to occupy an indispensable place within it. The necessary participation of a colonized other, as well as the repetition required for accumulation, unwittingly admits the performative "temporality" (Bhabha's word) of the mimicry, improvisation, and displacement already recommended as politically expedient by Lady Macbeth. Her edict of "look like the time to beguile the time" could easily be the blueprint for the colonial identities Sánchez portrays.

The performance of popular culture constantly interrupts the colonial historicism I have just described, through reiterative representation of traditional terms that consequently break down and have authoritatively to be reaffirmed again and again. Taking place in the gap between signifier and signified, such re-presentation engages with what would be the timeless authority of History only to denaturalize it, by highlighting and hijacking its discursive, inherently unstable instrumentality as a lever of colonialism. Consequently, the disruption wreaked by the Morrisons or Daniel Santos involves the renovation of Traditional identities into contingent identities. From there, they radically restage colonial struggles from the island's past, according to an insurgent strategy that evades incorporation by a colonial constitution or bourgeois paternalism. Evasion is made possible by the opportunity to rewrite the terms of a constantly renewable history, whose displacement offers the chance for new forms of political agency beyond the island's established terms of colonial dependency.

Sánchez's work which comes closest to exploding the very premises of colonialism is *Quíntuples*, a work which, at least, primes the fuse of explosive postcolonial possibilities. Joseph Chadwick (77-81) has suggested that *La guaracha del Macho Camacho* points to the possibility of meaningful sociopolitical action in Puerto Rico by means of an ironical re-staging of colonial capitalism that, initially, alienates its subjects from agency in their world, through the commodity fetishism it produces. However, not only does *Quíntuples* definitively discount the possibility of alienation, by showing that social life is inherently mediated by politico-economic structures that preclude a direct relation to the world. It also enacts, in real time, the possible elimination of oppressive models of identity, a more overtly political action than any I perceive in Sánchez's first novel.

As I have already affirmed, the possibilities offered by *Quíntuples* are not formulated as a coherent program but rather as the unforeseeable potentialities resulting from a committed search for a postcolonial sovereignty so far only hypothesized by politics but only undertaken culturally, as Arlene M. Dávila has demonstrated. In this, Sánchez's work shows affinities with the emancipatory projects of figures like José Martí and his Puerto Rican counterparts, Eugenio María de Hostos and Ramón Emeterio Betances (J. L. González, "El país" 14-15). These intellectuals viewed liberation from colonialism not as the teleological assertion of an already present concept of sovereignty but as the first step to establishing a national identity through the joint struggle for an unprecedented independence. In this sense, the identities that emerge through performance itself, in *Quíntuples*, only foresee the fluid process of cultural assertion out of which a constantly renewable and kaleidoscopic nationality may emerge (cf. Minh-ha 332). The fluidity of such cultural assertion paradoxically provides the element of constancy sustaining Puerto Rican identity: that is, the flux of a nationality characterized by the contingent interaction of heterogeneous interests and individual situations.

Thus, Sánchez draws on a radically progressive nineteenth-century project of nationality which, by the 1930s, had been redeployed in a reactionary rearguard action by a displaced Puerto Rican elite, the *hacendado* class. They promoted their interests under the guise of representing those of all Puerto Ricans. It was by these means that lost social authority was regained in the intellectual sphere. The *hacendados* displaced their dispossession as a class to a discourse that spoke of and for all Puerto Rican's supposed national dispossession, even if–as the cited case of José de Diego perfectly exemplifies–such a self-proclaimed position of representation is full of contradictions. While Sánchez rejects the messianic nationalism of the *hacendados*, and ironizes the nostalgic jingoism of their foundational discourses, his work still draws on the exemplarity of nationalist allegory. Only this time, he does not settle on representing Puerto Rico as an ailing body or a nuclear family. Instead, he draws our attention to the space of popular culture, as the perfect allegorical representation of Puerto Rico and the Caribbean; a popular culture whose everyday workings exemplify the democratic possibilities of a flexible and open nationality, that bypasses established political structures, perhaps marking their obsolescence.[5]

At this point, I am aware of the dangers of the "catastrofismo" described by Irma Rivera Nieves ("El orden"), to which I have already referred in my introduction. It should by now be clear by now that Sánchez's work is far from reductive in this respect, since if colonial dependency is the manifest context of his work, its exploration highlights a complex web of power relations and strategies that cannot be contained by a recourse to national politics or geopolitics and involve questions of sexuality, gender, class, and race. These generators of identity do not merely reflect Puerto Rico's political and economic status but suggest individual forms of survival whose public reverberations reach beyond given contingencies. In this optimistic sense, Luis Rafael Sánchez highlights public conflicts through the portrayal of indivi(dual) acts of survival and continues the work of another Caribbean intellectual, Frantz Fanon.

---

[5] On the problems of Latin American literature as "national allegory," Fredric Jameson's phrase, see Franco ("The Nation as Imagined Community").

In *Black Skin, White Masks* (1952), Fanon theorizes postcolonial struggle through the prism of psychoanalysis and suggests a politics of liberation, whose dynamism emerges in the complex psychic arena of ideological identification and subject formation. For Fanon, these are agonistic processes, where the imaginary proximity of the colonizer and colonized in discursive power relations admits the possibility of the subversive transformations already implied in my discussion of Homi Bhabha–who draws heavily on Fanon's work–and enacted by Sánchez's protagonists. By aligning itself with Fanon's view that colonial identities emerge out of the pregnable process of subject formation, as transformable cultural constructs, Sánchez's work is able to refute the racism of Antonio S. Pedreira and the pessimistic fatalism of René Marqués.

Transformation itself, as paranoid loss and collapse of authoritarianism, becomes the major term contested between these intellectuals and Sánchez. By embracing transformation as the sine qua non of Puerto Rican identity, he opposes the manipulation of transformation as a controlled crisis, whose threat could facilitate the reaffirmation of their local authority. Arnaldo Cruz-Malavé ("Toward an Art" 138-48) has shown how *hacendado* literary and political discourse has traditionally staged the collapse of paternal authority, as a form of spectacular, "abject transvestism." It has done so through a portrayal of threatening castration, impotence, death, homosexuality, effeminacy, or docility that "cunningly incite[s] us [Puerto Ricans] to close ranks around the father, with righteous indignation or with rage" (141). Thus, the indignant tone of Pedreira's or Marqués's work is a bugle call to Puerto Ricans manfully to ward off abjection in the reassertion of a national identity that must be defended. From this perspective, Sánchez's offensiveness lies in his transformation of crisis into a cause of celebration, where what is celebrated is the loss of control under the onslaught of mimicry, desire, and improvisation, or of any attempt to reinforce authority by staging its abjection (cf. Cruz-Malavé, "Toward an Art" 151).

A 1995 satirical essay by Sánchez, "Minga y Petraca al Nuevo Senado" [Minga and Petrarca for the New Senate], triggered a public carnival and a major media event on the island by setting the stage for transvestism to strike back against the indefensible authority of traditionally paternalistic government on the island. Using the pretext of imminent Senate elections there, Sánchez dryly nominated two popular and scandalously vulgar drag comedians, Minga and Petraca, for election to office. He suggested that all they lacked to be fit to hold public office was an easily acquired veneer of sophistication and an initiation into political sleaze.

Following the essay's publication, several editorials appeared and a lively public debate was generated in the press and television concerning the corruption and vulgarity of politics on the island, as well as the role of intellectuals in exposing such vice. But Sánchez's satirical broadside took on new proportions and exploded into a surreal media carnival when the comedians who play Minga and Petraca led a mock, fully televised campaign rally to the steps of the Senate itself.

Judging from the reaction to this essay, it is clear that Sánchez continues to sharpen the satirical edge of his essay writing. Moreover, an indication of his growing maturity as an essayist is his increasingly virtuoso use of dry wit and razor sharp observation instead of the shrill diatribe of many of his earlier essays.

Throughout his work, Sánchez relates cultural identity to processes typical of Puerto Rican popular culture. Though he has been joined by other writers in this enterprise, his perspective is still a distinctive one, whose dialogue with those of his contemporaries contributes to the vitality of Puerto Rican literature at the turn of the millenium. Certainly, the porous inclusiveness of popular culture, portrayed in a novel such as *La importancia de llamarse Daniel Santos*, initially contrasts with the popular culture portrayed by another brilliant Puerto Rican writer, Edgardo Rodríguez Juliá. In his urban chronicle, *El entierro de Cortijo* [*Cortijo's Funeral*] (1983), the funeral of another legendary musician, Rafael Cortijo, highlights what for Rodríguez Juliá are the irrevocable divisions of Puerto Rican society. The conspicuous absence of the middle classes from the funeral, or the discomfort of certain of their few members in attendance, undermine the hybrid inclusiveness proposed by Sánchez in his celebration of the bolero. In this sense, Rodríguez Juliá's perspective refutes the possibility of the relatively greater cohesion suggested by Sánchez's second novel and aligns him more closely with the perspective presented in *La guaracha del Macho Camacho*. Rodríguez Juliá suggests that the question posed by Pedreira in 1929, "¿Qué somos y cómo somos?," is irrevocably unresolved and perhaps unresolvable. For Rodríguez Juliá, popular culture serves to remind Puerto Ricans of their irreconcilable heterogeneity. Posed as a question without answer, in an ever more fragmented society, Ro-dríguez Juliá finally arrives, via an apparently less reconciliatory route, to Sánchez's position of wishing to defer to the unrepresentable autonomy of the subordinate groups whose liberation is founded on their irreconcilable affiliations in relation to popular culture. However, the difference of perspective between Sánchez and Rodríguez Juliá is ultimately not as great as it would at first seem. For instead of being mistaken as a wishful space of differentiated inclusion, it should be clear by now that popular culture is presented by Sánchez as a transforming mirror that creatively accentuates the divisions Rodríguez Juliá identifies. Refracted by popular culture, privileged histories and identities are constantly restaged and the lowly colonial inventively avoids being arrested by a binding authenticity.

For his part, Juan Duchesne Winter problematizes the term "popular culture" by highlighting its exclusive use in populist politics and high culture. According to Duchesne Winter, "popular culture" is often a buzz word permitting the academic or politician to speak for and represent non-elite groups, whose aspirations are thus, at best, hierarchically mediated or, at worst, arrested. For whom does popular culture exist and by whom is it recognized? Certainly, in Sánchez's case, his books—written by a successful writer and intellectual deeply rooted in the Afro-Antillean roots of his humble origins—are explorations of popular culture which primarily appeal to an educated, liberal readership, though the depiction of popular processes mediated by reference to learned literary tradition (e.g. Sarmiento, Marqués). However, this tradition may be contextualized in the politics of Puerto Rico, through figures such as Antonio S. Pedreira, whose influence on leaders such as Pedro Albizu Campos and Luis Muñoz Marín was immense. It is largely through an ironic engagement with the cultural baggage represented by the populism of a figure such as Muñoz Marín that Sánchez highlights the potential tyranny of those claiming to speak for the people. At the same time, Sánchez disowns the traditional authority of Puerto Rican writers such as René Marqués. By this means, Sánchez suggests limits to the authority of bourgeois politics and a bourgeois intelligentsia, and clears a space, as yet uncharted and unclaimed, for popular voices outside traditionally mediated parameters. It is for this reason that, in *Quíntuples*, the possibilities implied by the undoing of established terms of identity are unstated. Meanwhile,

as Agnes I. Lugo-Ortiz has observed in her study of the short story
"¡Jum!," the protagonist's defiant silence highlights the fragmented
boundaries of any concept of the Puerto Rican *pueblo*. By doing so
it "is a silence that does not predetermine the nature of the utterances to follow, but which opens the space for the act of utterance
itself" (Lugo-Ortiz 131-32).

Ultimately, Sánchez refuses to speak for the constituent groups
of the popular space he proposes. These groups include the blacks,
mulattoes, homosexuals, and women who emerge in his work.
Since the black, gay, and women's movements in the 1960s the voices of the latter undeniably enrich contemporary culture. By his pre-
meditated refusal to be a spokesman, however, Sánchez does not
merely propose to reverse the balance of power within an un-
changed order of cultural and political discourse in Puerto Rico. Instead, he imagines popular culture not as a series of group identities
to be represented but as an intermediary space in terms of which
tentatively privileged colonial classes as well as non-elite groups are
defined. This is a space where Puerto Rican identity may be negotiated through a multiple if not unproblematic cultural hybridity,
whose constitutional incorporation, discussed earlier, may be evad-
ed. Indeed Bhabha's faith in cultural hybridity gradually seems less
naive, for the openness portrayed in *La importancia de llamarse
Daniel Santos* and the unutterable dissipation of *Quíntuples* point
beyond Lamming's Caribbean horizon of authoritarian representation and hence incorporation of plural, often deviant, identities, beyond the difference Baudrillard criticizes.[6]

Sánchez's vision of popular culture allows Puerto Ricans to hollow out ideology in the improvisation of their daily lives. And so,
displaced by its relentless performance, ideology loses its footing
and falls into silence (Cf. Bhabha, "Dissemination" 154-55). Meanwhile, sustained by the dying echo of Puerto Rico's populist past
and feudal paternalism, the increasingly discreet silence of Luis
Rafael Sánchez's work testifies to an eloquent egalitarianism.

---

[6] Aurea María Sotomayor ("Daniel Santos" 318) discusses the openness of *La
importancia* in similar terms.

BIBLIOGRAPHY

1. SELECTED PLAYS, SHORT STORIES, AND NOVELS BY LUIS RAFAEL SÁNCHEZ[1]

"El trapito." *M* 22 June 1957: 23.

"La espera." *M* 28 Dec. 1957: 25.

Cuento de Cucarachita Viudita. Unpublished play. Ateneo Puertorriqueño, Festival de Navidad, San Juan, 1959.

"Destierro." *M* 4 July 1959: 9.

La espera [play]. *Cuadernos de Artes y Letras* [San Juan, PR] 37-38 (1960): 15-20 [act 1]; 39 (1960): 11-17 [act 2].

"Espuelas." *RICP* 3.6 (1960): 27-32.

La farsa del amor compradito. 1960. *Sol 13 interior.* 5-111.

Los ángeles se han fatigado. 1960. *Sol 13 interior.* 177-209.

La hiel nuestra de cada día. 1961. *Sol 13 interior* 113-75.

. . . *O casi el alma (auto da fe en tres actos). Teatro puertorriqueño (séptimo festival)* San Juan: Instituto de Cultura Puertorriqueña, 1965. 379-457. Republ. as *Casi el alma (auto da fe en tres actos).* Río Piedras, P.R.: Editorial Cultural, 1974.

"Ojos de sosiego ajenos." *SN* 5.4 (1975): 72.

Sol 13 interior. Río Piedras: Editorial Cultural, 1976.

Parábola del andarín. Unpublished play. Institute of Puerto Rican Culture, Twentieth Festival of Puerto Rican Theater, Tapia Theater, San Juan, June 1979.

Macho Camacho's Beat. Trans. Gregory Rabassa. New York: Pantheon, 1981. New York: Avon, 1982. Trans. of *La guaracha del Macho Camacho.* Buenos Aires: La Flor, 1976.

En cuerpo de camisa. 4th ed. Río Piedras: Editorial Cultural, 1984.

"Que sabe a paraíso." *En cuerpo de camisa* 1-9.

"La maroma." *En cuerpo de camisa* 11-15.

"Tiene la noche una raíz." *En cuerpo de camisa* 17-23.

"Aleluya negra." *En cuerpo de camisa* 25-32.

"Memoria de un eclipse." *En cuerpo de camisa* 33-42.

"¡Jum!" *En cuerpo de camisa* 53-60.

"Ejemplo del muerto que se murió sin avisar que moría." *En cuerpo de camisa* 67-72.

---

[1] For Sánchez's complete output to date, consult the bibliographies in Birmingham-Pokorny (125-30), Hernández Vargas and Caraballo Abréu (253-92), Vázquez Arce (*Por la Vereda* 233-44), and Perivolaris.

"La parentela." *En cuerpo de camisa* 73-80.
"Etc." *En cuerpo de camisa* 81-90.
"Los negros pararon el caballo." *En cuerpo de camisa* 91-96.
Quíntuples. Hanover, N.H.: Ediciones del Norte, 1985.
La importancia de llamarse Daniel Santos. Hanover, N.H.: Ediciones del Norte, 1988.
La pasión según Antígona Pérez. 11th ed. Río Piedras: Editorial Cultural, 1989.
La guaracha del Macho Camacho. 14th ed. Buenos Aires: La Flor, 1991.

2. SELECTED ESSAYS BY LUIS RAFAEL SÁNCHEZ

"Cine de nuestro tiempo: *La Dolce Vita*." *M* 14 Aug. 1961: 22.
"De James Baldwin: un ensayo profético." *M* 1 July 1963: 31.
"Un sedante colectivo." *Hora* [San Juan] Sept. 1971: 17.
"La gente de color: cariños y prejuicios." *C* 23 July 1972: 22-23.
"Literatura puertorriqueña y realidad colonial." *C* ("En Rojo") 30 Nov. 1974: 14-15.
"El debut en Viena." *C* ("En Rojo") 2 Aug. 1975: 10-11.
"Cinco problemas al escritor puertorriqueño." *Vórtice* [Stanford], 2.2-3 (1979): 117-21. Expanded version entitled 'Cinco problemas posibles para el escritor puertorriqueño' in *No llores por nosotros, Puerto Rico* 147-66.
"La guagua aérea." *ND* ("Domingo") 25 Sept. 1983: 6-10.
"Flying Bus." Trans. Elpidio Laguna-Díaz. Rodríguez de Laguna 17-25. Trans. of "La guagua aérea."
"Puertorriqueño he nacido." *ABC* ("Cumbre latinoamericana") [Madrid] 19 July 1991: xviii.
La guagua aérea. Río Piedras: Editorial Cultural, 1994.
"La generación o sea." 1972. *La guagua aérea* 51-54.
"La guagua aérea." 1983. *La guagua aérea* 11-22.
"Nuevas canciones festivas para ser lloradas." 1984. *La guagua aérea* 175-185.
"En busca del tiempo bailado." 1990. *La guagua aérea* 59-62.
"El cuarteto nuevayorkés." 1993. *La guagua aérea* 23-34.
"Preguntan por Ruth Fernández." 1993. *La guagua aérea* 37-40.
"Las señas del Caribe." 1993. *La guagua aérea* 41-45.
"Minga y Petraca al Nuevo Senado." *ND* 21 Mar. 1995: 51.
No llores por nosotros, Puerto Rico. Hanover, N.H.: Ediciones del Norte, 1997.
"El debut en Viena." 1975. Rev. version in *No llores por nosotros, Puerto Rico* 3-17.
"La gente de color." 1972. Rev. version in *No llores por nosotros, Puerto Rico* 19-29.
"Literatura puertorriqueña y realidad colonial." 1974. Rev. version in *No llores por nosotros, Puerto Rico* 167-79.
"Caribbeanness." Trans. Alfred MacAdam. *The Oxford Book of Latin American Essays*. Ed. Ilan Stavans. Oxford: Oxford UP, 1997. 418-21. Trans. of "Las señas del Caribe."

3. INTERVIEWS

"Los motivos del lobo." Interview with Mayra Montero. *La guagua aérea* 101-04.
"El lenguaje como juego malabar." Interview with Efraín Barradas. *La guagua aérea* 105-09.
"Nueva York es el gran sueño de Bolívar." Interview with Norberto Bogard. *El Diario/La Prensa* [New York] 11 Nov. 1994: 6-7.

"Wico en la intimidad." Interview with Julio Cordero Ávila. *ND* 23 Mar. 1980: 17.

"El oficio y la memoria: Luis Rafael Sánchez." Interview with Arcadio Díaz Quiñones. *SN* 12.1 (1981): 27-38.

"En palabras del escritor: entrevista a Luis Rafael Sánchez." Interview with Alida Millán Ferrer. *C* ("En Rojo") 20-26 Aug. 1993: 22-23.

"Luis Rafael Sánchez: el gozo redentor." Ortega, *Reapropiaciones* 237-43.

"De la guaracha al beat." Interview with Gregory Rabassa. *Espejo de escritores: entrevistas con Borges, Cortázar, Fuentes, Goytisolo, Onetti, Puig, Rama, Rulfo, Sánchez, Vargas Llosa.* Ed Reina Roffé. Hanover, N.H.: Ediciones del Norte, 1985. 173-94.

4. Secondary Texts

Alfonso, Vitalina. "Sátira, guachafita; diferentes expresiones de un mismo propósito." *Narrativa puertorriqueña actual. Realidad y parodia.* Pinos Nuevos. Havana: Letras Cubanas, 1994. 13-27.

Alonso, Carlos J. "*La guaracha del Macho Camacho*: The Novel as Dirge." *MLN* 100.2 (1985): 348-360.

Alvarado, Ana D., María Milagros López, and Wanda E. Ramos. "Celebrating Life and the Rearticulation of Mytho-Misogyny: Women Unearthing the 'Machosaurus.'" *S* 6 (1989): 1-7.

Aparicio, Frances R. "Entre la guaracha y el bolero: un ciclo de intertextos musicales en la nueva narrativa puertorriqueña." *RevIb* 59.162-63 (1993): 73-89.

Arrillaga, María. "Enajenación social y lingüística en *La guaracha del Macho Camacho* de Luis Rafael Sánchez." *Hispamérica* [Gaithersburg, MD] 12.34-35 (1983): 155-64.

Barradas, Efraín. *Para leer en puertorriqueño: acercamiento a la obra de Luis Rafael Sánchez.* Río Piedras: Editorial Cultural, 1981.

———. "Cuerpo que desgarra su camisa." *Cupey* [PR] 3.2 (1986): 27-33.

———. "La importancia de llamarse Luis Rafael Sánchez o permiso para un leve sobresalto crítico-literario." *T* 2.5 (1988): 191-203.

———. "Jangueando con el o sea: Luis Rafael Sánchez y el español puertorriqueño." *T* 6.22 (1992): 185-97.

Beauchamp, José Juan. "*La guaracha del Macho Camacho*: lectura política y visión del mundo." *REHPR* 5(1978): 105.

Ben-Ur, Lorraine Elena. "Myth Montage in Contemporary Puerto Rican Tragedy: *La pasión según Antígona Pérez.*" *LATR* 4.7 (1975): 15-21.

———. "Hacia la novela del Caribe: Guillermo Cabrera Infante y Luis Rafael Sánchez." Hernández Vargas and Caraballo Abréu 207-221.

Cachán, Manuel. "*En cuerpo de camisa* de Luis Rafael Sánchez: la antiliteratura alegórica del otro puertorriqueño." *RevIb* 59.162-63 (1993): 177-86.

Caraballo, Daisy. "Una lectura de *La hiel nuestra de cada día.*" Hernández Vargas and Caraballo Abréu 31-39.

Cerna-Bazán, José. "Lugar del narrador y discursividad social en *La guaracha del Macho Camacho. Nómada* [San Juan] 3 (1997): 61-67.

Chadwick, Joseph. "'Repito para consumo de los radioyentes': Repetition and Fetishism in *La guaracha del Macho Camacho.*" *REHPR* 21 (1987): 61-83.

Colón Zayas, Eliseo. "La problemática del ser puertorriqueño en los cuentos de Luis Rafael Sánchez." *PC,* 4.26 (1981): 21-25.

———. *El teatro de Luis Rafael Sánchez.* Madrid: Playor, 1985.

———. Rev. of *La importancia de llamarse Daniel Santos. RevIb* 55.146-47 (1989): 515 16.

Corral, Wilfrido H. "Humor y texto bailable en Luis Rafael Sánchez." Encuentro con América Latina: historia y literatura conference. Departamento de Filología Española & Departamento de Historia Contemporánea, University of Valencia, 1993. Photocopy to the author. 73-86.

Cruz-Malavé, Arnaldo. "Repetition and the Language of the Mass Media in Luis Rafael Sánchez's *La guaracha del Macho Camacho.*" *LALR* 13.26 (1985): 35-48.

———. 1995 "Toward an Art of Transvestism: Colonialism and Homosexuality in Puerto Rican Literature." Bergmann and Smith 137-67.

Dauster, Frank. "*La pasión según Antígona Pérez.*" *SN* 1.4 (1971): 85-86.

Feliciano Fabre, Mariano A. "Cuentos de asedio y soledad." Introduction. Sánchez, *En cuerpo de camisa* i-xx.

Fernández Olmos, Margarite. "Luis Rafael Sánchez and Rosario Ferré: Sexual Politics and Contemporary Puerto Rican Narrative." *H* 70 (1987): 40-46.

Fiet, Lowell A. "Luis Rafael Sánchez's *The Passion of Antígona Pérez*: Puerto Rican Drama in North American Performance." *LATR* 10.1 (1976): 97-101.

Figueroa, Armando. Rev. of *La importancia de llamarse Daniel Santos. Revista Hispánica Moderna* [Columbia UP] 2 (1989): 197-99.

Gelpí, Juan G. "La cuentística antipatriarcal de Luis Rafael Sánchez." *Hispamérica* 15.43 (1986): 113-20.

———. *Literatura y paternalismo en Puerto Rico.* Río Piedras: Universidad de Puerto Rico, 1993.

González, Aníbal. Rev. of *La guagua aérea. LALR* 23.45 (1995): 103-07.

González, José Emilio. "El primer libro de cuentos de Luis Rafael Sánchez." *RICP* 44 (1969): 7-15.

———. "La literatura dramática contemporánea de Puerto Rico." *Insula* [Madrid] 30.356-57 (1976): 4.

González Echevarría, Roberto. "La vida es una cosa *Phenomenal: La guaracha del Macho Camacho* y la estética de la novela actual." *Isla a su vuelo fugitiva.* Madrid: Porrúa, 1983. 91-102.

González Maldonado, Edelmira. "*La guaracha del Macho Camacho.*" *Estudios* [Duquesne UP] 45 (1977): 193-96.

Gozo, María Teresa. "Algunos aspectos de la carnavalización en *La guaracha del Macho Camacho* de Luis Rafael Sánchez." *Revista Chilena de Literatura* 26 (1985): 121-29.

Guinness, Gerald. "*La guaracha* in English: *Traduttore Traditore.*" *Here and Elsewhere: Essays on Caribbean Literature.* Río Piedras: Universidad de Puerto Rico, 1993. 59-84.

Hernández Vargas, Nélida. "Hoja biográfica." Hernández Vargas and Caraballo Abréu 1-4.

Hernández Vargas, Nélida, and Daisy Caraballo Abréu, eds. *Luis Rafael Sánchez: crítica y bibliografía.* Río Piedras: Universidad de Puerto Rico, 1985.

Huertas, Johanna Emmanuelli. "*Quíntuples*: las máscaras de la representación." *REHPR* 17-18 (1990-91): 339-51.

López-Baralt, Luce. "La prosa de Luis Rafael Sánchez escrita en puertorriqueño." *Insula* [Madrid] 31.356-57 (1976): 9.

———. "*La guaracha del Macho Camacho.* Saga nacional de la 'guachafita' puertorriqueña." *RevIb* 51.131 (1985): 103-123. [Already in his 1981 book, Barradas (13, 27) refers to this then unpublished study, allowing me to presume that López Baralt wrote it in around 1980].

Lugo-Ortiz, Agnes I. "Community at its Limits: Orality, Law, Silence, and the Homosexual Body in Luis Rafael Sánchez's '¡Jum!'." Bergmann and Smith 115-36.

Marín, María del Rosario. "Explotación publicitaria de la mujer en *La guaracha del Macho Camacho* de Luis Rafael Sánchez." *Prisma* [Caracas] 1 (1986): 9-24.

Martínez Capó, Juan. "Luis Rafael Sánchez, *En cuerpo de camisa*." *M* ("Puerto Rico Ilustrado") 9 Mar. 1968: 24.

Martínez López, Benjamín. "*La guaracha del Macho Camacho*." *C* ("En Rojo") 8-10 Oct. 1976: 6-7.

Meléndez, Priscilla. "El texto teatral como teoría: *Farsa del amor compradito* de Luis Rafael Sánchez." *REHPR* 13 (1986): 109-18.

———. "El espejo en las tablas: hacia una poética de la teatralidad en *Farsa del amor compradito* de Luis Rafael Sánchez." *La dramaturgia hispanoamericana contemporánea: teatralidad y autoconciencia.* Madrid: Pliegos, 1990. 80-106.

———. "Lo uno y lo múltiple: farsa e incesto en *Quíntuples* de Sánchez." *LATR* 26.1 (1992): 7-22.

Morales Faedo, Mayuli. "Variaciones sobre la relación público-actor/personaje en el teatro de Luis Rafael Sánchez." *Conjunto* [Havana] 80 (1989): 60-68.

Morell, Hortensia R. "El paraíso perdido en un cuento de René Marqués, reencontrado en un relato de Luis Rafael Sánchez." *T* 3.12 (1989): 651-70.

———. "*Quíntuples* y el vértigo del teatro autorreflexivo de Luis Rafael Sánchez." *LATR* 27.2 (1994): 39- 51.

Morfi, Angelina. "El teatro de Luis Rafael Sánchez." Hernández Vargas and Daisy Caraballo Abréu 5-29.

Ortega, Julio. *Reapropiaciones: cultura y nueva escritura en Puerto Rico.* Río Piedras: Universidad de Puerto Rico, 1991.

———. 1991 "Teoría y práctica del discurso popular (Luis Rafael Sánchez y la nueva escritura puertorriqueña)." *Reapropiaciones* 9-52. First published (1989) as a 'Research Paper' by the Centre for Latin American Cultural Studies (King's College, London UP).

Padua, Reinaldo Marcos. "*La guaracha del Macho Camacho*." *C* ("En Rojo") 27-29 Aug. 1976: 6-7.

Paravisini, Lizabeth. "Luis Rafael Sánchez and Norman Mailer: Puerto Rico and the United States as Heard on the Radio." *S* 1 (1984): 20-29.

Parkinson Zamora, Lois. "Clichés and Defamiliarization in the Fiction of Manuel Puig and Luis Rafael Sánchez." *Journal of Aesthetics and Art Criticism* 41 (1983): 421-436.

Perivolaris, John. "Luis Rafael Sánchez." V. Smith 749-51.

Rama, Ángel. "Dos narradores puertorriqueños." *El Universitat* [Caracas] 19 Feb. 1978: 1.

Ramos, Julio. "*La guaracha del Macho Camacho*: texto de la cultura puertorriqueña." Texto Crítico 8 (1982):24-25.

Ramos Rosado, Marie. *La mujer negra en la literatura puertorriqueña: cuentística de los setenta.* Río Piedras: Universidad de Puerto Rico, 1999. [Chapter on *En cuerpo de camisa*].

Robatto, Matilde Albert. "Antígona Pérez: heroicidad y fatalismo." Hernández Vargas and Caraballo Abréu 42-47.

Routte-Gómez, Eneid. "Documenting the Puerto Rican Psyche." *SJS* ("Venue") 23 May 1993: 4-5.

Santos Silva, Loreina. "*En cuerpo de camisa* o los malamañosos." *Renacimiento* [Puerto Rico] 1.2 (1981): 21-29.

Smith, Paul Julian. Letter to the author. 17 May 1993.

Sotomayor, Aurea María. "Daniel Santos es Daniel Santos es Daniel Santos." *Hilo de Aracne: literatura puertorriqueña hoy.* Río Piedras: Universidad de Puerto Rico, 1995. 313-18.

Umpierre, Luz María. "Critic fails to see literary growth." *SJS* 27 June 1979: 19.

Vaquero de Ramírez, María. "Interpretación de un código lingüístico: *La guaracha del Macho Camacho*." *REHPR* 5 (1978): 27-69.

Vázquez Arce, Carmen. "Salsa y control: el discurso expositivo de Luis Rafael Sánchez." Diss. Universidad Nacional Autónoma de México, 1984.
———. *Por la vereda tropical: notas sobre la cuentística de Luis Rafael Sánchez.* Buenos Aires: La Flor, 1994.
———. Letter to the author, 14 Mar. 1994.
Waldman, Gloria F. *Luis Rafael Sánchez: pasión teatral.* San Juan: Instituto de Cultura Puertorriqueña, 1988.

5. GENERAL STUDIES, BACKGROUND

Acosta Belén, Edna. "Spanglish: A Case of Languages in Contact." *New Directions in Language Learning, Teaching, and Bilingual Education.* Ed. H. Dulay and M.K. Burt. Washington D.C.: Tesol, 1975. 151-58.
———, ed. *La mujer en la sociedad puertorriqueña.* Río Piedras: Huracán, 1980.
Alonso, Manuel A. *El jíbaro.* Río Piedras: Edil, 1992.
Aparicio, Frances. "La vida es un Spanglish disparatero." *European Perspectives on Hispanic Literature in the US.* Ed. G. Fabre. Houston: Arte Público, 1988. 147-60.
———. *Listening to Salsa: Gender, Latin Popular Music and Puerto Rican Culture.* Middletown, Conn.: Wesleyan University Press, 1997.
Appignanesi, Lisa, and John Forrester. *Freud's Women.* London: Weidenfeld and Nicolson, 1992.
Apter, Emily. "Masquerade." Wright 242-44.
Bakhtin, Mikhail. 1973 *Problems of Dostoevsky's Poetics.* Trans. R. W. Rostel. Michigan: Ardis-Ann Arbor.
———. *Rabelais and his World.* Trans. Helene Iswolsky. Bloomington: Indiana UP, 1984.
Baralt, Guillermo A. *Esclavos rebeldes: conspiraciones y sublevaciones de esclavos en Puerto Rico (1795-1873).* 3rd ed. Río Piedras: Huracán, 1989.
Barradas, Efraín. "El machismo existencialista de René Márques: relecturas y nuevas lecturas." *SN* 8.3 (1977): 69-81.
———. "De lejos en sueños verla: visión mítica de Puerto Rico en la poesía neorrican." *RCR* 7.3 (1979): 46-56.
———. "Puerto Rico acá, Puerto Rico allá." *RCR* 8.2 (1980): 43-49.
Baudrillard, Jean. *Symbolic Exchange and Death.* Trans. Iain Hamilton Grant. London: Sage, 1993.
———. *The Transparency of Evil.* Trans. James Benedict. London: Verso, 1993.
Belaval, Emilio S. "María Teresa monta en calesa." 1946. *Cuentos para fomentar el turismo.* 4th ed. Río Piedras: Editorial Cultural, 1985. 77-89.
Belsey, Catherine. *Critical Practice.* London: Routledge, 1980.
Benítez Rojo, Antonio. *La isla que se repite. El Caribe y la perspectiva posmoderna.* Hanover, NH: Ediciones del Norte, 1989.
———. *The Repeating Island: The Caribbean and the Postmodern Perspective.* Trans. James E. Maraniss. Durham, NC: Duke UP, 1992. 2nd expanded ed., 1996.
Benjamin, Walter. "The Work of Art in the Age of Mechanical Reproduction." *Illuminations.* London: Fontana, 1992. 211-44.
Bergmann, Emilie L., and Paul Julian Smith, eds. *¿Entiendes?: Queer Readings, Hispanic Writings.* Durham, NC: Duke UP, 1995.
Bhabha, Homi K. *The Location of Culture.* London: Routledge, 1994.
———. "Locations of Culture." *The Location of Culture* 1-18.
———. "The Other Question." *The Location of Culture* 66-84.

Bhabha, Homi K. "Of Mimicry and Man: The Ambivalence of Colonial Discourse." *The Location of Culture* 85-92.

———. "Signs Taken for Wonders." *The Location of Culture* 102-22.

———. "Dissemination: Time, Narrative and the Margins of the Modern Nation." *The Location of Culture* 139-170.

———. "How Newness Enters the World: Postmodern Space, Postcolonial Times and the Trials of Cultural Translation." *The Location of Culture* 212-35.

Blanco, Tomás. *El prejuicio racial en Puerto Rico*. Río Piedras: Huracán, 1985.

Bondanella, Peter. *The Cinema of Federico Fellini*. Oxford: Princeton UP, 1992.

Bosch, Juan. *Hostos el sembrador*. 6th ed. Santo Domingo: Alfa & Omega, 1991.

Burke, Frank. *Federico Fellini:* Variety Lights *to* La Dolce Vita. London: Columbus, 1987.

Butt, John, and Carmen Benjamin. *A New Reference Grammar of Modern Spanish*. 2nd ed. London: Arnold, 1994.

Cabán, Pedro. "Redefining Puerto Rico's Political Status." Meléndez and Meléndez 19-39.

Carr, Raymond. *Puerto Rico: A Colonial Experiment*. New York: New York UP, 1984.

Carrión, Juan Manuel, "The Petty Bourgeoisie and the Struggle for Independence in Puerto Rico." *The Puerto Ricans: Their History, Culture, and Society*. Ed. Adalberto López. Cambridge, Mass.: Schenkman, 1980. 233-56.

———. "The National Question in Puerto Rico." Meléndez and Meléndez 67-75.

Centro: Journal of the Centre of Puerto Rican Studies [Hunter College, New York]. 56-77. "Race and Identity" issue. 8.1-2 (1996).

Cruz-Malavé, Arnaldo. "Teaching Puerto Rican Authors: Identity and Modernization in Nuyorican Texts." *ADE Bulletin* 91 (1988: 45-51).

Dávila, Arlene M. "Contending Nationalisms: Culture, Politics, and Corporate Sponsorship in Puerto Rico." Negrón-Muntaner and Grosfoguel 231-42.

———. *Sponsored Identities: Cultural Politics in Puerto Rico*. Philadelphia: Temple University, 1997.

Díaz Quiñones, Arcadio. "Recordando el futuro imaginario: la escritura histórica en la década del treinta." *SN* 14.3 (1984): 16-35.

———. "Tomás Blanco: racismo, historia, esclavitud." Introduction. Blanco 13-92.

———. "The Hispanic-Caribbean National Discourse: Antonio S. Pedreira and Ramiro Guerra y Sánchez." Hennessy 98-121.

———. *La memoria rota*. Río Piedras: Huracán, 1993.

———. "La vida inclemente." *La memoria rota* 17-66.

———. "Los años sin nombre." *La memoria rota* 109-34.

———. "Pedro Henríquez Ureña: modernidad, diáspora y construcción de identidades." *Modernización e identidades sociales*. Ed. Gilberto Giménez and Ricardo Rozas. Mexico City: Universidad Nacional Autónoma, 1994. 59-117.

Diederich, Bernard, and Al Burt. *Papa Doc: Haiti and its Dictator*. Harmondsworth: Penguin, 1972.

Doane, Mary Ann. *Femmes Fatales*. London: Routledge, 1992.

Rev. of *La Dolce Vita*. *Time* 21 Apr. 1961: N. pag.

Douglas, Mary. *Purity and Danger: An Analysis of the Concept of Pollution and Taboo*. London: Routledge, 1966.

Duchesne Winter, Juan. "Capa de Próspero, piel de Calibán." *P* 6-7 (1993): 71-79.

Dyer, Richard. *Only Entertainment*. London: Routledge, 1992.

Falcón, Rafael. *Lo afronegroide en el cuento puertorriqueño*. Miami: Universal, 1993.

Fanon, Frantz. *Black Skin, White Masks*. 3rd ed. London: Pluto, 1986.

Fava, Claudio G., and Aldo Vigano. *The Films of Federico Fellini*. Secaucus, NJ: Citadel, 1985.

Fernández, Ronald. *The Disenchanted Island: Puerto Rico and the United States in the Twentieth Century.* New York: Praeger, 1992.

———. *Cruising the Caribbean: US Influence and Intervention in the Twentieth Century.* Monroe, ME: Common Courage, 1994.

Fernández, Ronald, Serafín Méndez Méndez, and Gail Cueto. *Puerto Rico Past and Present: An Encyclopedia.* Westport, Conn., & London: Greenwood, 1998.

Fernández Retamar, Roberto. *Caliban: apuntes sobre la cultura en Nuestra América.* Mexico City: Diógenes, 1971.

———. "Caliban: Notes toward a Discussion of Culture in Our America." Trans. Edward Baker. *Caliban and Other Essays.* Minneapolis: Minnesota UP, 1989. 1-45.

Flores, Juan. *Divided Borders: Essays on Puerto Rican National Identity.* Houston: Arte Público, 1993.

———. "The Insular Vision: Pedreira and the Puerto Rican Misère." *Divided Borders* 13-57.

———. "Refiguring *La charca*." *Divided Borders* 71-84.

———. "'Bumbún' and the Beginnings of *Plena* Music." *Divided Borders* 85-91.

———. "Cortijo's Revenge: New Mappings of Puerto Rican Culture." *Divided Borders* 92-107.

———. "Puerto Rican Literature in the United States: Stages and Perspectives." *Divided Borders* 142-52.

———. "'Qué assimilated, brother, yo soy asimilao': The Structuring of Puerto Rican Identity in the US." *Divided Borders* 182-95.

Flores, Juan, John Attinasi, and Pedro Pedraza Jr. "'La Carreta Made a U-Turn:' Puerto Rican Language and Culture in the United States." *Divided Borders* 157-81.

Flores, Juan, and Ricardo Campos. "National Culture and Migration: Perspectives from the Puerto Rican Working Class." *Divided Borders* 111-41.

Franco, Jean. "The Nation as Imagined Community." *The New Historicism.* Ed. H. Aram Veeser. London: Routledge, 1989. 204-12.

———. "Beyond Ethnocentrism: Gender, Power and the Third-World Intelligentsia." Williams and Chrisman 359-69.

Freud, Sigmund. "Fragment of an analysis of a case of hysteria." *Standard Edition of the Complete Psychological Works of Sigmund Freud.* Trans. and ed. James Strachey. Vol. 7. London: Hogarth Press and Institute of Psychoanalysis, 1953. 7-122. 24 vols. 1953-74.

———. "Negation." *Standard Edition.* Vol. 9. 1961. 235-39.

Freud, Sigmund and Josef Breuer. *Studies on Hysteria. Standard Edition.* Vol. 2. 1955. 1-251.

García, Neftalí. "Puerto Rico Siglo XX: lo histórico y lo natural en la ideología colonialista." *PC* ("Documentos") [San Juan, PR] 1.8 (1978): 1-28.

Giusti Cordero, Juan A. "AfroPuerto Rican Cultural Studies: Beyond *Cultura Negroide* and *Antillanismo*." *Centro* 56-77.

González, Aníbal "To Write Iris Chacón: Puerto Rican Literature and the Mass Media Today." MLA Convention, 1982. [no more information available].

———. "(D)escribir a Iris Chacón: la literatura puertorriqueña y los medios de comunicación masiva." *Eco: Revista de la Cultura de Occidente* [Bogotá] 44.1 (1983): 12-21.

González, José Luis. 1989 *El país de cuatro pisos y otros ensayos.* 7th ed. Río Piedras: Huracán.

———. "El país de cuatro pisos: notas para una definición de la cultura puertorriqueña." *El país de cuatro pisos* 11-42.

González, José Luis. "Literatura e identidad nacional en Puerto Rico." *El país de cuatro pisos* 43-84.

———. "Plebeyismo y arte en el Puerto Rico de hoy." *El país de cuatro pisos* 85-97.

———. "Bernardo Vega: el luchador y su pueblo." *El país de cuatro pisos* 107-29.

———. "Sobre la literatura puertorriqueña de los cincuenta." *El país de cuatro pisos* 139-49.

González Echevarría, Roberto. "The Case of the Speaking Statue: *Ariel* and the Magisterial Rhetoric of the Latin American Essay." *The Voice of the Masters: Writing and Authority in Modern Latin American Literature*. Austin, TX: Texas UP, 1985. 8-32.

Grosfoguel, Ramón. "Puerto Rico in the World System: The Different Modes of Incorporation in the Twentieth Century (1898-1995)." 19th Annual Conference of the Society for Caribbean Studies. Institute of Commonwealth Studies, London, 7 July 1995.

Grosfoguel, Ramón, Frances Negrón-Muntaner, and Chloé S. Georas. "Beyond Nationalist and Colonialist Discourses: The *Jaiba* Politics of the Puerto Rican Ethno-Nation." Negrón-Muntaner and Grosfoguel 1-36.

Grosz, Elizabeth. "The Body of Signification." *Abjection, Melancholia, and Love: The Work of Julia Kristeva*. Ed. John Fletcher and Andrew Benjamin. London: Routledge, 1990. 80-103.

Hennessy, Alistair, ed. *Unity in Variety: The Hispanic & Francophone Caribbean*. London: MacMillan, 1992. Vol 2 of *Intellectuals in the 20th Century Caribbean*. 2 vols.

hooks, bell. "Postmodern Blackness." Williams and Chrisman 421-27.

Hutcheon, Linda. *A Poetics of Postmodernism: History, Theory, Fiction*. London: Routledge, 1988.

Jackson, Richard L. *The Black Image in Latin American Literature*. Albuquerque: New Mexico UP, 1976.

James, C. L. R. *The Black Jacobins: Toussaint L'Ouverture and the San Domingo Revolution*. 3rd ed. London: Allison and Busby, 1980.

Jiménez Román, Miriam. "*Un hombre (negro) del pueblo*: José Celso Barbosa and the Puerto Rican 'Race' toward Whiteness." *Centro* 8-29.

Kinsbruner, Jay. *Not of Pure Blood: The Free People of Color and Racial Prejudice in Nineteenth-Century Puerto Rico*. Durham, NC: Duke UP, 1996.

Kristeva, Julia. *Powers of Horror. An Essay on Abjection*. Trans. Leon S. Roudiez. New York: Columbia UP, 1982.

———. *Revolution in Poetic Language*. Trans. Margaret Waller. New York: Columbia UP, 1984.

Kutzinski, Vera M. *Sugar's Secrets: Race and the Erotics of Cuban Nationalism*. Charlottesville, Virginia: UP of Virginia, 1993.

Lacan, Jacques. "Bisexualité et différence des sexes." *Scilicet* 1 (1968): 85-96.

———. *Encore*. Ed. Jacques-Alain Miller. Le Séminaire. 20. Paris: Seuil, 1975.

Laplanche, J., and J. B. Pontalis. *The Language of Psychoanalysis*. Trans. Daniel Lagache. London: Hogarth, 1980.

———. "Foreclosure (Repudiation)." *The Language of Psychoanalysis* 166-69.

———. "Projection." *The Language of Psychoanalysis* 349-56.

Lechte, John. *Julia Kristeva*. London: Routledge, 1990.

Leprohon, Pierre. *The Italian Cinema*. London: Secker and Warburg, 1972.

Lincoln, C. Eric. "Black Religion and Racial Identity." *Racial and Ethnic Identity*. Ed. Herbert W. Harris, Howard C. Blue, and Ezra E. H. Griffith. London: Routledge, 1995. 209-221.

López Cantos, Ángel. "Aproximación al hombre de color puertorriqueño: siglo XVIII." Sued Badillo and López Cantos 241-310.

Lyotard, Jean-François. *The Postmodern Condition: A Report on Knowledge.* Trans. Geoff Bennington and Brian Massumi. Manchester: Manchester UP, 1986.

McAnany, Emile G. "Television and Cultural Discourses: Latin American and United States Comparisons." *Studies in Latin American Popular Culture* 8 (1989): 1-21.

McNamee Alemañy, John. "El status jurídico y político de Puerto Rico." *Pl* 6-7.1-2 (1987-88): 207-11.

Maldonado Denis, Manuel. *Puerto Rico y Estados Unidos: Emigración y colonialismo.*Mexico City: Siglo XXI, 1976.

———. *Puerto Rico: mito y realidad.* 3rd ed. San Juan: Antillana, 1979.

Marqués, René. *El puertorriqueño dócil y otros ensayos: 1953-71.* 3rd ed. San Juan: Antillana, 1977.

———. "El problema del idioma en Puerto Rico." *El puertorriqueño dócil* 131-149.

———. "El puertorriqueño dócil: literatura y realidad psicológica." *El puertorriqueño dócil* 151-215.

Márquez, Juan Luis. "Crítica y teatro en Puerto Rico: una propuesta para su revitalización." *RICP* 59 (1973): 9-14.

Martin, Gerald. *Journeys Through the Labyrinth: Latin American Fiction in the Twentieth Century.* London: Verso, 1989.

Martín-Gamero, Amalia, ed. *Antología del feminismo.* Madrid: Alianza, 1975.

Mattos Cintrón, Wilfredo. "The Struggle for Independence: The Long March to the Twenty-First Century." Meléndez and Meléndez 201-14.

Mayne, Richard. "Rome Sweet Rome." *The Sunday Telegraph* 4 October 1987: 17.

Meléndez, Edgardo. "Colonialism, Citizenship, and Contemporary Statehood." Meléndez and Meléndez 41-52.

Meléndez, Edwin, and Edgardo Meléndez, eds. *Colonial Dilemma: Critical Perspectives on Contemporary Puerto Rico.* Boston: South End, 1993.

Meléndez Dávila, María del C. "Análisis de las alternativas de Status en Puerto Rico." *Pl* 6-7.1-2 (1987-88): 213-17.

Minh-ha, Trinh T. "Cotton and Iron." *Out There: Marginalization and Contemporary Cultures.* Ed. Russell Ferguson, Martha Gever, Trinh T. Minh-ha, and Cornel West. London: The New Museum of Contemporary Art, New York; MIT, 1990.

Minority Rights Group. *No Longer Invisible: Afro-Latin Americans Today.* London: Minority Rights Publications, 1995.

Mintz, Sidney W. "Haiti's Class Warfare." *Foreign Affairs.* 74.1 (1995): 73-86.

Mohr, Nicholasa. "Puerto Ricans in New York: Cultural Evolution and Identity." Rodríguez de Laguna 157-60.

Moliner, María. *Diccionario de uso del español.* Vol. 1. Madrid, Gredos, 1988. 2 vols.

Morales Carrión, Arturo. *Puerto Rico: A Political and Cultural History.* New York: Norton, 1983.

Moreno Fraginals, Manuel, ed. *África en América Latina.* Mexico City: Siglo XXI.

Neate, Wilson. "US Puerto Rican Literature." V. Smith 686-88.

Negrón-Muntaner, Frances. "English Only Jamás but Spanish Only Cuidado: Language and Nationalism in Contemporary Puerto Rico." Negrón-Muntaner and Grosfoguel 257-85.

Negrón-Muntaner, Frances, and Ramón Grosfoguel, eds. *Puerto Rican Jam: Essays on Culture and Politics.* Minneapolis: UP of Minnesota, 1997.

O'Callaghan, Evelyn. *Woman Version: Theoretical Approaches to West Indian Fiction by Women.* London: Macmillan, 1993.

Ortega, Julio. "Conversaciones en San Juan." *Reapropiaciones* 67-85.

Palés Matos, Luis. *Poesía completa y prosa selecta.* Caracas: Ayacucho, 1978.

Palés Matos, Luis. *Tuntún de pasa y grifería*. Ed. Mercedes López Baralt. San Juan: Instituto de Cultura Puertorriqueña; Universidad de Puerto Rico, 1993.

Pantojas-García, Emilio. *Development Strategies as Ideology: Puerto Rico's Export-Led Industrialization Experience*. Boulder: Lynne Rienner, 1990.

Pedreira, Antonio S. *Insularismo*. 2nd ed. Río Piedras: Edil, 1973.

Quintero Rivera, A. G., ed. *Identidad nacional y clases sociales*. Río Piedras: Huracán, 1979.

———. *Conflictos de clase y política en Puerto Rico*. 3rd ed. Río Piedras: Huracán, 1981.

———. *Conflictos de clase y política en el Puerto Rico del siglo XIX*. 5th ed. Río Piedras: Huracán, 1986.

———. *Plebeyos y patricios: burgueses, hacendados, artesanos y obreros: las relacions de clase en el Puerto Rico de cambio de siglo*. Río Piedras: Huracán, 1988.

Ragland-Sullivan, Ellie. "Dora and the Name-of-the-Father: the Structure of Hysteria." *Discontented Discourses*. Ed. Marleen Barr and Richard Feldstein. Urbana: Illinois UP, 1989. 208-40.

———. "Hysteria." Wright 163-64.

Ridgeway, James. *The Haiti Files: Decoding the Crisis*. Washington DC: Essential; Azul, 1994.

Ríos, Palmira N. "Export-Oriented Industrialization and the Demand for Female Labour." Meléndez and Meléndez 89-101.

Rivera de Álvarez, Josefina. *Diccionario de literatura puertorriqueña*. 2nd ed. San Juan: Instituto de Cultura Puertorriqueña, 1970.

———. *Literatura puertorriqueña. Su proceso en el tiempo*. Madrid: Partenón, 1983.

Rivera Nieves, Irma. *El tema de la mujer en el pensamiento social de Hostos*. Río Piedras: Universidad de Puerto Rico, 1992.

———. "El orden del discurso en Puerto Rico." *P* 6-7 (1993): 54-70.

Rodríguez, Clara E. "Puerto Ricans: Between Black and White." *The Puerto Rican Struggle: Essays on Survival in the US*. Ed. Clara E. Rodríguez, Virginia Sánchez Korrol, and José Óscar Alers. Maplewood, N.J.: Waterfront, 1980. 20-30.

Rodríguez Beruff, Jorge. *Política militar y dominación: Puerto Rico en el contexto latinoamericano*. Río Piedras: Huracán, 1988.

Rodríguez de Laguna, Asela, ed. *Images and Identities: The Puerto Rican in Two World Contexts*. New Brunswick, N.J.: Transaction, 1987.

Rodríguez Juliá, Edgardo. *La renuncia del héroe Baltasar*. 2nd ed. Río Piedras: Editorial Cultural, 1986.

———. *El entierro de Cortijo* 4th ed. Río Piedras: Huracán, 1988.

———. *Puertorriqueños: álbum de la sagrada familia puertorriqueña a partir de 1898*. 2nd ed. Madrid: Playor, 1989.

———. *La noche oscura del Niño Avilés*. 2nd ed. Río Piedras: Universidad de Puerto Rico, 1991.

———. Interview. *Reapropiaciones: cultura y nueva escritura en Puerto Rico*. By Julio Ortega 123-62.

Rojas Osorio, Carlos. "La mujer en el pensamiento de Hostos." *P* 6-7 (1993): 137-39.

Rowe, William, and Vivian Schelling. *Memory and Modernity: Popular Culture in Latin America*. London: Verso, 1991.

Sánchez Korrol, Virgina E. *From Colonia to Community: The History of Puerto Ricans in New York City*. London: University of California, 1993.

Sandoval Sánchez, Alberto. "Puerto Rican Identity Up in the Air: Air Migration, its Cultural Representations, and Me 'Cruzando el Charco.'" Negrón-Muntaner and Grosfoguel 189-208.

Santiago-Valles, Kelvin A. *"Subject People" and Colonial Disourse: Economic Transformation and Social Disorder in Puerto Rico*. New York: New York State UP, 1994.

Santiago-Valles, Kelvin A. "Puerto Rico." Minority Rights Group 139-61.

Santos, Mayra. "Puerto Rican Underground." *Centro* 216-31.

Scarano, Francisco A. *Puerto Rico: cinco siglos de historia.* San Juan: McGraw Hill Interamericana, 1993.

Silvestrini, Blanca G. "La mujer puertorriqueña y el movimiento obrero en la década de 1930." Acosta Belén, *La mujer* 67-90.

Smith, Paul Julian. *Laws of Desire: Questions of Homosexuality in Contemporary Spanish Writing and Film.* Oxford: Clarendon, 1992.

Smith, Verity, ed. *Encyclopedia of Latin American Literature.* London: Fitzroy Dearborn, 1997.

Sommer, Doris. *Foundational Fictions: The National Romances of Latin America.* Berkeley: California UP, 1991.

Sotomayor, Aurea María. "La mujer ideal según Hostos: reflexiones en torno al libro de Irma Rivera Nieves." *El tema de la mujer en el pensamiento de Hostos.* 6-7 (1993): 121-23.

Suárez Radillo, Carlos Miguel. "Panorama del teatro hispanoamericano contemporáneo." *Urogallo* [Madrid] 6. 35-36 (1975): 135-45.

Sued Badillo, Jalil, and Ángel López Cantos. *Puerto Rico negro.* Río Piedras: Editorial Cultural, 1986.

Thom, Martin. "*Verneinung, Verwerfung, Ausstossung*: A Problem in the Interpretation of Freud." *The Talking Cure: Essays in Psychoanalysis and Language.* Ed. Colin MacCabe. London: Macmillan, 1981. 162-87.

Torres, Andrés. *Between Melting Pot and Mosaic: African Americans and Puerto Ricans in the New York Political Economy.* Philadelphia: Temple UP, 1995.

Torres-Saillant, Silvio. *Caribbean Poetics: Toward and Aesthetic of West Indian Literature.* Cambridge: Cambridge UP, 1998.

Trías Monge, José. *Puerto Rico: The Trials of the Oldest Colony in the World.* New Haven: Yale UP, 1997.

Vázquez Arce, Carmen. "Luis Palés Matos y su papel en la formulación del proyecto nacional del treinta." Spanish Caribbean Culture: Subjectivity and Nationality conference. Cambridge University, England. 2 June 1995.

Vega, José Luis. "La nieve del trópico." *Techo a dos aguas.* Río Piedras: Plaza Mayor, 1998. 25-29.

Waugh, Patricia. "Postmodernism." Wright 341-45.

Williams, Patrick, and Laura Chrisman, eds. *Colonial Discourse and Postcolonial Theory: A Reader.* London: Harvester Wheatsheaf, 1994.

Williamson, Edwin. *The Penguin History of Latin America.* Harmondsworth: Penguin, 1992.

Woodyard, George W. "Toward a radical theatre in Latin America." *Contemporary Latin American Literature.* Ed. Harvey L. Johnson and Phillips B. Taylor Jr. Houston: Latin American Studies Committee, 1973. 93-102.

———. 1994 "Puerto Rican drama." *The Cambridge Guide to African and Caribbean Theatre.* Ed. Martin Banham, Errol Hill, and George Woodyard. Cambridge: Cambridge UP. 219-24.

Wright, Elizabeth, ed. *Feminism and Psychoanalysis: A Critical Dictionary.* Oxford: Blackwell, 1992.

Young, Robert J. C. *Colonial Desire: Hybridity in Theory, Culture and Race.* London: Routledge, 1995.

Zavala, Iris M. *El bolero: historia de un amor.* Madrid: Alianza, 1991.

———. *Culture and Colonialism: Hispanic Modernisms and the Social Imaginary.* Bloomington: Indiana UP, 1992.

Zenón Cruz, Isabelo. *Narciso descubre su trasero (el negro en la cultura puertorriqueña).* 2 vols. Humacao, PR: Furidi, 1974-75.

NORTH CAROLINA STUDIES IN THE ROMANCE LANGUAGES AND LITERATURES

I.S.B.N. Prefix 0-8078-

Recent Titles

When ordering please cite the *ISBN Prefix* plus the last four digits for each title.

Send orders to: University of North Carolina Press
P.O. Box 2288
CB# 6215
Chapel Hill, NC 27515-2288
· U.S.A.